# Philippians,
# Colossians,
# Philemon

✠ Catholic Commentary on Sacred Scripture

SERIES EDITORS
**Peter S. Williamson**
**Mary Healy**

ASSOCIATE EDITOR
**Kevin Perrotta**

CONSULTING EDITORS
**Scott Hahn**, Franciscan University of Steubenville
**Daniel J. Harrington, SJ**, Weston Jesuit School of Theology
**William S. Kurz, SJ**, Marquette University
**Francis Martin**, Sacred Heart Major Seminary
**Frank J. Matera**, Catholic University of America
**George Montague, SM**, St. Mary's University
**Terrence Prendergast, SJ**, Archbishop of Ottawa

# Philippians, Colossians, Philemon

Dennis Hamm, SJ

Baker Academic

a division of Baker Publishing Group
Grand Rapids, Michigan

© 2013 by Dennis Hamm, SJ

Published by Baker Academic
a division of Baker Publishing Group
P.O. Box 6287, Grand Rapids, MI 49516-6287
www.bakeracademic.com

Printed in the United States of America

Library of Congress Cataloging-in-Publication Data

Hamm, M. Dennis.
    Philippians, Colossians, Philemon/Dennis Hamm, SJ; Peter S. Williamson and Mary Healy, general editors.
       p.  cm.—(Catholic commentary on sacred Scripture)
    Includes bibliographical references and index.
    ISBN 978-0-8010-3646-0 (pbk. : alk. paper)
    1. Bible. Philippians—Commentaries. 2. Bible. Colossians—Commentaries. 3. Bible. Philemon—Commentaries. 4. Catholic Church—Doctrines. I. Title.
BS2705.53.H34  2013
227'.607—dc23
                                     2013027280

*Nihil obstat:*
Rev. Lam T. Le, STL
Censor Deputatus
January 30, 2013

*Imprimatur:*
Most Rev. Walter A. Hurley, DD
Bishop of Grand Rapids
February 28, 2013

The *nihil obstat* and *imprimatur* are official declarations that a book or pamphlet is free of doctrinal or moral error. There is no implication that those who have granted the *nihil obstat* or the *imprimatur* agree with the content, opinions, or statements expressed therein.

# Contents

# Illustrations

# Editors' Preface

The Church has always venerated the divine Scriptures just as she venerates the body of the Lord. . . . All the preaching of the Church should be nourished and governed by Sacred Scripture. For in the sacred books, the Father who is in heaven meets His children with great love and speaks with them; and the power and goodness in the word of God is so great that it stands as the support and energy of the Church, the strength of faith for her sons and daughters, the food of the soul, a pure and perennial fountain of spiritual life.

Second Vatican Council, Dei Verbum 21

Were not our hearts burning [within us] while he spoke to us on the way and opened the scriptures to us?

Luke 24:32

The Catholic Commentary on Sacred Scripture aims to serve the ministry of the Word of God in the life and mission of the Church. Since Vatican Council II, there has been an increasing hunger among Catholics to study Scripture in depth and in a way that reveals its relationship to liturgy, evangelization, catechesis, theology, and personal and communal life. This series responds to that desire by providing accessible yet substantive commentary on each book of the New Testament, drawn from the best of contemporary biblical scholarship as well as the rich treasury of the Church's tradition. These volumes seek to offer scholarship illumined by faith, in the conviction that the ultimate aim of biblical interpretation is to discover what God has revealed and is still speaking through the sacred text. Central to our approach are the principles taught by Vatican II: first, the use of historical and literary methods to discern what the biblical authors intended to express; second, prayerful theological reflection to understand the sacred text "in accord with the same Spirit by whom it was written"—that is, in light of the content and unity of the whole Scripture, the living tradition of the Church, and the analogy of faith (*Dei Verbum* 12).

The Catholic Commentary on Sacred Scripture is written for those engaged in or training for pastoral ministry and others interested in studying Scripture to understand their faith more deeply, to nourish their spiritual life, or to share the good news with others. With this in mind, the authors focus on the meaning of the text for faith and life rather than on the technical questions that occupy scholars, and they explain the Bible in ordinary language that does not require translation for preaching and catechesis. Although this series is written from the perspective of Catholic faith, its authors draw on the interpretation of Protestant and Orthodox scholars and hope these volumes will serve Christians of other traditions as well.

A variety of features are designed to make the commentary as useful as possible. Each volume includes the biblical text of the New American Bible, Revised Edition (NABRE), the translation approved for liturgical use in the United States. In order to serve readers who use other translations, the most important differences between the NABRE and other widely used translations (RSV, NRSV, JB, NJB, and NIV) are noted and explained. Each unit of the biblical text is followed by a list of references to relevant Scripture passages, Catechism sections, and uses in the Roman Lectionary. The exegesis that follows aims to explain in a clear and engaging way the meaning of the text in its original historical context as well as its perennial meaning for Christians. Reflection and Application sections help readers apply Scripture to Christian life today by responding to questions that the text raises, offering spiritual interpretations drawn from Christian tradition, or providing suggestions for the use of the biblical text in catechesis, preaching, or other forms of pastoral ministry.

Interspersed throughout the commentary are Biblical Background sidebars that present historical, literary, or theological information, and Living Tradition sidebars that offer pertinent material from the postbiblical Christian tradition, including quotations from Church documents and from the writings of saints and Church Fathers. The Biblical Background sidebars are indicated by a photo of urns that were excavated in Jerusalem, signifying the importance of historical study in understanding the sacred text. The Living Tradition sidebars are indicated by an image of Eadwine, a twelfth-century monk and scribe, signifying the growth in the Church's understanding that comes by the grace of the Holy Spirit as believers study and ponder the Word of God in their hearts (see *Dei Verbum* 8).

A map and a Glossary are located in the back of each volume for easy reference. The glossary explains key terms from the biblical text as well as theological or exegetical terms, which are marked in the commentary with a cross (†). A list of Suggested Resources, an Index of Pastoral Topics, and an Index of Sidebars are included to enhance the usefulness of these volumes. Further resources, including questions for reflection or discussion, can be found at the series website, www.CatholicScriptureCommentary.com.

It is our desire and prayer that these volumes be of service so that more and more "the word of the Lord may speed forward and be glorified" (2 Thess 3:1) in the Church and throughout the world.

Peter S. Williamson
Mary Healy
Kevin Perrotta

## Note to Readers

The New American Bible, Revised Edition differs slightly from most English translations in its verse numbering of the Psalms and certain other parts of the Old Testament. For instance, Ps 51:4 in the NABRE is Ps 51:2 in other translations; Mal 3:19 in the NABRE is Mal 4:1 in other translations. Readers who use different translations are advised to keep this in mind when looking up Old Testament cross-references given in the commentary.

# Abbreviations

| | |
|---|---|
| † | Indicates that a definition of the term appears in the glossary |
| ACCS 8 | Ancient Christian Commentary on Scripture, New Testament, vol. 8, *Galatians, Ephesians, Philippians*, ed. Mark J. Edwards (Downers Grove, IL: InterVarsity, 1999) |
| ACCS 9 | Ancient Christian Commentary on Scripture, New Testament, vol. 9, *Colossians, 1–2 Thessalonians, 1–2 Timothy, Titus, Philemon*, ed. Peter Gorday (Downers Grove, IL: InterVarsity, 2000) |
| BDAG | *A Greek-English Lexicon of the New Testament and Other Early Christian Literature*, 3rd edition; revised and edited by Frederick William Danker, based on the 6th edition of Walter Bauer's *Griechisch-Deutches Wörterbuch* (Chicago: University of Chicago Press, 2000) |
| Catechism | *Catechism of the Catholic Church* (2nd edition) |
| CBQ | *Catholic Biblical Quarterly* |
| CCSS | Catholic Commentary on Sacred Scripture (Grand Rapids: Baker Academic, 2008–) |
| Lectionary | *The Lectionary for Mass* (1998/2002 USA edition) |
| LXX | Septuagint |
| NABRE | New American Bible, Revised Edition |
| NIV | New International Version |
| NJB | New Jerusalem Bible |
| NRSV | New Revised Standard Version |
| NT | New Testament |
| OT | Old Testament |
| RSV | Revised Standard Version |

## Books of the Old Testament

| | | | | | |
|---|---|---|---|---|---|
| Gen | Genesis | Josh | Joshua | 1 Kings | 1 Kings |
| Exod | Exodus | Judg | Judges | 2 Kings | 2 Kings |
| Lev | Leviticus | Ruth | Ruth | 1 Chron | 1 Chronicles |
| Num | Numbers | 1 Sam | 1 Samuel | 2 Chron | 2 Chronicles |
| Deut | Deuteronomy | 2 Sam | 2 Samuel | Ezra | Ezra |

| Neh | Nehemiah | Wis | Wisdom | Obad | Obadiah |
| Tob | Tobit | Sir | Sirach | Jon | Jonah |
| Jdt | Judith | Isa | Isaiah | Mic | Micah |
| Esther | Esther | Jer | Jeremiah | Nah | Nahum |
| 1 Macc | 1 Maccabees | Lam | Lamentations | Hab | Habakkuk |
| 2 Macc | 2 Maccabees | Bar | Baruch | Zeph | Zephaniah |
| Job | Job | Ezek | Ezekiel | Hag | Haggai |
| Ps | Psalms | Dan | Daniel | Zech | Zechariah |
| Prov | Proverbs | Hosea | Hosea | Mal | Malachi |
| Eccles | Ecclesiastes | Joel | Joel | | |
| Song | Song of Songs | Amos | Amos | | |

## Books of the New Testament

| Matt | Matthew | 1 Tim | 1 Timothy |
| Mark | Mark | 2 Tim | 2 Timothy |
| Luke | Luke | Titus | Titus |
| John | John | Philem | Philemon |
| Acts | Acts of the Apostles | Heb | Hebrews |
| Rom | Romans | James | James |
| 1 Cor | 1 Corinthians | 1 Pet | 1 Peter |
| 2 Cor | 2 Corinthians | 2 Pet | 2 Peter |
| Gal | Galatians | 1 John | 1 John |
| Eph | Ephesians | 2 John | 2 John |
| Phil | Philippians | 3 John | 3 John |
| Col | Colossians | Jude | Jude |
| 1 Thess | 1 Thessalonians | Rev | Revelation |
| 2 Thess | 2 Thessalonians | | |

# Introduction to the Prison Letters

We are about to read together three of the four letters of St. Paul commonly known as the Prison Letters—Ephesians, Philippians, Colossians, and Philemon. These four are clustered under that label because they state that Paul writes them from some place of confinement. A fifth letter, 2 Timothy, also presents Paul as writing from prison, but because it has been traditionally categorized with 1 Timothy and Titus as a set of three called the Pastoral Letters, it is not usually grouped with the other Prison Letters. This commentary treats only three of the traditional Prison Letters—Philippians, Colossians, and Philemon—because the Catholic Commentary on Sacred Scripture devotes a separate volume to Ephesians, which is so comprehensive as a summary of Paul's theology that it warrants a commentary of its own.

I will provide a separate introduction to each of the three letters. But before we begin to read individual letters, it seems useful to address a number of general questions these letters naturally raise—questions like the following: Where was Paul imprisoned when he wrote? Why was he imprisoned? Did the people of the first-century Mediterranean world write and read letters the way we do—and if not, how can we adjust our reading of these letters to better understand them? How do we make sense of somebody else's mail? How did someone's †occasional correspondence come to be recognized as the Word of God for all Christians?

To begin with that last question, we get our main picture of Paul's place in the growth of the early Church from Luke's portrayal of him in the Acts of the Apostles. There we meet him as the zealous Pharisee Saul of Tarsus, who is part of the crowd stoning the first Christian martyr, Stephen (Acts 7–8). Though he is not himself throwing the stones, he is minding the cloaks of those who do.

Soon he becomes so convinced that the Jesus movement among his fellow Jews is a threat to Judaism that he seeks and obtains authorization to block the progress of "the Way," as it was coming to be called (see Acts 9:2), by seeking out and imprisoning its promoters. Heading for Damascus on such a mission, he has his famous experience on the road, an encounter with the risen Jesus, who identifies himself with the very communities Paul seeks to eliminate (Acts 9). Shortly thereafter, this persecutor of "the Way" becomes its best evangelist. Luke spends the rest

Fig. 1. Gustave Doré's graphic interpretation of Saul/Paul's conversion.

of Acts telling how this Saul of Tarsus, eventually better known as Paul the Apostle, uses his talents for preaching, teaching, and organizing Christian communities. He soon takes his place next to the Rock himself, Peter, as one of the great leaders of the early Church. In highly abbreviated form, Luke sketches the story of Paul's mission journeys, mainly among the Gentiles in the areas we now call Turkey and Greece. Finally, Luke shows how Paul imitates his Master by ending his days under persecution, including interrogations and incarcerations by Jewish and Roman authorities.

While Luke says nothing about Paul's letter writing, Paul put the faith and practices of these first Christians into such moving and memorable words that his letters were early recognized as having a value far beyond the occasions that prompted them and the particular churches and persons to whom they were first addressed. They were recognized as inspired by the Holy Spirit—even as the Word of God.

## Where Was Paul Imprisoned?

None of Paul's Prison Letters names the locations of his various imprisonments. As disappointing as this is to us history detectives, the failure to mention these locations is perfectly understandable. Does a student attending Creighton

University, writing home, include a sentence like, "I am writing to you from Creighton University, in Omaha"? Just as the student's parents know perfectly well where their child is going to school, so also Paul's addressees knew where the Apostle was imprisoned. It was, no doubt, the talk of the church.

Reading his letters two millennia later, we are out of the loop. But we can make educated guesses. First, we can look for clues in the letters themselves. If, for example, Paul mentions "the praetorium" as part of the neighborhood, as he does in Philippians 1:23, then we know he is in a major city that has a Roman governor's residence, or at least an imperial guard, for these are meanings of "praetorium." That narrows down the possible candidates but still allows for a number of major cities as the possible location. Or, if Paul mentions several comings and goings between the place of the addressees and the place where he is in custody, our guess should favor a shorter rather than a longer distance between those places. We shall review some of the details of these educated guesses as we deal with the individual letters.

Second, we can seek information in the Acts of the Apostles, which speaks of Paul imprisoned in four different locations—

1. Philippi, overnight, after an illegal beating (16:23–30);
2. Jerusalem, in the temple compound, under Roman protective custody when threatened by some of his fellow Jews (21:27–23:30);
3. Caesarea Maritima, first for two years under Governor Felix (23:34–24:26) and then under Governor Festus (24:27–25:32); and finally
4. Rome, under imperial house arrest for two years, awaiting trial before the emperor (28:16–31).[1]

It is easy to understand why the traditional presumption has been that Paul wrote the Prison Letters from Rome. The very brief incarcerations in Philippi and Jerusalem did not allow time for the writing of letters. The Caesarean incarceration afforded plenty of time but presented a formidable distance from Ephesus, Philippi, or Colossae. However, Paul is portrayed in the book of Acts as receiving visitors "in great numbers" and proclaiming the kingdom of God and teaching about the Lord Jesus Christ while under house arrest in Rome (Acts 28:23, 31), which presents an attractive solution to the question of location.

1. When Christians today think of Paul in prison, our cultural experience may lead us to think of him as "serving time," sitting out a "term" assigned by a judge as punishment for a crime. This list of Paul's time "in chains" serves to remind us that in the first-century Roman Empire, incarceration was always a matter of being *held in custody* until official judgment led either to death or freedom, not a matter of serving a term.

Consequently, preachers and commentators have for centuries presumed Rome to be the site for Paul's writing the Prison Letters. But in Paul's list of exploits in 2 Corinthians 11 there is a strong reminder that Paul's Letters and the book of Acts tell only part of the story. Parodying the boasting of the "super-apostles" (see 11:5 and 12:11), Paul lists as his "credentials" his apostolic sufferings:

> far greater labors, *far more imprisonments*, far worse beatings, and numerous brushes with death. Five times at the hands of the Jews I received forty lashes minus one. Three times I was beaten with rods, once I was stoned.
>
> 2 Cor 11:23–25

The mention of "far more imprisonments" surely reaches beyond the four narrated in Acts. The mention of five Jewish and three Roman beatings, while not necessarily tied to imprisonments, refers to punishments that were usually a prelude to imprisonment in first-century Jewish and Roman practices. Luke shows how Saul himself, in his zeal, could imprison fellow Jews he considered heretical (Acts 8:3; 9:1, 14; 22:4). After his conversion, Paul experienced the same from his peers.

In recent scholarship, a new candidate for location has emerged. The city of Ephesus has been proposed as a likely place of the writing of at least the letters to Philemon, Colossians, and even Philippians. While neither Paul's Letters nor Acts explicitly mentions Ephesus as a place where Paul was confined, both provide data that make Ephesus a plausible venue. I consider Ephesus the likely location in which Paul wrote the letters to Philemon and Colossians, and Rome the venue for writing to the Philippians. But discussion of these details can wait for the introductions of the individual letters. It is enough to note here that the question of where Paul was when he wrote the Prison Letters is a matter of educated guesswork. As we will see, the guessing process itself is illuminating.

## Why Was Paul Imprisoned?

A far more significant issue than the locations, and therefore the timing, of Paul's imprisonments and writing is the question of *why* he was held in custody. Paul is almost as uninformative about the ostensible reasons for his arrests as about the locations. As in the case of *where*, the question of *why* was needless for his addressees, who likely knew his situation. Again, we who are out of the loop need to guess at the reasons as well as we can from the available clues.

The reasons for Paul's incarcerations mentioned in Acts are clear enough. During the uproar created in Philippi, when Paul and Silas (and possibly Luke)

Fig. 2. A denarius coin struck circa 18 BC. Left: the inscription around the coin reads CAESAR AVGVSTVS ("Caesar Augustus"). The other side reads DIVVS IVLIVS ("divine Julius"). The image is "the Julian star," the comet that appeared in the evening sky shortly after the assassination of Julius Caesar in 44 BC. The star was taken as a sign of his divinity. [Info taken from NumisBid.com]

threaten the livelihood of the owners of a slave girl by freeing her from a demonic spirit, the city magistrates strip, beat, and lock them up, apparently to pacify the boisterous crowd (Acts 16:16–24). The incarcerations by Roman officials in Jerusalem and Caesarea are a matter of protective custody against Jerusalem vigilantes who appear to be threatening this Saul of Tarsus, whom the Romans know to be a citizen of the empire. The house arrest in Rome is a matter of custody pending trial. In the letters to the Philippians and Philemon, the closest Paul comes to an explanation of the cause of his imprisonment is in referring to himself as "a prisoner for Christ" (Philem 1 and 9) or as suffering "imprisonment for the gospel" (Philem 13) or "for the defense [*apologia*] of the gospel" (Phil 1:16).

But what was it about Paul's presentation of the gospel that provoked imprisonment? The Roman Empire had, after all, come to terms with Judaism as a religion whose practices did not threaten Roman law and order. What in Paul's preaching gave pause to the local custodians of social order? The complaint of some Thessalonian Jews against Paul and company may hold a clue. Luke writes that they dragged Jason and some of the brothers before the city magistrates, shouting, "These people who have been creating a disturbance all over the world have now come here, and Jason has welcomed them. They all *act in opposition to the decrees of Caesar and claim instead that there is another king, Jesus*" (Acts 17:6–7). Like the members of the Sanhedrin who brought Jesus to Pilate with the charge that he was challenging Caesar's authority (Luke 23:1–2), these people knew that the Roman officials in Thessalonica would be disturbed by the Christian claim that Jesus is Lord, with its implication that the emperor is not. As we will see in our study of Philippians, Paul proclaimed exactly such an interpretation, though his challenge to Roman domination was spiritual, not military or political. Any Roman official with a concern for imperial law and order ("homeland security" in our terms) would become suspicious of a traveling teacher exciting groups with talk about the "kingdom of God" and claiming that a Jewish anointed one was "Lord and Savior"—language used in Roman emperor worship. While Paul taught cooperation with secular officials (see Rom 13), his talk about an alternative kingdom and the sovereignty of one Jesus would have made him, to use an expression from modern law enforcement, a "person of interest," and even someone to take into custody for closer scrutiny.

## Letter Writing in the Ancient World: Oral Scripts

Although email, instant messaging, and texting now dominate the majority of the world's written correspondence, we still do enough traditional letter writing for formal invitations, important legal transactions, and key moments in relationships (love letters, condolences, congratulations, wedding invitations) to know what is involved in writing and reading a letter. We have *something* in common with the ancients in this matter. Yet when we read the letters of the New Testament, it is necessary to note some differences in the letter writing of the first-century Mediterranean world.

(1) The skills of reading and writing were much further from universal than they are in our world. Good writers and readers were rare enough to warrant the social role of the scribe, a professional who was really good at taking dictation. Some scribes were trusted enough to take a general idea or intent and put it into their words for the author's approval before sending, as many executive assistants do today. We have good reason to assume that Paul was an able writer and reader of Greek, but we know he often used a scribe. For example, while he clearly identifies himself as the author of the Letter to the Christians in Rome (Rom 1:1), just before the close of the letter we read, "I, Tertius, the writer of this letter, greet you in the Lord" (16:22). No one speaks of Tertius as the *author* of the Letter to the Romans; the author is Paul, who in identifying himself as the sender claims authorship (1:1). Yet the scribe Tertius can call himself the letter's *writer*, the one who actually put pen to parchment. This fact reminds us not to make too much of stylistic variations among letters attributed to Paul.

(2) Before the development of rapid transportation and electronic media, a good deal of time could elapse between the writing and the reading of a letter. This meant a couple of things: you only took the time and effort to write (or hired a scribe to write) a letter when it was a matter of importance to you and your addressees, and you wrote in a way that you expected to be intelligible some weeks or months in the future.

(3) Letters were read aloud. (That is true of virtually every document in the Bible—a fact that is important to keep in mind.) While today we mainly

Fig. 3. Papyrus 46, with the text of 2 Cor 11:43–12:2, the oldest copy of a Letter of Paul (ca. 220 AD), showing what the script of a Greek text looked like to the original readers. Note the space-saving merging of the words into an unbroken sequence of letters.

read texts silently, in the very oral world of the first century, people considered a written text as a score intended for oral performance, that is, as a script meant for some literate person to read aloud. Thus we can expect in the Letters of Paul the kind of wordplay that comes naturally in oral communication (we'll find several examples of this in the Letter to Philemon). We can also expect first-century letters to be organized in a way that helps a listening audience follow and remember what is being said. Thus what is said early in a document prepares for what comes later. This affected the format of ancient letters.

(4) Most of us use a particular format and set of conventions when we write a standard letter, as opposed to an email message or a Post-it note. Our letter format involves

(a)   the date of writing at the top; then, in more formal letters,

(b)   the name and address of the intended receiver;

(c)   a salutation in the form of the word "Dear" followed by the name of the addressee, where *Dear* usually works simply as a pointer, not necessarily as a term of affection;

(d)   the body of the letter, carrying the main communication (e.g., information, request, or agreement);

(e)   a closing, like "Sincerely yours"; and

(f)   the signature of the sender.

Placing the signature at the end certifies that the sender stands behind all that has been written above. This letter format is indicative of a text-centered culture interested in archiving communications, agreements, and information.

The first-century Greco-Roman letter, the kind Paul wrote, had a slightly different format. Letter writers in the ancient world did not seem to be much interested in dating their correspondences; this may simply be due to the unpredictable and often lengthy lapse between the time of the letter's writing and time of its reception. Thus, first-century letters usually begin with

(a) a *prescript* identifying the sender, the intended addressee, and some conventional greeting; then, instead of moving immediately into the business of the correspondence, the author uses the device of

(b) a *thanksgiving*, often in the form of a prayer, to communicate something that affirms the personal relationship between sender and receiver—something like, "I thank Zeus that your ankle sprain is healed and you are back on the handball court";

(c) then comes the body, the business of the letter; finally,

(d) to reaffirm that the relationship between sender and receiver is more than the business of the letter, the author usually has a personal note, often about travel plans that will afford face-to-face communication between the parties involved, sometimes followed by greetings from others known to the addressee.

The format of ancient letters reflects the oral nature of the culture in which they were written. If that format seems familiar, it may be that it is close to the shape of a typical phone call, a contemporary form of oral communication. Although no one formally taught us this format, our phone calls typically follow a similar format:

(a) *Greeting.*

(b) *Self-identification,* unless we are calling someone who we know will recognize our voice.

(c) *Specification of addressee.* If we are not familiar with the voice of the one who answers the phone call, we usually make sure we are talking to the intended addressee by saying something like, "Am I speaking with Amelia?"

(d) *Small talk, part one,* functioning like the thanksgiving part of the ancient letter. If I am talking to someone with whom I have a relationship that goes beyond the business at hand, I instinctively affirm that relationship by making small talk about the weather or something else we have in common ("Have you recovered from Saturday's party?") before addressing the reason for the call.

(e) *The business.* Now it is time for the transaction, which is signaled by a phrase like, "Well, the reason I'm calling. . . ."

(f) *Small talk, part two.* Just as it is a bit abrupt to charge into the business at hand without a personal segue, it is also rather abrupt to end the call without another personal acknowledgment that there is more to the relationship than the immediate occasion of the call. This is similar to Paul's mention of travel plans toward the end of his letters.

(g) *Sign-off.* Often, we reiterate the agreement ("OK then, I'll come by to pick you up at six Saturday"), but the termination of an encounter requires the following element.

(h) *Some personal valedictory,* if only a simple "Good-bye."

Our reflection on the format of the phone call in our culture helps make sense of the ancient letter—especially the need for self-identification at the start, the cushion of small talk before the business (handled nicely by the epistolary thanksgiving), and something similar ("So-and-so sends greetings") before the closing.

## How to Read Someone Else's Mail

No matter how much the media of communication have changed since the first century, a message is still a message. When we recognize a particular text as representing an act of communication between specific persons, we know what is involved in understanding that text. Furthermore, if we are the intended receiver, we usually know or recognize the sender, and the text draws on the preexisting relationship we have with the sender. Local and current-events references do not require explanation. Allusions suffice. Jokes come easily. Much is reasonably presumed. We catch the meaning of a friend's communication because we inhabit the same thought world and share a common history.

Understanding a message that was not originally intended for us is quite another matter. In a very real sense, when we read Paul's Letters we are reading someone else's mail. That is, we are not the addressees the author originally intended. That means we do not inhabit the same thought world and set of experiences as the author. And so we need to do what we would do if we found an opened letter on the sidewalk and dared to enter into the privacy of that correspondence: we examine the text imaginatively to see what the text implies about the relationship between sender and receiver. This is guesswork, but it is guesswork based on the language of the text, which, if it is a contemporary text written in our native tongue, we have a good chance of understanding.

Now, if the text is archived material—say, part of a collection of letters written by the novelist Henry James—if we cared enough, we would use everything we could learn about James's world, especially what we learn from his other letters.

These strategies—figuring out what the text implies about the sender and receivers and learning about the thought world from other texts and contemporary information—are necessary in the project of understanding Paul's Letters.

There is, however, an important sense in which the letters of the New Testament are *not* someone else's mail. Very soon after their writing, these bits of correspondence were recognized as having value beyond their original occasion and context. For example, even though it is obvious that what we call the First Letter to the Corinthians addresses a very specific set of pastoral problems besetting the Christian community of Corinth in the 50s of the first century AD, it speaks powerfully to the challenges and the faith shared by Christians of any era. The early Church recognized that all Christians could consider themselves addressed by Paul's letter to the local church in Corinth. Indeed, the Church recognizes this text as the inspired Word of God.

This insight can lead contemporary readers to expect a passage from a New Testament letter to speak to them directly, without considering what it meant to the original readers. And often a passage may do that quite powerfully. But recent Catholic teaching—for example, *Divino afflante Spiritu* (1943), *Dei Verbum* (1965), and *Verbum Domini* (2010)—has emphasized the importance of attending first to what a given biblical text meant in the time, culture, and literary form in which it was written. Paradoxically, we scholars find that the more seriously we take that task, that is, looking for the original meaning, the more we discover what that original meaning implies for living the faith today.

## Why Are Some of Paul's Letters "Disputed"?

Anyone who sits down to read scholarly discussions about the writings of Paul soon encounters references to the seven "undisputed" letters (Romans, 1 Corinthians, 2 Corinthians, Galatians, Philippians, 1 Thessalonians, and Philemon) and the six "disputed" letters (Ephesians, Colossians, 2 Thessalonians, 1 Timothy, 2 Timothy, and Titus). What scholars are disputing is Pauline authorship. (The Letter to the Hebrews, which has sometimes been attributed to Paul, carries no claim in the text to Pauline authorship, is usually considered anonymous, and therefore is not included among the Letters of Paul.) Since one of the three letters studied in this commentary, Colossians, is among the "disputed" letters, it is good to say something here about that potentially disconcerting label. Most importantly, what is disputed is not their validity and authenticity as inspired Scripture conveying the apostolic tradition, but rather the more specific technical issue of authorship: Is Paul in fact the author of this particular letter? Or does this text give evidence of having been written at a later time by another Christian schooled in the Pauline tradition? What gives rise to this dispute is the notable variation in vocabulary, style, and formulation of Christian doctrine that recent generations of scholars have found among six of the letters attributed to Paul. Some scholars attribute those variations to a mix of various causes: the work of Paul's scribes, the development of his own thought over his missionary life, and the diversity of the problems addressed. Others see clues to †pseudonymous writing in such things as the apparent dependency of some letters on others (e.g., Ephesians on Colossians) or an apparent development of thought that seems to require a longer time period than Paul's relatively short career as a Christian missionary.

Since some scholars dispute the Pauline authorship of Colossians, we shall explore this topic more fully in the introduction to that book.

## What Is Special about These Three Letters?

Enforced confinement can foster reflection and introspection. Thus letters from prison often reveal much about their writers. This is surely true of Philippians and, to a lesser extent, Philemon. The same is true of Colossians: even if Colossians is pseudonymous, it reveals Paul's followers' understanding of their model and mentor. So coming to know Paul and, possibly, the early Church's appreciation of him, is clearly one way in which these Prison Letters are of particular interest.

Of special value are the two famous hymns or poems embedded in Philippians and Colossians—the "Christ hymn" of Phil 2:6–11 and the cosmic song of Col 1:15–20. Some scholars have thought that one or both of these passages had an existence prior to the writing of the letters, perhaps as songs sung in the earliest Christian liturgies. And it is undeniable that these pieces have had a life of their own in the centuries *after* the writing of the letters—in private prayer, in eucharistic worship, in the Liturgy of the Hours, and especially in development of the Church's doctrine of the divinity and humanity of Jesus Christ—what we call Christology. These days, scholars are beginning to appreciate more and more how these hymns fit into the letters that contain them. Whether Paul composed the poems himself or inherited them, these songs are not simply pasted into the letters; he integrates their vision and imagery fully into the fabric of his respective argument. Each is the kernel of the organic whole of the respective letter. This commentary will give special attention to this aspect of these great sources of the Church's prayer, celebration, and theology.

There are, of course, further important features of these letters that invite our careful study. We learn much about the early churches in Philippi and Colossae that can illuminate and inspire our own participation in church life today. All three letters speak powerfully of how Christians experience salvation in daily life. The robust prayer that introduces and permeates each document demonstrates the vital part prayer has always played in Christian living.

## A Word about Words

Even though I am not presuming much if any technical knowledge of biblical scholarship, I am presuming that the readers of this commentary are curious and eager to consider the results of the work of biblical scholars. And while I presume no knowledge of Greek on the part of my readers, I think they share my interest in the original Greek words that underlie the English translations. When a passage employs a Greek word or phrase that carries an important resonance from the Greek Old Testament (called the †Septuagint) or in first-century Greco-Roman culture, I will insert the Greek word (in familiar Latin letters, not the Greek alphabet) and will explain what I find especially meaningful, or perhaps hard to put into English, regarding that word or phrase.

For example, it may be a simple matter to translate *kyrie* as "Lord," which many English-speaking readers recognize as a title for addressing God in the Old Testament. But it is helpful to learn that the Greek word was also used to mean "master" in the context of master-slave relationships. Further, it is important to know that in the eastern part of the Roman Empire *kyrie* was used in worship of the emperor as divine. These associations for the Greek word *kyrios* (or *kyrie* in direct address) cannot be expressed in any single word available in English, so we sometimes need to spell out what the original readers and auditors grasped spontaneously. This is something like our need for footnotes to understand the jokes, wordplay, and topical allusions in Shakespeare's plays—meanings that the original audiences caught immediately, without any need for explanation.

These letters may be, in an important way, other people's mail. But they are also *our* letters in that, from early on, our now two-millennia-old community of faith has recognized them as the inspired Word of God. As the house churches of Philippi and Colossae lived in the presence of Jesus whom they recognized as Messiah and risen Lord, so do we. If the times and cultures have changed, the life and mission of the Church we share has much in common with the life and mission of the early churches.

# Paul's Letter to Philemon

Philemon, the shortest of Paul's letters, is a little gem. A mere twenty-five verses, it nonetheless reveals much about the Apostle's pastoral vision and method, and it provides a privileged glimpse into the life of the early Church.

It is clear from the text that Paul writes from prison, though he does not tell us where. The main addressee, Philemon, is a convert of Paul's, apparently living in Colossae. We surmise this from the reference to Philemon's slave Onesimus as "one of you" in Col 4:9. Given that Onesimus has come to Paul on his own, and given that Ephesus is a mere hundred miles from Colossae, Ephesus is a good guess regarding the location of Paul's imprisonment. Paul writes Philemon (1) to inform him that his missing slave has become a fellow Christian and (2) to persuade him to receive Onesimus in mercy as the brother in Christ that he has become, and to do "even more" (perhaps emancipate him?).

A careful reading reveals a fascinating and complex set of relationships between Paul, the slave-owner Philemon, the slave Onesimus, and the church that meets at Philemon's house. As a piece of correspondence meant to deal with a specific need on a specific occasion, it is highly unlikely that Paul ever thought this letter was destined to a permanent afterlife as a part of the Scriptures. Yet, as we will discover, this piece of †occasional writing exemplifies such wisdom regarding the life and mission of the Church that it was eventually recognized as the Word of God. It also provides a marvelous example of how attending to what seems to have been the *original* meaning of the letter (what it meant *then*) turns out to be the best way to understand what it can mean for Christians today (what it means *now*).

Fig. 4. A Roman home big enough to host the weekly gathering of a "house church."

## Ephesus as the Place of Writing: A Reasonable Guess?

Given that neither Paul's Letters nor the Acts of the Apostles explicitly mentions that Paul was imprisoned at Ephesus, it may seem odd to suggest that he wrote Philemon during an imprisonment there. However, a number of facts point toward this capital of the Roman province of Asia as a likely place for Paul to have found himself in chains.

1. Acts 19 describes the uproar Paul's ministry caused in Ephesus, when silversmiths with a vested interest in the reputation of the goddess Artemis and her temple (models of which they made and sold to tourists) accused Paul of speaking against worship of the local idol. The intervention of the town clerk during a riot in the theater, urging the craftsmen to bring charges against Paul in the courts to pursue their grievances, could have led to his incarceration (Acts 19:35–40).

2. Paul's decision to bypass Ephesus on his return from the third mission trip (Acts 20:16–17), asking the Ephesian elders to meet him at Miletus instead, suggests he may have been avoiding further friction (entailing incarceration?) with the civic authorities in Ephesus.

28

3. In his First Letter to the Corinthians, exemplifying how he and his co-workers "are endangering ourselves all the time," he makes a passing reference to how "at Ephesus I fought with beasts, so to speak," a strong metaphor for facing resistance in that town, language that could well include incarceration (1 Cor 15:32). And even when, a little later in the letter, he speaks more positively about ministry in Ephesus, he still mentions strong opposition there: "I shall stay in Ephesus until Pentecost, because a door has opened for me wide and productive for work, *but there are many opponents*" (1 Cor 16:8–9).

4. The reference in 2 Timothy 1:18b to the "services [Onesiphorus] rendered in Ephesus," paralleling his visit to Paul during his Roman imprisonment (v. 17), could easily refer to an Ephesian incarceration.

5. Along with this circumstantial support for the plausibility of an Ephesian imprisonment is the relative proximity of Ephesus to Colossae (around a hundred miles). Thus, given that the Letter to Philemon entails a slave who makes his way on his own to Paul, Ephesus is a more likely venue for Paul's imprisonment than the far more distant sites of Rome or Caesarea.

## Literary Features

So short that it does not even call for chapter divisions, this letter still exhibits the epistolary format we considered in the general introduction: a prescript which identifies senders and intended addressees, and proffers a greeting (vv. 1–3); a thanksgiving (4–7); the body (8–20); travel talk (21–22); and final greetings and blessing (23–25).

That this is a communication between friends comes through in Paul's use of wordplay—for example, in his allusion to the literal meaning of the slave name Onesimus ("useful," v. 11) and to its sound (*onaimēn* = "profit," v. 20), and in the punning on "heart," sometimes meaning the *source* of affection (vv. 7 and 20) and sometimes the *object* of affection, Onesimus (vv. 12 and 20).

## Theological Themes and Meaning for Today

This letter has a specific purpose, to reconcile a fractured relationship between master and slave, and probably to free up Onesimus to join Paul's mission project. It is not a teaching letter. At the same time, the communication presumes and implies some profound theological themes. A Christian finds his or her identity first of all in being an adopted child of the ultimate Father, God, in being a servant of the ultimate Lord, Jesus, *and* in being brother or sister to all other Christians. This identity, which Paul refers to as being "in Christ," supersedes all other social roles, such as master and slave (as in 1 Cor 7:21–24). Paul's way of communicating here, both authoritative and loving, exemplifies a pastoral style that remains a perennial model for leadership in the Church.

# Outline of Paul's Letter to Philemon

It is reasonable enough to outline this brief letter more or less as the NABRE editors do, simply naming the conventional parts: Address and Greeting (1–3); Thanksgiving (4–7); Body (8–22); Final Greetings (23–25). This four-part division names the obvious segments. But other scholars, noticing recurrences of words and phrases, have sensed a more elaborate design connecting those segments. The most satisfying and fruitful one is the †chiastic structure described by John Paul Heil.[1]

A  Opening Address and Greeting (1–3)
   Paul begins with a framework of imprisonment and partnership under grace
  B  Thanksgiving (4–7)
     From love, Philemon's partnership can result in doing good for Christ
    C  Appeal (8–10)
       Paul appeals to Philemon for Onesimus
      D  Onesimus (11–13)
         Paul wanted to keep Onesimus, his heart, to serve on behalf of Philemon
        E  Philemon's consent (14), a "free-will offering"
           The good that Philemon can do in regard to Onesimus must be from benevolence

---

1. "The Chiastic Structure and Meaning of Paul's Letter to Philemon," *Biblica* 82 (2001): 178–206. Accessible online at www.bsw.org/Biblica/Vol-82-2001. For details regarding the verbal parallels that join the parallel members in the chiastic structure, see the article.

      D′ Philemon's beloved brother (15–17)

         Paul wants Philemon to welcome Onesimus as a beloved brother and partner

    C′ Philemon's debt to Paul (18–19)

      Paul wants Philemon to charge him for any debt Onesimus may owe

  B′ What Philemon will do (20–22)

    From obedience, Philemon will do good in benefiting Paul with Onesimus

A′ Closing Greetings (23–25)

  Paul closes with a framework of imprisonment and partnership under grace

# Paul's Letter to Philemon and Everyone Else at His House

This letter's brevity is an asset for students of Paul. Its shortness makes it easy to slow down and linger over each word—to listen carefully for Paul's implied meaning. If we take it seriously as an ancient letter and do our best to imagine the original situation, we will be surprised by what it says to us today. For anyone just beginning a serious study of Paul, it might help to think of it as a training letter, the study of which will provide preparation for reading other, lengthier pieces of Paul's correspondence.

When we struggle with the meaning of a word or phrase, we should first attend to the immediate context, that is, the rest of the letter at hand—in this case a mere twenty-five verses. But since we do learn something of Paul from his other letters, we will draw on whatever light they cast on Paul's style, vocabulary, and themes. There is, of course, the still fuller context of the Greco-Roman world of the first century AD to draw upon as well. For example, what scholars have learned about first-century slavery will also throw light on this ancient text about a master and his slave.

My sometimes-lengthy explanations of the elements of this very short letter may surprise you. My intent is to fully explain the Pauline expressions I know we will meet again in his other letters. Let us begin.

## Who's Writing to Whom? Where? (1–3)

¹Paul, a prisoner for Christ Jesus, and Timothy our brother, to Philemon, our beloved and our co-worker, ²to Apphia our sister, to Archippus our

Fig. 5. Cast of the corpse of slave (as evidenced by the manacles that remain on his ankles) found at the ruins of Pompeii from the Mt. Vesuvius eruption, 79 AD.

**fellow soldier, and to the church at your house. ³Grace to you and peace from God our Father and the Lord Jesus Christ.**

**OT:** Num 6:24–26
**NT:** Matt 12:46–50 // Mark 3:31–35 // Luke 8:19–21
**Catechism:** meaning of the title Christ, 436–40; meaning of Lord, 446–51

1      The first four words of the letter present our first translation challenge; **Paul** calls himself a **prisoner for Christ Jesus,** literally, "a prisoner *of* Christ Jesus," which is indeed the rendering of the JB, NJB, NIV, and NRSV. The literal rendering sounds like Paul is saying that Jesus has imprisoned him—which might appear to contradict Paul's celebration of Jesus as his liberator! The NABRE translation, "prisoner for Christ Jesus," is true enough, but may obscure some of Paul's meaning. Paul can also describe himself as a *"slave of* Jesus Christ" (Rom 1:1; Phil 1:1; see also Gal 1:10), and he uses this bold imagery to affirm his radical allegiance to and love for Jesus. As we will see, Paul is literally imprisoned in the *cause* of Jesus, but he also claims, in effect, "Jesus has captured me," reflecting a sentiment expressed explicitly in Phil 3:12: "I have indeed been taken possession of by Christ." One suspects that Paul deliberately chose an ambiguous phrase that would be open to the latter meaning.

Why does he include **Timothy** as a cosender of this letter? We know from the Acts of the Apostles that Timothy was a traveling companion and coworker of Paul; indeed, he is the sole *addressee* of two of the Pastoral Epistles (1 and 2 Timothy). Timothy is also named as coauthor of five other Pauline Letters (2 Cor 1:1; Phil 1:1; Col 1:1; 1 Thess 1:1; and 2 Thess 1:1). Since this letter will turn out to be primarily addressed to one individual, **Philemon,** mentioning a cosender may seem a needless addition. But as we will see, Paul means this message to be a rather public communiqué. And this well-known companion of Paul, **our brother** Timothy, serves as a weighty witness to the request Paul

---

## St. Ambrose on the Paradox of True Freedom

St. Ambrose of Milan, writing in the fourth century, caught the paradox of Paul's identification as "prisoner of Christ." To be "imprisoned" by Christ is to be bound to a master who liberates in that union. There is no other such Master to escape to.

> How many masters has one who runs from the one Lord. But let us not run from him. Who will run away from him whom they follow bound in chains, but willing chains, which loose and do not bind? Those who are bound with these chains boast and say: "Paul, a prisoner of Christ Jesus, and Timothy." It is more glorious for us to be bound by him than to be set free and loosed from others.

---

is about to make. It is possible, too, that Timothy is acting as Paul's scribe in the writing of this letter. Verse 19—"I, Paul, write this in my own hand: I will pay"—besides being an IOU note, may also indicate Paul's intervention in the physical writing process done by another hand.

When he calls Philemon **beloved** and **our co-worker**, Paul is more than simply acknowledging him as a colleague, the way we today might use "coworker" to refer to a person in the next office cubicle. For Paul, the mission of the Church is the *work of the Lord*. Indeed, he writes to the Corinthians, "If Timothy comes, see that he is without fear in your company for he is doing the work of the Lord" (1 Cor 16:10; literally, "for he *works the work* of the Lord"). "Coworker" is a name Paul reserves for those who have labored at the work of the Lord, that is, spreading the gospel—people like Aquila and Priscilla, Urbanus, Timothy (Rom 16:3, 9, and 21), Epaphroditus (Phil 2:25), Euodia, Syntyche, and Clement (Phil 4:2–3). So "coworker" here identifies Philemon as a key leader in the Christian mission.

Calling Apphia **our sister** is similar to calling Timothy "our brother." This is the kinship language with which members of the Christian community referred to one another. It is rooted in Jesus' way of referring to his disciples as his true family (see Mark 3:31–35). Paul calls Archippus **our fellow soldier**, the same epithet he uses for Epaphroditus (Phil 2:25), drawing on the metaphor of Christian mission as a battle, as in 2 Cor 10:3–6 and Eph 6:10–17.

Along with the three individuals named as addressees, Paul includes **the church at your house**. The word "church" here translates the Greek term *ekklēsia*, which in the New Testament always refers to a community, not a building. It

---

## Roman Custody: What Kind of Confinement for Paul?

When we twenty-first-century readers, schooled in the imagery of cops-and-robbers films and television crime shows, read Paul's references to being imprisoned, we readily picture him confined behind bars in something like a modern jail. This picture is anachronistic. Roman custody came in three versions. (a) The harshest form was confinement in a quarry or *carcer* (from which we derive our word "incarceration"). An abandoned quarry was typically a pit easily transformed into a place of confinement. This severe situation did not allow for ready access for visitors. (b) A more humane form of Roman confinement was *custodia militaris* ("military custody"). In this form of custody, confinement was ensured by the supervision of military personnel and, usually, chaining to the guard on duty. The location was a secondary consideration; it could be an ordinary dwelling. Paul's "house arrest" in Rome, described at the end of the Acts of the Apostles (Acts 28:16–31), is an example of military custody. (c) The third kind was *custodia libera* ("free custody"), where supervision was provided by nonmilitary personnel, sometimes even family, and chaining was not employed.

Given that Paul was a Roman citizen, and therefore likely to be treated with restraint (see Acts 16:35–39; 24:23; 27:3), and in regular communication with friends, he does not seem to be confined to a *carcer* (quarry). But since he refers regularly to being "in chains," he does not appear to be in *custodia libera*. Military custody, then, best describes his situation when he communicates with Philemon.[a]

a. Richard J. Cassidy, *Paul in Chains: Roman Imprisonment and the Letters of St. Paul* (New York: Crossroad, 2001), 37–43, 69–76.

---

shows up in our English words "ecclesiastical" and "ecclesial," and it has venerable Old Testament roots. In the Greek version of the Old Testament (the †Septuagint), *ekklēsia* translates the Hebrew word for the "assembly" of the people of Israel gathered for worship, especially at Mount Sinai and in the Jerusalem temple. So in the New Testament the very term implies that a Christian community is the gathered people of God. In Paul's writing, the word almost always refers to a particular local Christian community.

In whose house does this *ekklēsia* gather? We readers of the English translation might take **your** (in "your house") as referring to Philemon, Apphia, and Archippus, as if they were a family who owned the house. But the possessive pronoun is singular, not plural, in the Greek. That leaves the question, which

## The House Church in Early Christianity

**BIBLICAL BACKGROUND**

We noted that "the church at your house" refers to the community that gathers in Philemon's home. This is a helpful reminder that, in the early days of the Christian movement, Christian communities had not yet built special buildings in which to gather for worship. (These buildings eventually came to be called "churches.") Rather, they gathered in homes with a space large enough for a group to assemble.

How large a group a first-century-AD villa might accommodate, we can only guess from the available archaeological remains in eastern Mediterranean sites. Here is how one scholar summarizes the archaeological data from places like Corinth, Thessalonica, and Pompeii:

> If we averaged out these sizes, we would arrive at a villa with a *triclinium* [dining room] of some 36 square meters and an *atrium* of 55 square meters. If we removed all the couches from the *triclinium*, we would end up with space for perhaps 20 persons. If we included the atrium, minus any large decorative urns, we could expand the group to perhaps 50 persons, provided people did not move around, and some did not mind getting shoved into the shallow pool. The maximum comfortable group such a villa could accommodate would most likely be in the range of 30 to 40 persons.[a]

Such dimensions give us reason to picture the church that meets at Philemon's place as a community of some thirty-five persons. Luke gives us a glimpse of this practice when he describes the life of the early Jewish-Christian community in Jerusalem in Acts 2:46: "Every day they devoted themselves to meeting together in the temple area and to breaking bread in their homes." In his greetings to the Christian community in Rome, Paul refers to three such house churches in that city (Rom 16:5, 14, 15). The phrase "house church" refers not to the house but to the community that meets there.

a. Vincent Branick, *The House Church in the Writings of Paul* (Wilmington, DE: Michael Glazier, 1989), 39–40.

one of the three is the owner? Some scholars, noting that Archippus is the last person named before the reference to the house, take him to be the owner. But the fact that Paul names Philemon first and dubs him **co-worker** identifies *him* as the primary addressee and the owner of the house. As we will see, Philemon is also the leader of the community that meets at his house.

We might be tempted to bypass the greeting—**Grace to you** (plural) **and peace from God our Father and the Lord Jesus Christ**—as a pious formula of no particular importance. Yet for Paul the greeting is never mere convention. The usual salutation in a Greek letter in those days was simply "Greetings," as in the apostolic letter in Acts 15:23 and at the head of the Epistle of James. But

3

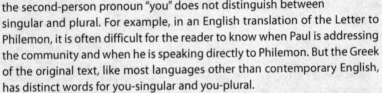

## "You" in Greek: Singular or Plural?

**BIBLICAL BACKGROUND**

In a classroom situation, when I say something like "Are you still with me?" the class does not know if I am addressing the whole class or if I am singling out the sleepy student in the third row. They need a contextual clue, like the focus of my eyes or a pointed finger, to understand how I mean "you." Similarly, when we read "you" in a letter of Paul or a saying of Jesus in the Gospels, it is sometimes not clear whether the speaker or writer is addressing an individual or a group. It is a peculiarity of modern English that the second-person pronoun "you" does not distinguish between singular and plural. For example, in an English translation of the Letter to Philemon, it is often difficult for the reader to know when Paul is addressing the community and when he is speaking directly to Philemon. But the Greek of the original text, like most languages other than contemporary English, has distinct words for you-singular and you-plural.

The Sermon on the Mount (Matt 5–7) provides another example of the importance of knowing whether the "you" in the text is individual or communal. Jesus' teaching takes on a fresh meaning when one learns that most of the "yous" in Matt 5–7 are plural, signaling that the speech is addressed to the community of those who follow Jesus.

When the context does not make it clear whether Paul addresses an individual or the whole community, this commentary will note whether Paul is using singular or plural "you."

Paul always Christianizes the conventional salutation, as he does here. **Grace** is the free gift of God by which Christians are saved, and **peace**, coming from this Jewish teacher, surely entails the Hebrew sense of *shalom*, the peace and fullness of life whose source is God. Paul may well be alluding to the priestly blessing of Numbers 6:24–26: "The LORD bless you and keep you! The LORD let his face shine upon you and be *gracious* to you! The LORD look upon you kindly and give you *peace*!"[1] That Paul speaks of "peace from . . . the Lord Jesus Christ" might well be heard as a deliberate contrast to the *pax Romana*, the imperial "peace" established coercively by the Lord Caesar. The Greek second-person pronoun is precise: Paul addresses his greeting to you-plural, that is, the church that meets in Philemon's house.

The titles for God and Jesus, **God our Father and the Lord Jesus Christ**, which we may hear as conventional formulas, also deserve our attention

1. Noted by Joseph A. Fitzmyer, *The Letter to Philemon: A New Translation with Introduction and Commentary*, Anchor Bible 34c (New York: Doubleday, 2000), 90.

here. For Paul, to call God "Father" was already part of his pre-Christian Jewish heritage; the Lord God is called "Father" some fifteen times in the Old Testament, though only rarely in direct address (Isa 63:16; 64:7). The paternal title takes on a fresh dimension for Christians; it seems to have been Jesus's habitual way of praying (see Mark 14:36, "Abba, Father"), the form of divine address he taught disciples in the Our Father (Matt 6:9; Luke 11:2), and the common Christian way of praying, even among Gentiles, to which Paul alludes in Rom 8:15 and Gal 4:6. Indeed, understanding God as Father grounds Jesus' own reference to his disciples as a new family of brothers and sisters (Matt 12:50). That background in Jesus' ministry and in the life of the early Church clarifies why Paul, and the early Church generally, uses the kinship language of brother and sister to describe the relationships of Christians to one another.

Paul's use of titles for **Jesus** also entails more than conventional formulas. **Christ** is the English transliteration of the Greek word *Christos*, which means "anointed one." "Christ" is therefore the equivalent of the Hebrew word *messiah*, which also means "anointed one." In Jewish tradition, the anointed one was God's special agent in the glorious events of the age to come. Some thought of the anointed one as a king descended from David; others, as a temple priest; still others as a "prophet like Moses" (see Deut 18:15–18). When the Christian tradition applies the title "Christ" or "Messiah" to Jesus, it acclaims him as the fulfillment of all these expectations, especially in the role of king. This is surely true in the case of Paul. He uses the title "Christ" in other letters where he emphasizes Jesus' fulfillment of the biblical promises of an anointed one, a royal agent of God who would lead a restored Israel (the twelve tribes reunited, as promised in Isa 49:5), the end-time people of God. Far from being a solitary figure, the messiah is a king who rules a people (see the oracle of Nathan in 2 Sam 7). That vision of a people united around, and even *in*, the Messiah is a crucial aspect of the message of this letter, which so emphasizes community. *Christos* occurs eight times in this brief document of twenty-five verses. It frames both the letter's opening and its final greeting, in each case with "Christ Jesus" at the beginning (vv. 1 and 23) and "the Lord Jesus Christ" at the end (vv. 3 and 25).[2]

---

2. Some scholars hold that when Paul writes to Gentiles, the title Christ devolves into something like a second name, with little emphasis on the Jewish tradition regarding the messiah. However, it should be noted that people in Greco-Roman culture placed great stock in antiquity. Living in such a culture, Paul's readers would have appreciated that Jesus fulfilled ancient prophecies. On this, see N. T. Wright, "*Christos* as 'Messiah' in Paul: Philemon 6," in *The Climax of the Covenant: Christ and the Law in Pauline Theology* (Minneapolis: Fortress, 1993), 41–55.

Finally, the inclusion of the title "Lord" with Jesus Christ has its own special importance. Occurring five times in the letter, "Lord" (*kyrios* in Greek)[3] translates the unspeakable name of God, in Hebrew †YHWH. To apply it to Jesus is to confess that he is divine. But there are other dimensions, obvious to ancient Greek speakers and readers but not obvious to contemporary readers of English translations: *Kyrios* meant "master" with reference to slaves, and it was also a title for the Roman emperor. We shall see that these dimensions of "Lord" pertain to the letter's message in powerful ways.

### Reflection and Application (1–3)

*The individual and the community.* One might not expect the address and greeting of a letter to warrant much reflection and pastoral application. But the exegesis above suggests that there is plenty in these first three verses to ponder and apply. First, there is Paul's sense of the network of relationships entailed in Christian community. Even in a message primarily addressed to an individual, Paul implies right from the start that the news of Onesimus's conversion and his request of Philemon are matters of interest to the whole community. In the shared life of the Christian community, which Paul elsewhere calls "the body of Christ," the quality of any relationship within that community has implications for the rest.

*Church as community and as edifice.* The fact that the word "church" (*ekklēsia*) applied first to the community and only later to a special building in which the community gathers can help us understand the relationship between community and architecture. Today we are likely to link the sacredness of a church building to the fact that the Lord is present there in the reserved Eucharist. This is a reasonable and valid connection, but the church space was considered sacred even before the practice of reserving the Eucharist developed.

Paul teaches that the community itself is the temple of the Holy Spirit (see 1 Cor 3:16–17; 2 Cor 6:16–18; and also Matt 16:18), and the building eventually called "church" was first understood to be sacred because it was the space that housed the temple of the community when it gathered for the celebration of the Lord's Supper (1 Cor 11:18–22).

When it became the practice of the church to reserve the Eucharist after the liturgy for distribution to the sick or to those who were otherwise unable

---

3. Some Catholics will be familiar with praying the Greek prayer *Kyrie eleison* in the Latin Mass. And the Kyrie is sometimes heard in musical settings at English-language Masses today.

to participate directly in the community's celebration of the Eucharist, that ongoing presence of the Lord added a further dimension to the sacredness of the building. This history and these realities are part of what warrants the primacy of altar and pulpit in churches and, in many churches, a separate space or chapel for the reservation of the Eucharist for the sacrament of the sick, and as a special space for prayer and meditation.

*The Church, a new family.* The repetition of titles for Jesus and the parity of the Lord Jesus Christ with God our Father as source of grace and peace serve to underscore what makes the *ekklēsia* a "household" or a new "family." A Christian community is never simply a group of like-minded individuals who decide to join together for a common purpose. The people gathered for worship are there in response to God's initiative. They are "called out" (the root sense of *ekklēsia*) through faith and incorporation into the people of the Messiah. That, and nothing less, is what makes them a community. That they call God "Father" is no accident of patriarchal culture but an affirmation of what makes them a new family united with the risen Son, Jesus. Jesus already anticipates this later reality in his ministry (Matt 12:50). This understanding of Christian community and its source form an important background for the message to follow in the Letter to Philemon.

These considerations have practical implications regarding how we think about "going to church," how we design churches, and how we respond to varieties of church architecture. (1) The process of gathering to celebrate Eucharist is never simply a matter of convenience or efficiency—for example, a single Mass serving the maximum number of people. To gather for Mass is to enact the reality that in the celebration of the Lord's Supper we are indeed being "called out" at the initiative of God the Father to join his Son in serving him together in the Spirit. (2) Attention to the physical structure that houses the church, which is the community, can help our worship. Finding ourselves in a church building whose structure gives us a sense of being joined as one to focus ahead helps us respond to a transcendent God, one who calls us to stretch beyond ourselves and our immediate concerns to relate to the Source of all, whom we cannot see. And when we worship in a structure—a half circle, say, or in the round—we are reminded that the community itself is the new temple and that Jesus the incarnate Word is Emmanuel, God with us, and that we are indeed the body of Christ. Whether the architecture emphasizes the transcendent or immanent aspect of the eucharistic liturgy, we do well to respond to the truth that it conveys and appreciate what it says rather than criticize it for what our taste may find wanting.

## Thanksgiving, with a Rhetorical Purpose (4–7)

[4]I give thanks to my God always, remembering you [singular] in my prayers, [5]as I hear of the love and the faith you have in the Lord Jesus and for all the holy ones, [6]so that your partnership in the faith may become effective in recognizing every good there is in us that leads to Christ. [7]For I have experienced much joy and encouragement from your love, because the hearts of the holy ones have been refreshed by you, brother.

OT: Deut 28:9
NT: 2 Cor 7:13–15; Eph 4:12–13
Catechism: prayer of thanksgiving, 2637–38; Christian holiness, 2013–14; saints, 823

4–5     Even though Paul has joined himself with Timothy as cosender, has included the whole community in his address and greeting, and will allude to still others who are somehow privy to this communication, he moves right to I-you language in the singular as he begins the thanksgiving: **I give thanks to my God always, remembering you** (singular) **in my prayers.** This Paul-to-Philemon communiqué introduces the main business of the letter, which the rest of the community is meant to overhear. All of the "yous" in the thanksgiving are singular—the only cue for the non-Greek reader being "brother" in verse 7—and pertain to Philemon. Paul has heard about Philemon's **love and faith** both toward Jesus and toward his fellow Christians—"faith," of course, pertaining to **the Lord Jesus** and "love" toward Jesus but especially toward **all the holy ones.**

That last phrase, also commonly translated "the saints" (RSV, NIV, NRSV, and JB), is an expression Paul often uses in his letters, not referring to exceptional persons but to all members of the local church. "The holy ones," or "the saints," is a term used in the †Septuagint (the Greek Old Testament) to refer to the covenant people of God as a whole. They are "holy" not necessarily in exemplary behavior but as a people dedicated to, in the sense of "set apart for," the service of God. This meaning reflects the word's original use in the context of Israel's liturgy, for example in Exodus 19:6, "You will be to me a kingdom of priests, a holy nation" (spoken at Sinai), and Deut 7:6, "You are a holy people to the LORD, your God; the LORD, your God, has chosen you from all the peoples on the face of the earth to be a people specially his own."

Although it is God who chooses and sets apart a people for himself, to be called "holy" implies a moral challenge, as shown in Deut 28:9 LXX: "The Lord will raise you up for himself a holy people, as he swore to your ancestors, if you will hear the voice of the Lord your God and go in his ways." Along with other New Testament authors, Paul uses the term to refer to any and all baptized

Christians. The best rendering of the phrase "all the holy ones" may well be "all God's dedicated people," which catches both the passive idea of being set aside for a divine purpose and the consequent ethical challenge to live according to that purpose.[4] The phrasing of the sentence implies that Philemon loves and believes in the people of his community just as he loves and believes in Christ Jesus.

With verse 6 Paul's prayer moves from thanksgiving to petition. The blessing he prays for Philemon could be translated "that the sharing of your faith may become effective" (NRSV), but I find the rendering of the NABRE more consonant with the thrust of the letter: **so that your partnership in the faith may become effective.** For, as we will see, the substance of the letter has more to do with Philemon's *living* the fullness of the community's shared faith than with the *communication* of his personal faith to the community.

The adjective translated "effective" (*energēs*) is wonderfully apt. A rare word (used in the New Testament only here and in 1 Cor 16:9 and Heb 4:12), *energēs* connects with the term *synergos* ("coworker"), with which Paul honored Philemon in the prescript and which Paul will use again to describe his companions in the closing (v. 24). *Energēs* is also a reminder that Paul and Philemon are both involved in the work (*ergon*) of God. What Paul is about to ask Philemon to do will further that work, enabling the faith that he shares to become truly *energēs*.[5] This kind of verbal echo speaks more to the ear than to the eye.

And just how is Philemon's effective participation in the faith to show itself? Paul prays that it will be effective **in recognizing every good there is in us that leads to Christ.** If that language comes across as a rather vague prayer, it is because this is the NABRE's solution to a phrase that has constantly stymied translators. A literal rendering of the last phrase would be "in recognition of every good in us *toward Christ* [*eis Christon*]." Compare:

the acknowledgement of every good work that is in you in Christ Jesus.

Douay-Rheims

so that you will have a full understanding of every good thing we have in Christ.

NIV

when you perceive all the good that we may do for Christ.

NRSV

<hr/>

4. The phrase "all God's dedicated people" is the happy solution of Fitzmyer's translation in *Letter to Philemon*, 93.

5. Note the relationship of *energēs* to our words "energy" and "energetic."

may come to expression in full knowledge of all the good we can do for Christ.

NJB

The main problem here is unpacking what is implied in the simple word *eis*, which can mean "toward" or "with respect to" or "in honor of" or "for the sake of." It seems to me that the most satisfying solution is to translate the phrase as "toward Christ," taking it as shorthand for the building up of Christ's body, the church—the end-time people of God that Christ has inaugurated through his life, death, and resurrection.[6] This process is later spelled out in Eph 4:12–13, which describes the purpose of the gifted roles within the community: "to equip the holy ones for the work of ministry, for building up the body of Christ, until we all attain to the unity of faith and knowledge of the Son of God, to mature manhood, to the extent of the full stature of Christ." What Paul is about to ask of Philemon in verses 8–14 will exemplify precisely the kind of community-building that should come from his gifts as leader of the church that meets at his house. Paul, in other words, is about to request that Philemon recognize "the good" they have "toward Christ" (that is, toward the further growth of Christ's body, the church) in the new convert Onesimus.

7        **For I have experienced much joy and encouragement from your love.** This reference to Philemon's effective leadership—his joy and encouragement—indicates Paul's motivation in his prayer for Philemon. Paul affirms the way Philemon has built up this community; and he will ask of him another expression of that gifted leadership.

Paul brings his praise of Philemon to a climax by saying **the hearts of the holy ones have been refreshed by you, brother.** Paul's wording is a bit gutsier than the English overtones of "heart-refreshing" imply. The word translated "hearts," *splanchna*, literally means "innards" or "bowels," and was used in the Greek Old Testament to name the seat of emotions, especially compassion (e.g., Prov 12:10; see 2 Cor 7:15 for a New Testament example). The KJV and the Douay-Rheims both have "bowels of the saints" here. But since the biblical imagery has to do with feelings and not the gastrointestinal references evoked today by the words "guts" and "bowels," contemporary translators rightly choose "heart," which catches the meaning nicely. Aware of the strength of this earthy image, Paul will use it playfully two more times in this brief and personal letter.

6. This is the solution offered by N. T. Wright in "*Christos* as 'Messiah' in Paul." Wright's point is that "Christ/Messiah" always entails the end-time people of God over which the Anointed One reigns.

## The Septuagint

The Septuagint is the name of the Greek translation of the Old Testament made around 250 BC for use in the Greek-speaking Jewish Diaspora—the scattering of Jews throughout the eastern Mediterranean world. The name Septuagint, from the Latin for seventy, alludes to the legend that the translation was made by seventy translators, who, working independently, turned the Hebrew Scriptures into seventy identical versions in Greek. The Septuagint was the main version of the Scriptures used by the Greek-speaking church and also, therefore, the version mainly used by the writers of the New Testament. Consequently, the words of the New Testament, including of course the Letters of Paul, often derive shades of meaning from how they are used in the Septuagint. As a result, the Septuagint actually functions as our best dictionary for New Testament Greek. That is why this commentary sometimes refers to the use of a particular word in the Septuagint. We have already had occasion to profit from the Septuagint in our treatment of the words for "church," "work," "holy ones," and "heart." The sign "LXX" (the Roman numeral for seventy) refers to the Septuagint.

Most editions of the Septuagint contain seven books not contained in the Hebrew Bible—Tobit, Judith, Wisdom, Sirach, Baruch, 1 and 2 Maccabees, plus some additions to Daniel and Esther. The Church accepted these books as Scripture by the fourth century, a reality reaffirmed formally at the Council of Trent. The main reason that Catholic Bibles are longer than most Protestant ones is that Martin Luther, when he made his translation into German, chose not to include in the main body of his translation the seven Greek books that do not have counterparts in the Hebrew Bible. He left them for others to translate and gave them the now-familiar title "Apocrypha," holding them "not equal to the Scriptures, but useful and good to read."

## Reflection and Application (4–7)

As in the case of the address and greeting of this letter, when he comes to the epistolary convention of the thanksgiving, Paul manages to infuse this standard element with Christian feeling and purpose. From the first word, *eucharistō* ("I give thanks"), Paul reminds his readers, including us, that thanksgiving is the very foundation of our faith and relationship to God and one another. For us, as well as for our Jewish ancestors, gratitude for what God has first done for us is the primary motive for our own actions. That is as true of the New Covenant as it was of the first one. Indeed, since the early centuries we have called our celebration of the Lord's Supper "the Eucharist," that is, "thanksgiving." When we want to refresh our motivation as we make our way to participate in the weekly or daily Eucharist, a simple and effective way is to ask oneself, "What am I especially grateful for today?"—and then to make one's participation in the liturgy an expression of that gratitude.

Paul's way of summing up Philemon's pastoral leadership with the striking phrase "you have refreshed the hearts"—or even more strikingly, "refreshed the bowels"—"of the holy ones" is a reminder that good leadership in the community of faith, whether on the level of church or family, is not simply a matter of providing direction and a sense of order. Ideally, it will be deserving of that stunning description. Have I refreshed the hearts of my congregation? Have I refreshed—with affection, affirmation, and encouragement—the hearts of my family or my friends or my coworkers or my clients or my students or my customers?

## I Return Your Onesimus, a Changed Man (8–14)

[8]Therefore, although I have the full right in Christ to order you to do what is proper, [9]I rather urge you out of love, being as I am, Paul, an old man, and now also a prisoner for Christ Jesus. [10]I urge you on behalf of my child Onesimus, whose father I have become in my imprisonment, [11]who was once useless to you but is now useful to [both] you and me. [12]I am sending him, that is, my own heart, back to you. [13]I should have liked to retain him for myself, so that he might serve me on your behalf in my imprisonment for the gospel, [14]but I did not want to do anything without your consent, so that the good you do might not be forced but voluntary.

OT: Num 15:3; Sir 33:30–31
NT: 1 Cor 4:15; 7:20–24; 9:12–23
Catechism: slavery, 2414; human equality, 1934–38

8    The word **therefore** is a clear signal that the contents of the thanksgiving—that is, the qualities of Philemon's leadership and of the community that he has nurtured—are the things that encourage Paul to make his request. The thanksgiving was not a mere pleasantry but a preparation for what he is about to say.

Paul alludes to a **right** to **order** Philemon, but claims he will *not* use it. The word for "right" (*parrēsia*) is rare in Paul's writing and refers more to confidence and boldness than to the right that underlies that attitude (NRSV has "although I am bold enough"). And the word for "order" is a strong one, used in the New Testament mainly for Jesus' commanding of demons (e.g., Mark 1:27;

9:25) and only here in Paul's writings. Where does Paul get this confidence to order Philemon to do the right thing? The most likely answer is that Paul was instrumental in Philemon's Christian conversion and mentored him in Christian leadership. Further, while he could claim his authority as an apostle (see Rom 1:1; 1 Cor 1:1; 2 Cor 1:1; Gal 1:1), he chooses not to exploit the power of this relationship as he makes his request. Paul expresses the same attitude in a more developed way in 1 Cor 9:12–23, where he explains why he does not insist on his "rights" as an apostle but chooses rather to make himself "a slave to all" (v. 19; and see 1 Thess 2:6–8).

**I rather urge you out of love.** Rather than pull rank Paul elects to lean on   **9** his relationship with Philemon as a fellow Christian. But he also enlists the emotional appeal of his condition as **a prisoner for** (literally, "of") **Christ Jesus**, repeating what he said in verse 1. His characterization of himself as **an old man** underscores the indignity of his confinement, and possibly his seniority over Philemon. "Old man" evokes for us twenty-first-century Western readers someone in his eighties or nineties, but scholars note that in the Greco-Roman world the word *presbytēs* could refer to someone between fifty and fifty-six years of age.[7]

At last Paul introduces the name of the person who will be the subject of his   **10–11** request—**Onesimus**. The original addressees would have recognized the name of a member of Philemon's household. Even those who did not know the man would have recognized the name, which means "useful," as a common slave moniker. It is much like the name Onesiphorus (2 Tim 1:16; 4:19), which means "profit-bearing."[8] Paul describes Onesimus as **my child . . . whose father I have become in my imprisonment** (or "while I was in chains," NIV). Having heard Paul describe his relationships with fellow Christians with similar metaphors in verses 1–2—"brother," "sister," "fellow soldier"—we are not surprised to hear "my child" and "whose father I have become" as another figure of speech. Indeed, Paul speaks elsewhere in his letters of his paternal role in the new birth of Christian conversion. A good example is 1 Cor 4:15: "Even if you should have countless guides to Christ, yet you do not have many fathers, for I became your father in Christ Jesus through the gospel."

This Christian conversion of the slave Onesimus has wonderful implications, which Paul proceeds to describe in a marvelous bit of wordplay, when he refers to Onesimus as the one **who was once useless** (*achrēston*) **to you but is now**

---

7. Fitzmyer (*Philemon*, 105) cites this example from Philo but notes other instances that use the word of older persons.

8. Fitzmyer (*Philemon*, 107) supplies other examples of slave names: *Karpos* (= fruit[ful]), *Chrēstos* (= good, profitable), and *Symphoros* (= suitable, profitable).

**useful** (*euchrēston*) **to [both] you and me.** There are two kinds of wordplay here. First, Paul alludes to the literal meaning of the name: Your man Useful became quite useless to you while absent from your household; but now I'm sending him back to you as truly useful. Second, those who heard the letter read aloud would have noticed a pun in the contrast between *a-chrēston* and *eu-chrēston*. For these words can sound like *a-Christon* and *eu-Christon*, which can be heard as "not-Christ-ed" and "well-Christ-ed"; that is, Onesimus was previously without Christ, but now he has become a Christian.

How is Onesimus useful to Paul? Possibly, he served as a messenger and "gofer" for the confined Paul. Further, Paul may be alluding to the service Onesimus may provide in the future as fellow evangelist, should Philemon take the hint and emancipate his slave.

12–13      **I am sending him, that is, my own heart, back to you.** Paul has already called Onesimus his child. Now he refers to him as his "heart," which again translates the word *splanchna*, the strong intestinal image he used above in complimenting Philemon for refreshing the *splanchna* of the holy ones (v. 7).[9] So in this clever word choice, Paul manages (a) to assert his bond of affection for Onesimus and (b) to suggest that Philemon should extend to this new Christian Onesimus the pastoral care he typically extends to the community in his house church.

The expression "to send back" seems to say that Philemon had first *sent* Onesimus to him, though the remainder of the letter suggests otherwise. Notice Paul's gentle and affectionate arm-twisting here. Paul knows full well that Philemon did not send the slave, but he also knows that Philemon would do anything for him—for Paul—to whom he owes his salvation. Perhaps with a touch of humor and irony, Paul is speaking as if Philemon actually sent Onesimus as a help in his imprisonment. The whole letter presupposes a deep affection between Paul and Philemon.

14      With the mention of **the good** that Paul is about to ask of him, we now see that "the good" he was praying that Philemon would "recognize" in verse 6 pertains to a concrete deed he is about to request. And he is careful to state that he wants Philemon's **consent** so that the good he does **might not be forced but voluntary.** The phrase that "voluntary" translates is *kata hekousion*, which carries a significant connotation from its use in the Greek Old Testament. Occurring only here in the New Testament, *hekousios* is used twelve times in the Septuagint, mainly in reference to the kind of temple sacrifice known as a "free-will offering" (e.g., Lev 7:16; 23:38; Num 15:3; 29:39). Paul's use of the phrase here, then, may well be an allusion to that temple sacrifice, so that

9. The Douay-Rheims version renders the sentence, "And do thou receive him as my own bowels."

Paul's final clause in verse 14 might be rendered, "not by compulsion but as a free-will offering," implying he knows it would be a sacrifice for Philemon to free an able-bodied slave who has not yet completed his peak years of service.[10] Verse 14 sits at the center of Heil's chiastic outline, which suggests that Paul has chosen to use this rare phrase quite deliberately. The sacrificial connotation also supports the idea that Paul is not here making an ethical argument about the institution of slavery. He is asking Philemon to sacrifice a legal right in order to serve the Christian mission.

## Finally, the Request (15–20)

[15]Perhaps this is why he was away from you for a while, that you might have him back forever, [16]no longer as a slave but more than a slave, a brother, beloved especially to me, but even more so to you, as a man and in the Lord. [17]So if you regard me as a partner, welcome him as you would me. [18]And if he has done you any injustice or owes you anything, charge it to me. [19]I, Paul, write this in my own hand: I will pay. May I not tell you that you owe me your very self. [20]Yes, brother, may I profit from you in the Lord. Refresh my heart in Christ.

**NT:** Rom 8:14–17; 12:4–5; 1 Cor 7:22; Gal 3:28
**Catechism:** slavery, 2414

The delicate ambiguity in the expression "I am sending him back" continues    **15–17** in verse 15: **Perhaps this is why he was away from you for a while.** The verb for "was away" can be rendered either actively ("went away," in this case imply-ing an illegal departure) or passively ("was separated," a euphemistic way of referring to the absence)—which the vagueness of "was away" captures well. The passive option leaves room for the interpretation that the separation was a matter of divine providence, as if God had good things in mind when he al-lowed this separation to occur.[11]

Paul's statement of the consequence that Philemon **might have** Onesimus **back forever** is wonderfully ironic. On the one hand, Paul knows full well that, if his request succeeds, Philemon will lose the service of his slave Onesimus.

10. Several scholars have noted the Septuagint background of this phrase, but John Paul Heil, in *The Letters of Paul as Rituals of Worship* (Eugene, OR: Wipf and Stock, 2011), 98–99, was apparently the first to draw the inference that Paul means Philemon would be making a free-will offering to God by allowing Onesimus to return to Paul.

11. So Fitzmyer, *Philemon*, 112, compares Paul's statement to that of Joseph to his brothers, who had sold him into slavery in Egypt: "God sent me here before you to preserve life" (Gen 45:5).

But on the other hand, now that the slave is his brother in Christ, he will indeed have that relationship with him forever.

Most commentators over the centuries have considered Onesimus a runaway slave on the presumption, apparently, that a slave away from his master's household is de facto a runaway, with no plan to return. However, it is unlikely that a man who wanted to entirely escape the control of a slave master would present himself to a close friend of that master. Further, given the qualities of Philemon and of the community that meets regularly in his house, and given that the slave has not simply left his master but has deliberately sought Paul out, there is another possible scenario: that he has had some kind of falling out with Philemon and has sought Paul out, as a friend of his master, to mediate a reconciliation.[12] The letter does not provide enough information to warrant a definitive judgment on this question, but this scenario seems to make better sense of the text than the runaway hypothesis.

In verse 16 Paul twice uses the word **slave** (*doulos*) of Onesimus (the only time he does so in this letter), thereby affirming what the slave name already implied. Onesimus is still legally Philemon's slave, but he has recently received an identity that transcends, without eliminating, that legal status. By virtue of his baptism into Christ Jesus, Onesimus has now become Philemon's **brother** in Christ. This single word carries a powerfully countercultural principle: baptism into Christ creates an identity that transcends all forms of social and cultural discrimination. Paul develops this principle elsewhere and in a variety of ways (Rom 8:14–17; 12:4–5; 1 Cor 7; Gal 3:28).

The phrase **as a man** (literally "in the flesh") raises the possibility for some interpreters that Onesimus was Philemon's blood brother. But that Philemon would have enslaved his blood brother is hardly likely. A more plausible meaning is this: Onesimus was already **beloved** "in the flesh" in the sense that he was a favored slave of Philemon; but now he is beloved as a brother **in the Lord**.

**So if you regard me as a partner, welcome him as you would me.** Some scholars take "partner" (*koinōnon*) to be a clue that Paul was some kind of business partner. The word seems to have that meaning in Luke 5:10, where it refers to partners in a fishing business, but it is a word Paul uses for fellow missioners (see 2 Cor 8:23, in which he calls Titus his "partner" and "co-worker"), as in the case of Philemon in verses 1 and 17. This understanding of partner (*koinōnos*) links nicely with the prayer about Philemon's "partnership [*koinōnia*] in the faith" in verse 6. For Paul, *koinōnos* has a much richer meaning than "partner"

---

12. See Fitzmyer (*Philemon*, 20–23) for a discussion of first-century texts that acknowledge cases of such *amicus domini* ("friend of the master") intercessions for an errant slave.

usually carries in our vocabulary. Now that Onesimus, too, is a partner in the faith that Philemon already shares with Paul, the master should welcome the slave as he would welcome Paul. This is another example of Paul's careful choice of words. Of course Philemon would roll out the red carpet for Paul. For Philemon to welcome the errant slave in this way, however, would be a shockingly countercultural exercise in hospitality. And that, it seems, is exactly what Paul intends.

In a very explicit way, Paul takes responsibility for any debt Onesimus has **18** incurred with Philemon: **And if he has done you any injustice or owes you anything, charge it to me.** Exactly *how* Onesimus has done injustice to Philemon or has incurred a debt has been a topic of speculation. Did Onesimus steal something—a vase, say—to sell to provide himself with bread for the road? Or might Paul be referring to the fact that a slave who has taken off from his master's household for whatever reason has stolen many days of work from his master? Possibly the slave has caused some damage on the job and now seeks Paul's mediation as a trusted friend of his master. Whatever the damage, Paul promises to cover it: **I will pay.**

Declaring **in [his] own hand** his promise to pay, Paul may be simply affirm- **19** ing that he is indeed the writer of the letter, including this specific promise. But it is also possible that he here interrupts the writing of a scribe, who has been taking dictation, and now scribbles verse 19 in his own hand. Recall that in the Letter to the Romans, Paul can name himself as the "author" of the letter (Rom 1:1), but in the series of greetings that ends the letter, a certain Tertius can describe himself as the one who has "written" it (16:22). In any case, this personalized promise turns the letter into what we call an IOU. Whatever its legal status within the customs of the day, this statement would surely have taken on a kind of testimonial value when read to the assembled community gathered at Philemon's place. One can sense more friendly irony here, as if Philemon would ever dream of making the great Apostle, his father in faith, pay the debt incurred by his slave!

In reminding Philemon that he owes Paul his **very self,** Paul lays it on thick, harking back to the relationship he first alluded to in verse 8: that he has the confidence to *command* Philemon to do what is right, that is, the authority that comes from being his Christian mentor and catechist, his father in the faith.

Paul draws his persuasion to a conclusion with yet one more punning refer- **20** ence to the slave's name. When he says **may I profit from you in the Lord,** he uses a rare verb, *onaimēn* (occurring only here in the New Testament), which resonates with the sound and meaning of the name Onesimus, which had already prompted wordplay in verse 11. In addition, when he says **refresh my heart in Christ**, he echoes the two previous uses of that strong image (*splanchna*: "innards, bowels, heart"), applied first to Philemon's pastoral care of the church that meets at his house in verse 7 ("the hearts of the holy ones have been refreshed by you") and then to Paul's own affection for Onesimus in verse 12 (calling the slave "my own heart"). Thus, when he says, "Refresh my heart in Christ," he is referring both to Onesimus and himself, thereby paralleling what he said in verse 17, "Welcome him as you would me." The phrase "in Christ" is a gentle reminder that the context for Paul's request and Philemon's expected response is their union in Christ and his Church.

### Reflection and Application (8–20)

*Why didn't Paul condemn the institution of slaveholding?* Why didn't Paul simply state that the ownership of human beings is intrinsically wrong and unacceptable, especially for Christians? This question arises quite spontaneously from readers of this letter today. This is because we happen to live at a moment in history when the majority of the world has come to a consensus that the ownership of one human being by another is a violation of human rights, even though various kinds of criminal enslavement still survive in our day (for example, the trafficking of women and children for sexual exploitation and enforced labor). It should be noted that, even though the New Testament does not deal with the institution of slavery as such, the scriptural teaching of the inherent dignity of the human person was nevertheless largely responsible for the change of attitude toward slaveholding, especially during the nineteenth century.[13]

In the Roman Empire of the first century AD, slavery was simply an accepted fact of life. It has been estimated that in the urban populations of the eastern Mediterranean, roughly a third were slaves (most commonly debtors, booty from war, or children born to slaves), another third freedmen (having worked off debt, or been manumitted—typically by the time they were thirty, when they could become citizens), and the remaining third freeborn. Faced with this reality, the members of the early Christian movement, perhaps a few

---

13. Papal teaching against slavery involving kidnapping and sale of persons began with Pope Eugene IV, *Sicut Dudum* (1435), and continued through the following centuries. The popes condemned not only the slave trade but also this kind of slavery itself, although they did allow for "just title" enslavement, which included forms of indentured servitude. See Joel S. Panzer, *The Popes and Slavery* (New York: Alba House, 1996). The popes' teaching was widely ignored and misrepresented, but it did ultimately have an effect.

# Church Teaching on Slavery

The *Catechism of the Catholic Church* (formally approved by Pope John Paul II June 25, 1992) is straightforward in its condemnation of slavery:

> The seventh commandment forbids acts or enterprises that for any reason—selfish or ideological, commercial, or totalitarian—lead to the *enslavement of human beings*, to their being bought, sold and exchanged like merchandise, in disregard for their personal dignity. It is a sin against the dignity of persons and their fundamental rights to reduce them by violence to their productive value or to a source of profit. St. Paul directed a Christian master to treat his Christian slave "no longer as a slave but more than a slave, as a beloved brother, . . . both in the flesh and in the Lord." (*Catechism*, 2414)

In the context of clearly asserting the evil of slavery, the authors of the *Catechism* refer to Paul's Letter to Philemon, because Paul's implied request for Onesimus's freedom highlights the slave's dignity; but it took centuries before people in general, and the Church in particular, came to a broad consensus regarding the immorality of slavery as a social structure. Indeed, the very concept of social structures as human constructs is a modern insight. Nowhere in this letter does Paul address the ethical issue of slavery as an institution. Philemon could respond to Paul's implied request by releasing Onesimus as an exception—indeed, a free-will offering—while retaining other slaves, if he had them. Paul emphasizes this slave's baptism, not simply his human dignity, as what makes him a brother.

The history of Christian practice and teaching regarding slavery is a good illustration of the development of doctrine. While aspects of the Old Testament laws on slavery mitigated somewhat the laws and customs around slavery in the ancient Near East, nothing in the Scriptures would have prompted Paul to challenge the institution of slavery per se as he encountered it in the Roman Empire. It was simply part of an apparently permanent social fabric.

Regarding the Church's approach to slavery in the development of moral doctrine, Pope John Paul II, in another context, makes an interesting observation. In his discussion of Paul's teaching on spousal relationships (*mutual submission, not simply wife to husband*) in the cultural context of first-century patriarchy, the pope observes:

> Saint Paul not only wrote: "In Christ Jesus . . . there is no more man or woman," but also wrote: "There is no more slave or freeman" [Gal 3:28]. Yet how many generations were needed for such a principle to be realized in the history of humanity through the abolition of slavery! And what is one to say of the many forms of slavery to which individuals and peoples are subjected, which have not yet disappeared from history? (*Mulieris dignitatem*, 24 [Aug. 15, 1988])

Just as Paul could teach that the new family relationships within the Christian community trump the conventional gender roles of the larger culture without at the same time challenging the patriarchal family structure in the culture of the Roman Empire, so he could advocate a Christian way of being master and slave without directly confronting the imperial institution of slavery itself.

thousand in all (including slaves) at the time of Paul's career (mainly the 50s), would not have thought it possible to alter this basic institution of the empire.

For Paul and his disciples, it was already a countercultural and revolutionary thing that members of the Christian community should treat one another as equals despite their respective places in society. This conviction is reflected in Paul's statement about the equality and unity of the baptized in Gal 3:28: "There is neither Jew nor Greek, there is neither slave nor free person, there is not male and female; for you are all one in Christ Jesus." For a fuller elaboration of this principle, see 1 Cor 7:17–23; Col 3:11.

As surprising as it may seem to us twenty-first-century readers, for Paul the important issue in the relationship between Philemon and Onesimus is not slavery but baptism. The issue is not that one is master and the other his slave; it is rather that, now that Onesimus has become a fellow Christian, they are brothers in Christ. That membership in the *koinōnia* ("communion") of the new family does not change the legal master-slave status of each before the Roman law, but it transcends that legal relationship, whether Onesimus is freed or not.

*In writing to a slaveholder without condemning slavery itself, is Paul, in this letter to Philemon, sending a false message to today's readers?* Only if today's reader ignores Church teaching. This question demonstrates well the value of the Catholic insistence that Scripture requires Tradition to be properly understood. The sidebar on Church doctrine and slavery adverts to the Catechism and Pope John Paul II on this issue. Much more can be said about the Church's contemporary awareness of both the utter incompatibility of slavery with the dignity of human beings, as well as the persistence of slavery in today's world. For example, the Compendium of the Social Doctrine of the Church (2003) laments, "The solemn proclamation of human rights is contradicted by a painful reality of violations, wars and violence of every kind, in the first place, genocides and mass deportations, the spreading on a virtual worldwide dimension of ever new forms of slavery, such as trafficking in human beings, child soldiers, the exploitation of workers . . . prostitution" (section 158).[14]

*Love of fellow Christians, a special duty?* This letter, which presents an example of a specific relationship in the early Church, highlights a perennial Christian reality: as baptized Christians, we have a special relationship with all other baptized Christians. Jesus' command to love our neighbor as ourselves is a call

---

14. The Office to Monitor and Combat Trafficking in Persons of the US State Department provides an overview of contemporary types of slavery (http://www.state.gov/j/tip/). The International Labor Organization of the UN estimates that there are at least 12 million persons in some form of slavery around the world.

to *universal* love, especially as understood in the light of the call to love enemies (Matt 5:44–48) and the good Samaritan parable (Luke 10:25–37). But Paul is careful to emphasize that, within that call to universal love, there is a special call to care for fellow Christians, much as the love command is phrased in the Gospel of John: "I give you a new commandment: Love one another. As I have loved you, so you also should love one another. This is how all will know that you are my disciples, if you have love for one another" (John 13:34–35). It can come as a surprise that we have a special obligation to love our fellow Christians. If this seems to privilege a kind of group selfishness, we need simply reflect on how much easier it is to relate to *like*-minded people *outside* of our community of faith than it is to relate to those of our community with whom we differ.

## Conclusion: Final Request (Hinted), Greetings, Blessing (21–25)

[21]**With trust in your compliance I write to you, knowing that you will do even more than I say. [22]At the same time prepare a guest room for me, for I hope to be granted to you through your prayers. [23]Epaphras, my fellow prisoner in Christ Jesus, greets you, [24]as well as Mark, Aristarchus, Demas, and Luke, my co-workers. [25]The grace of the Lord Jesus Christ be with your spirit.**

**NT:** 2 Cor 11:23–25; Col 4:7–17
**Catechism:** prayer of intercession, 2634–36

The word behind **compliance** is a weighty term in the New Testament usu-　**21–22** ally rendered "obedience." Used in the New Testament mainly by Paul, it refers most frequently to obedience to God and God's commands (Rom 5:19; 6:16; 15:18; 16:19) or to God's chosen representatives (2 Cor 7:15; 10:6; and here in Philem 21). So, for all his talk of preferring not to command but rather to "urge" Philemon "out of love," Paul reveals here that he is in fact expecting obedience. At this point in the letter, however, it is clear that Philemon's compliance is not simply to Paul but to the larger community in Christ and to the mutual love that this new family entails.

But exactly what action does this obedience require of Philemon? First, Paul's mandate that Philemon welcome Onesimus as he would welcome Paul implies at least that the master not punish his slave, either physically or financially. Second, Paul's desire in verse 13 that Onesimus "serve" (*diakoneō*) him (Paul) raises the possibility that he would like Useful to help him in ministry (*diakonia*)—a usefulness that was unavailable before the slave's Christian conversion. Third, the **even more** that he *knows* Philemon **will do** is most likely the early release of the slave, probably to serve Paul in his work of evangelization. Since it was common in the first-century Roman Empire for slaves to be manumitted eventually, when their usefulness diminished with age, the implied request is that he be released soon rather than later. The "even more" picks up on the sacrificial "good" that Paul had requested in verse 14.

**At the same time prepare a guest room for me.** Paul's request for eventual hospitality in Philemon's household exerts a further personal pressure on the primary addressee: Paul will have the opportunity to check up on Philemon's obedience—or failure to comply—regarding the explicit and implicit requests in this letter. By using the plural "you"—**for I hope to be granted to you** (plural) **through your** (plural) **prayers**—Paul refers again to the ecclesial context of this communication. Paul's release from prison and future personal presence with them is a matter for community intercessory prayer. The phrase "to be granted to you" is an example of the "divine passive," meaning that God is the one doing the granting. This way of putting it acknowledges that every good thing in the Christian life can be understood as a matter of divine providence.

**23–24**    Whether or not Paul intends it, his inclusion of greetings from five other named Christians puts yet further persuasive pressure on Philemon: these men, apparently well known and respected by Philemon and household—otherwise why mention them?—are party to Paul's now increasingly public request to Philemon. The particular names in this list of greeters hold special interest for

---

## Paul's Way of Pastoral Practice as *Imitatio Dei*

The early Christian commentator Origen saw in Paul's gentle way of pastoring nothing less than an imitation of God:

> God does not tyrannize but rules, and when he rules, he does not coerce but encourages. He wishes that those under him yield themselves willingly to his direction, so that one may do good not out of compulsion but out of his free will. This is what Paul with understanding was saying to Philemon in the letter to Philemon concerning Onesimus: "So that your good be not according to compulsion but according to free will." Thus, the God of the universe hypothetically might have produced a supposed good in us so that we would give alms by "compulsion" and we would be self-controlled by "compulsion." But he has not wished to do so.[a]

a. *Homilies on Jeremiah* 20.2.

---

readers of the New Testament. Mark and Luke have long been identified as the famous Mark and Luke, the traditional authors of two of the canonical Gospels. Their appearance as present with Paul comports with the accounts of Paul's travels in the Acts of the Apostles. John Mark, son of Mary of Jerusalem (Acts 12:12, 25), assisted Saul and Barnabas on the first mission (13:5) but departed from them at Pamphylia (13:13) and returned to Jerusalem. Because of that departure, Paul did not want John Mark to travel with him and Barnabas on the second mission journey (15:5, 13). Yet 2 Tim 4:11 portrays Paul as affirming Mark ("He is helpful to me in the ministry"), so there may have been a reconciliation after that initial rift. As for Luke, while his name does not come up in Acts, as presumed author of that document he is implicitly included as accompanying Paul in the so-called we-sections (Acts 16:10–17; 20:4–15; 21:1–18; 28:1–16), which recount Paul's second and third mission journeys and his voyage under Roman custody to Rome.

**Epaphras** is singled out as a **fellow prisoner**, which translates a rare word in the New Testament—*synaichmalōtos*.[15] The root word *aichmalōtos* means "captive," as in prisoner of war, a word that appears in Jesus' quotation of Isaiah in Luke 4:18. Thus *synaichmalōtos* means "fellow prisoner of war." Epaphras is Paul's fellow prisoner in both a literal and spiritual sense. Literally, he shares Paul's fate of confinement. And spiritually he is a fellow prisoner just as Archippus is a "fellow soldier" in verse 2, that is, a fellow fighter in the war against the powers of evil in the world. The allusion to Isaiah may also convey the sense that these Christians have experienced the messianic liberation prophesied in Isa 61:1.

Since Epaphras alone is called co-captive while the other four are coworkers, it is possible that the latter are not imprisoned with Paul and Epaphras but are visitors or are simply in the neighborhood.

It is notable that all five greeters named in verses 23–24, **Mark, Aristarchus, Demas, and Luke,** as well as Epaphras, also turn up in the Letter to the Colossians. This suggests the possibility that Colossians was written close in time to the Letter to Philemon, since the same companions surround Paul. But even if Colossians was written by a later disciple rather than by the Apostle himself, the information it contains has a good chance of being historical. It only stands to reason that a †pseudonymous writer, in his effort to be faithful to the Pauline tradition, would build on well-known facts regarding these key companions of Paul. And what Colossians tells us about Epaphras gives us our best clue regarding the location of the addressees of the Letter to Philemon. For in Col

---

15. It occurs elsewhere in the New Testament only in Rom 16:7, of Andronicus and Junia, and in Col 4:10, of Aristarchus.

4:12 Epaphras is called "one of you," that is, a resident of Colossae and member of the church that meets at Philemon's place. Moreover, Epaphras is the one who first brought the word of the gospel to Colossae:

> Just as in the whole world it [i.e., the word of truth, the gospel] is bearing fruit and growing, so also among you, from the day you heard it and came to know the grace of God in truth, as you learned it from Epaphras our beloved fellow slave, who is a trustworthy minister of Christ on your behalf and who also told us of your love in the Spirit.
>
> Col 1:6–8

The fact that the author of Colossians can also say of Onesimus that he is "one of you," that is, a Colossian, makes it all the more plausible that Philemon was addressed to Christians in Colossae. Once the location of the addressees has been established, it is easier to focus one's guesses regarding the geographical location of Paul's imprisonment. In the introduction to this commentary, we reviewed the various issues entailed in scholarly guesswork and why Ephesus seems the most likely place of origin for this letter.

**25**  **The grace of the Lord Jesus Christ be with your** (plural) **spirit**. The titles applied to Jesus in the closing echo the titles used of Jesus in the initial address:

prisoner of *Christ Jesus* (vv. 1 and 23)
grace of *the Lord Jesus Christ* (vv. 2 and 25)

It is no accident that references to Jesus as both Messiah and risen Lord frame this letter to an individual and a community whose identity consists in being a new family under the one Father, God.

The shuttling between the singular and plural in the final four verses (apparent in Greek but not in English translations) shows that Paul is aware his personal address to Philemon occurs in a public context and is sent with the knowledge of a number of other people on the sending end. In any community, even private decisions have communal consequences.

### Reflection and Application (21–25)

*Personal transactions and communal consequences.* The conclusion of this letter, with its further references to the network of persons that Paul has nurtured in his ministry, can issue a healthy challenge to our North American notions of individualism and privacy. In US culture, one's religion is often thought of as a private matter—"nobody's business but my own." Indeed, it is not uncommon to hear the statement, "I'm spiritual but not religious," where "religious" refers to membership in a worshiping community that meets regularly, expresses itself in common prayer and worship, and shares a common creed and tradition. How different is that individualist way of thinking from the shared faith community (_koinōnia_) of the church that meets at Philemon's house. They are part of an extended network of relationships with others who belong to the people "called out" (the _ekklēsia_), a new family under the one Father who is the God of Israel, now known as the Father of Jesus. As risen Lord, Jesus is acknowledged as Israel's Messiah, who presides over the restored people of God. In that context, there is no way Philemon could consider the conversion of a household slave and its consequences as "nobody's business but my own." Because of this network of persons "in Christ," everyone has an interest in how this new relationship is worked out. To be sure, there are individual decisions that need to be made in freedom, but the context and consequences are communal.

In our own day, we rightly privilege certain communications and transactions as private. For example, the Church protects what is said in the sacrament of Reconciliation with the seal of confession. And it is part of a professional code of ethics for a counselor to keep matters that are discussed in personal and group counseling sessions confidential. But these special situations of privacy are only a small part of the shared life that is Christian community. The sense of being part of an extended household—or, as Paul expresses it in other letters, a member of a body, for which Paul uses the shorthand expressions "in Christ" and "in the Lord"—has always been part of authentic church life.

People who gather regularly to acknowledge how God has revealed himself in the life, death, and resurrection of Jesus and who aspire to participate in his mission of being light for the world have much more in common than strangers stopping by a fast-food joint.

If the picture of community implied in Paul's Letter to Philemon seems utterly other than our culture, then it simply alerts us to one of the ways our Christian lives must become countercultural. Paul and his addressees took for granted the kind of bonding people discover today in renewal movements like Cursillo groups, Christian Life Communities, prayer groups, and social advocacy groups. It also happens through involvement in well-led parishes. Reading Paul's letter as a real letter, looking for what it implies about the faith and life of the persons involved—what the letter meant _then_—teaches us a lot about what it means to be church today. That is why this †occasional letter is the enduring Word of God, even for us in our own day.

What have we learned from studying this short letter of Paul? Let me list a few things.

1. Even when he is not directly quoting Scripture, Paul's thought and language are deeply rooted in his Jewish tradition.
2. Paul may be the most influential letter writer ever to put pen to parchment.
3. The Word of God sometimes comes in the form of ordinary and practical human communication.
4. Quite apart from the various roles that Christians might play in society and in the faith community, Paul was clear that baptism makes us profoundly united in the call to serve Christ and one another in the body of Christ.
5. For Paul, the greatest possible human fulfillment is the transformation of a person in Christian community, begun in baptism and lived out in faith, hope, and love. This is something Paul will spell out in other letters as imitation of the self-giving love of Jesus (see Phil 2).
6. For Paul, Christian authority serves the growth of the faith community with loving persuasion and readiness to challenge.
7. Paul took seriously Jesus' teaching that those who would be his disciples in doing the will of God form a family deeper than blood.
8. Christian moral teaching on slavery developed slowly. Even though Paul himself did not condemn slavery as an institution, his communication with Philemon regarding Onesimus touched on the topic in a way that contributed to slavery's eventual condemnation.

# Paul's Letter to the Christians in Philippi

Saint Paul's Letter to the Christians at Philippi has been a favorite down through the centuries. As in the Letter to Philemon, Paul writes with great affection and self-revelation. As in the case of other famous prisoners—think of Nelson Mandela or Martin Luther King Jr.—confinement led Paul to reflect on big questions. For example, What if I die here? What comes after death? Has my life been worthwhile? What can I hope for the people I would leave behind? Jesus has made all the difference in my life—how can I best communicate him to others? What do I make of my enemies? How do I make sense of suffering? How can I encourage my friends in their own suffering? What have I learned here that might help them? The life-giving truths Paul conveys about these things have encouraged millions ever since, far beyond his original addressees.

The general introduction to this volume took up some general issues regarding the Prison Letters. This specific introduction to Philippians will address these more immediate issues:

1. the location of the authors,
2. the location and social context of the recipients,
3. the letter's structure,
4. the occasion and genre of the letter,
5. its theological themes,
6. the relationship of Philippians to the other Pauline Letters, and
7. the letter's pastoral relevance today.

## From Where Did Paul Write?

Where was Paul confined when he wrote this letter? Ephesus has been a popular candidate in recent commentaries because of its relative proximity to Philippi, compared with the much farther distances of other places where Paul was known to have been imprisoned, Caesarea and Rome. While neither his other letters nor the Acts of the Apostles explicitly mention an imprisonment in Ephesus, it is possible given Paul's general references to "far more imprisonments" (2 Cor 11:23) and to trouble in Ephesus (1 Cor 15:32; 16:8–9). However, a closer scrutiny of Paul's travel references in Philippians and his mention of imperial institutions—"the whole praetorium" (1:13) and "Caesar's household" (4:22)—have made the traditional location, Rome, quite plausible again. I find Rome the most convincing venue, as the commentary on these passages will show. Philippi's location on the Via Egnatia (or Egnatian Way), Rome's main highway to the East, would allow for the comings and goings mentioned in the letter, making calculations about hypothetical sea travel irrelevant. At the end of the day, however, the location of the church *to* which Paul writes is far more important than the place *from* which he writes.

## The Historical and Social Context of the Recipients

Philippi was a major city in the Roman province of †Macedonia, in the northeastern arm of today's Greece. It sat on the Via Egnatia, the major east-west road across the southern part of the Balkan Peninsula, joining Byzantium in the east (today's Istanbul) to the Adriatic Sea in the west. Across the water, the road continued up the boot of Italy to Rome. Philippi lay some eighty miles to the east of Thessalonica, Macedonia's capital. Adjoined to a fertile plain and near the gold deposits of the Pangaion Hills, Philippi gets its name from Alexander the Great's father, Philip of Macedon, who took it over around 360 BC, especially to mine the gold. Some three centuries later, Octavian, later called Caesar Augustus, made it a Roman colony and a settlement for retired Roman veterans. Colonizing the place with former Roman soldiers meant the takeover of Greek farmland and, eventually, the concentration of more and more land into the ownership of Roman colonizers. This resulted in an increasingly powerful urban elite and a growing number of wealthy colonist farmers.

Since we are reading a letter addressed to a small Christian minority in a mainly non-Christian, Gentile population, it is helpful to try to form a concrete picture of the social situation of Paul's addressees. Using the data of archaeology, ancient history, profiles of other first-century Roman and Greek towns, and clues from the letter itself, Peter Oakes, in a recent study, has attempted to reconstruct the demographics of Philippi in the mid-first century AD.[1] Granting

1. *Philippians: From People to Letter* (Cambridge: Cambridge University Press, 2001).

that such a reconstruction is hypothetical, the effort to create the picture helps the contemporary reader listen to the text from the point of view of the original recipients.

The following picture emerges from Oakes's study. At the time Paul wrote, the population of Philippi was around fifteen thousand, judging from such things as the size of its theater (seating eight thousand).

- The wealthy Roman elite constituted around 3 percent.
- Roman farmers living in the city and working land outside the walls, some 20 percent.
- Service groups (shopkeepers, bakers, hunters, entertainers, and so on—a third of them Roman citizens, two-thirds Greek), around 37 percent.
- The poor (people living below subsistence level, selling marginal goods or begging), 20 percent.
- Slaves, about 20 percent of the population.

Since slaves were embedded in households (*familiae*), their situation varied according to the household of their master. Roughly a third of the slave population was in the households of the Roman elite; a quarter was in the households of the commuting colonist farmers; and the rest were in families of the service groups. The families of the poor could not afford to own slaves. Thus, while slaves had the lowest social status, they were not among the poor. And although Roman citizens constituted only around a third of the population, their power and social status in this special colony made them the dominant cultural influence. The Roman atmosphere, focused on empire and emperor, prevailed.

Even though the Greeks were in the majority, the Roman citizens—especially the elite and the colonist farmers—held the wealth and power and so dominated the culture. Roman society has been characterized as the most status-symbol-conscious culture of the ancient world. It was a highly stratified society in which the elite especially thought of their lives as an "honors race" (*cursus honorum*), which is abundantly reflected in the inscriptions on public monuments detailing the various offices each civic benefactor held in his or her lifetime. Honor meant both esteem and public office. Thus to seek honor and to seek office were one and the same thing; one held office in order to gain honor.

Roman municipalities in the provinces replicated this social stratification, where wealth was mainly important for the civic honor one could accrue by underwriting public works.[2] The many honorific inscriptions unearthed in Philippi demonstrate that, after the city of Rome itself, this colony was perhaps the most status-conscious place in the empire. The general population of Philippi would have been confronted with this *cursus honorum* culture at every turn—in the Roman forum at the center of the city, in the honorific inscriptions in public places, in emperor worship, in the images on Roman coins, in the lineup of civic processions, and in the lifestyle of Roman veterans and their descendants. This background illuminates much of the language and imagery Paul uses when he writes to the church in this city.

Jewish presence in Philippi was apparently minute. There is no first-century archaeological evidence for a Jewish synagogue there. The account of Paul and Silas's first visit to the area (with Timothy and Luke?) in Acts 16:12–16 simply mentions a "place of prayer" with a small gathering of women, whereas Paul finds flourishing synagogue communities in Thessalonica and Beroea (Acts 17:1–10) farther down the road to the west.

So much for the general population of Philippi. The little Christian community within Philippi would, of course, have reflected the complex composition of the population as a whole, but in different proportions. The research I am summarizing proposes the following composition for the local church:

- Christians from households of Roman elite: around 1 percent (+ 3 percent slaves) = 4 percent
- Christians from colonist farmers: around 15 percent (+ 4 percent slaves) = 19 percent
- Christians from service groups: around 43 percent (+ 9 percent slaves) = 52 percent
- Christian poor: 25 percent[3]

Thus over three-fourths of the Christian community was from the service groups and the poor, and sixteen percent were slaves. The economic picture of the Philippian church, then, is of a small group made up mainly of landless noncitizens who were somewhat financially insecure. Certain passages in Paul's Letters give evidence that the Macedonian churches, of which the Philippians

2. In quite another context, the Gospel of Luke provides an example of how Roman benefaction brings honor, when the Jewish residents of Capernaum say, regarding the Roman centurion who had requested healing for his slave, "He deserves to have you do this for him, for he loves our nation and he built the synagogue for us" (Luke 7:4b–5).

3. It is important to keep in mind that these figures are educated guesses, the best we can do with the data supplied by the archaeology and documentary evidence from the first-century Mediterranean world.

and the Thessalonians were chief, did indeed experience poverty. He reminds the Thessalonians, "You recall, brothers, our toil and drudgery. Working night and day in order not to burden any of you, we proclaimed to you the gospel of God" (1 Thess 2:9). In the present letter, he refers to aid that came to him from the Philippians during that same period of ministry:

> You Philippians indeed know that at the beginning of the gospel, when I left Macedonia, not a single church shared with me in an account of giving and receiving, except you alone. For even when I was at Thessalonica you sent me something for my needs, not only once but more than once.
>
> Phil 4:15–16; and see 2 Cor 9:1–4

How big is the community to which Paul writes? We can only guess, but the reference to local harassment (1:28) suggests they are a distinct minority. If the community was, say, between 150 and 300, the Philippian Christians would constitute 1–2 percent of the population of the town of Philippi.[4]

The courts favored the Roman colonists over the Greeks, and those colonists owned most of the land and wielded the power, even though they only made up around a third of the population. Public inscriptions, including those on coins, were in Latin, and Latin books would have dominated the texts in the public library. We saw how the primarily agricultural economy of Philippi put the wealth and power in the hands of the elite landowners and the colonist farmers. This was bound to magnify the difference in status between rich and poor. Yet citizenship versus noncitizenship was also an issue. Even the brief account in Acts of Paul and Silas's time in Philippi highlights this fact. The masters of the slave girl with the oppressive spirit complain that Paul and company are "advocating customs that are not lawful" for Roman citizens. But when Paul later reveals that the magistrates have beaten and jailed him and Silas without trial even though they are Roman citizens, those same magistrates are alarmed (Acts 16:19–39).

## The Structure of Philippians: One Letter or Several?

Some scholars have argued that Philippians is not a single letter but a composite of several. Since a composite would imply a mix of more than one occasion and genre, it is important to address the issue of structure before we take up other questions.

---

4. The fact that Philippians mentions only one Latin name, Clement (4:3), along with the three Greek names in verse 2 (plus a fourth if *Syzygos*, translated "yokemate" in the NABRE, is a personal name), reflects the Greek majority in the Philippian church expressed in the hypothetical model.

The idea that the canonical Letter to the Philippians is actually a composite of several letters or fragments springs from what appear to be interruptions and abrupt shifts of focus within the letter. For example, 4:10–20 can be read as a self-contained thank-you note for the aid brought by Epaphroditus, and 2:19–30 comprises updates about Timothy and Epaphroditus that appear to interrupt the flow. And the "Beware of the dogs!" imperative at 3:2 can seem a startling intervention just when Paul seems to be concluding the letter at 3:1.

However, further study has led to a growing awareness that the parts and arrangement of this letter can indeed be read as a coherent whole. For instance, a recent study demonstrates the unity of Philippians by analyzing it according to †chiastic structures, showing that the letter appears to be designed on a pattern of ten elements, forming concentric parallels (A–B–C–D–E–E′–D′–C′–B′–A′), with each of these parts containing its own minichiasm.[5] Moreover, when one sees that one of the primary purposes of the letter is to present models for imitation—Christ in particular, but Paul, Timothy, and Epaphroditus as well—the passages about Timothy and Epaphroditus fit in quite appropriately. It is hoped that the unity of the letter will become evident in the details of this commentary.

Part of the discussion about the unity of Philippians centers on what is sometimes called "the Christ hymn"—the famous passage about Christ's emptying himself (2:6–11) introduced by the words, "Have among yourselves the same attitude that is also yours in Christ Jesus, / Who, though he was in the form of God . . ." Due to its power and elegance, this passage has taken on a life of its own, including becoming a canticle used strategically in the Liturgy of the Hours and in the lectionary for key eucharistic celebrations. Many commentators have made the case that these six verses are essentially a pre-Pauline hymn, sung by early Christians at worship, which Paul has incorporated into his letter. This passage may thus provide both a window on how the earliest Christians worshiped and evidence of perhaps the earliest efforts at †Christology—that is, thinking through the relationship between the Son and the Father and between Christ's humanity and his divinity. This hypothesis has led to an enormous body of literature studying possible backgrounds to the passage as a free-standing, pre-Pauline work.

The passage surely reflects early Christology, but that it is necessarily a pre-Pauline composition is no longer a consensus view among scholars. The passage is so integral to the language and thought of the letter and resonates so well

---

5. John Paul Heil, *Philippians: Let Us Rejoice in Being Conformed to Christ*, Early Christianity and Its Literature 3 (Atlanta: Society of Biblical Literature, 2010). Heil's outline appears under the heading "Chiastic Outline of the Letter to the Philippians," below.

with the rest of the †undisputed letters of Paul that a good case can be made that Paul wrote it. Even if the passage is indeed the work of a prior author, Paul has clearly made it his own and integrated it seamlessly into the fabric of his letter. It is part of the structure created by the author. This is the perspective this commentary takes regarding the famous Christ hymn of 2:6–11.

## The Occasion and Genre of the Letter

The Letter to the Philippians is best described as a letter of friendship. That is, its purpose is mainly to further an ongoing relationship with the recipients, entailing self-disclosure and expressions of concern, encouragement, and gratitude. A man who is forcibly detained naturally wants to let good friends know how it goes with him. The concern and encouragement that Paul extends to them is not prompted by a particular crisis. Rather, it seems that this little Christian church is challenged by the ongoing coldness and hostility they meet in an urban setting that has little sympathy for their peculiarly non-Roman ways. Paul's strategy is to encourage them by sharing the example that so inspires him, the self-emptying love of Christ, in the "hymn" of 2:6–11. He also presents his own experience, along with that of Timothy and Epaphroditus, as a model of God's power enabling them to follow the example of the incarnate, crucified, and risen Christ.

The occasion for Paul's writing at *this* particular time is the need to send back the Philippians' emissary, Epaphroditus, sooner than they might have expected. Having fallen sick on his mission to bring help to Paul, Epaphroditus has regained sufficient health to travel again, but he needs to go home to recover fully. Paul wishes to smooth his welcome home by explaining the early return and commending his service (2:25–30). This communication also provides the opportunity to include his heartfelt thanks for the financial aid that Epaphroditus brought to him from them (4:10–20).

## Theological Themes

This letter of friendship occasions some profound self-revelation from Paul, its principal author. Apart from 2 Corinthians and parts of Galatians and Romans, nowhere else in the letters we have does Paul share so candidly his motivation for following Jesus. In doing so, he explores several key themes that have instructed and inspired Christian disciples ever since: Christ as judge (implied in "the day of Christ" in 1:6, 10; 2:16); the joy of sharing Christian life (the noun "joy" occurs five times in the letter, and forms of the verb "rejoice" eleven times); the grace of serenity in the face of rejection and death (1:15–26), abasement or abundance (4:11–13); the incarnation, death, and exaltation of God's eternal Son as Messiah and Lord of all (2:6–11); Christian discipleship as the imitation of the self-emptying of Christ (1:27–2:18) and as "the fellowship of his suffering" and "the power of his resurrection" (3:7–11); the ongoing maturation of the Christian community (1:6–11; 2:12–13) and of individual Christians (3:12–16); and the place of financial aid in the life of the Church (4:15–18).

## Philippians among the Other Pauline Letters

If indeed this letter was written from Rome, it gives us a glimpse of Paul's thought toward the end of his career. Whatever part Timothy played as coauthor, the voice of Paul as we know him from the other letters is unmistakably audible here as well. As in the other undisputed letters, we meet again Paul's stress on God's initiative and the lordship of the risen Jesus, and his focus on the unity of the local church as the work of God. Paul does not directly quote Scripture in this letter as he does in Romans, Galatians, and 1 Corinthians; yet his Jewish roots show in his deft *allusions* to biblical tradition (e.g., Job 13:16 at 1:19; Isa 45:23 at 2:10).

Whereas 1 Corinthians, Galatians, and Colossians are written to address specific pastoral issues, Philippians has more in common with Romans in that it reveals more deeply Paul's sense of the universal aspects of Christian faith and life. Even when Paul brings up the issue of "the dogs" in chapter 3 he does so mainly to exemplify his newfound freedom and joy in Christ. Philippians offers a depth of self-revelation that is rare among Paul's Letters. But his references to his experience are never self-indulgent; they always serve to illustrate the good news of God in Christ.

## Pastoral Pertinence Today

The famous Christ hymn celebrating the self-emptying of the eternal Son and his present exaltation (2:6–11), with its introduction (1:27–2:5) and its application to community life (2:12–18), illustrated by the examples of Timothy, Epaphroditus, and Paul himself (3:4–16), remains a classic expression of Christian spirituality. The vision of the Christ hymn—that following Jesus is a matter of imitating his own self-emptying service to the Father and to other human beings—still animates Christian discipleship. It has rightly been described as the master story that energized Paul's own life and led him to the conviction that his own experience of God's grace in Christ was available to all followers of Jesus.[6] It is therefore permanently inspiring for catechesis and preaching.

---

6. The notion of the hymn as master story is that of Michael J. Gorman, as elaborated in several of his writings, e.g., *Inhabiting the Cruciform God: Kenosis, Justification, and Theosis in Paul's Narrative Soteriology* (Grand Rapids: Eerdmans, 2009).

# Outline of the Letter to the Philippians

1. Greetings, thanksgiving, and joyful intercession (1:1–11)
   Senders, receivers, and greeting (1:1–2)
   Thanksgiving (1:3–8)
   Intercession (1:9–11)
2. Paul's captivity as exemplary (1:12–26)
   How Paul's chains advance the gospel (1:12–18a)
   Facing the future (1:18b–26)
3. A call to conduct worthy of the gospel (1:27–2:4)
   The thesis: strive together to be faithful citizens of the Lord's commonwealth (1:27–30)
   Qualities required for a Christian community to live that way (2:1–4)
4. The best example of all: Christ's self-emptying and service (2:5–18)
   Christ's example celebrated: the "Hymn" (2:5–11)
   Christ's example applied to Christian living (2:12–18)
5. Two more examples: Timothy and Epaphroditus (2:19–3:1a)
   The incomparable Timothy, "slaving" for the gospel (2:19–24)
   Epaphroditus, faithful "unto death" (2:25–3:1a)
6. Paul himself as an example of the joy of "faithful citizenship" in Christ (3:1b–4:1)
   Rehearsing a familiar issue to illustrate the source of Christian freedom and joy (3:1b–7)
   Paul's righteousness from God and the faithfulness of Christ (3:8–11)
   We are, each and all, a work in progress (3:12–16)

Our identity, our citizenship, our goal: conformation to *our* Lord and Savior, Christ (3:17–4:1)

7. A Final call to unity and joy: Reconcile! Rejoice! Pray! (4:2–9)

   Euodia and Syntyche, Reconcile in the Lord! (4:2–3)

   Rejoice in what is good, true, beautiful! (4–9)

8. Thanks and final greetings (4:10–23)

   A delicate thank you (4:10–14)

   Further thanks, greetings, and a blessing (4:15–23)

# Chiastic Outline of the Letter
# to the Philippians

This outline is from the recent study by John Paul Heil.[1]

A  Grace from the Lord Jesus Christ to the holy ones (1:1–2)

  B  My prayer that you abound and be filled to glory and praise of
      God (1:1–11)

    C  I rejoice and I will be joyful (1:12–18)

      D  Death in my body is gain but remaining is for your faith
          (1:19–30)

        E  Joy in humility for the day of Christ who humbled
            himself to death (2:1–16)

        E′  Rejoice with those who neared death for the work of
            Christ (2:17–30)

      D′  Gain in faith in the death of Christ and the body of his
          glory (3:1–21)

    C′  Rejoice in the Lord, rejoice (4:1–5)

  B′  Glory to God who will fulfill you as I am filled and abound
      (4:5–20)

A′  Greeting from holy ones and grace from the Lord Jesus Christ
    (4:21–23)

1. Heil, *Philippians*, 30.

# Greeting, Thanksgiving, and Joyful Intercession

## Philippians 1:1–11

Paul begins this letter with the standard Greek format we met in the Letter to Philemon—first, the identification of the senders; second, the naming of the intended recipients; and third, a greeting. Then comes the expected thanksgiving. As in the Letter to Philemon, Paul invests these ordinary elements with Christian language that prepares his readers for the message he intends to convey. Already in these preliminaries the careful, clever writer we met in that shorter letter shows his skills and affection once again.

### Senders, Receivers, and Greeting (1:1–2)

¹Paul and Timothy, slaves of Christ Jesus, to all the holy ones in Christ Jesus who are in Philippi, with the overseers and ministers: ²grace to you and peace from God our Father and the Lord Jesus Christ.

OT: Dan 7:18
NT: Rom 1:1

Mentioning the name of **Timothy** prepares the way for Paul's reference to him later in the letter (2:19–24), where he will serve as one of several examples of self-giving service according to the mind of Christ. When Paul characterizes himself and Timothy as **slaves of Christ Jesus**, that term for their subservience to Jesus as Lord and Master would carry a powerful resonance for a community that

1:1

surely included a number of actual slaves. Later Paul will speak, even more surprisingly, of the Lord himself as having taken on the form of a slave.[1]

As in Philemon, Paul applies a biblical term for the people of God, **the holy ones** (e.g., Ps 34:10; Isa 4:3; Dan 7:18), to the Christian community. This phrase, sometimes translated "saints," is

Fig. 6. A capital in the forum of Philippi, suggesting the local cultural dominance of pagan worship.

for Paul a common epithet for Christians. It refers not to their heroic virtue, as in canonized saints, but to their status as the covenant people of God. What is unusual here is his explicit mention of those in leadership positions—**overseers and ministers** (*episkopoi* and *diakonoi*), traditionally translated "bishops and deacons" (RSV; NIV, "overseers and deacons"; NJB, "presiding elders and deacons"). Our NABRE translation acknowledges that in the mid-first century these roles had not yet developed into the full hierarchical form that was evident later. By the second century, St. Ignatius of Antioch refers to a local church administered by a single bishop, supported by presbyters (later called priests) and deacons. Nevertheless, these words in Philippians are clearly role designations and may indicate Paul's courteous attention to the fact that leadership titles are especially important to the status-conscious people of Roman Philippi.

The parallel expressions **in Christ Jesus** and **in Philippi** may seem at first a simple reference to the Christians in Philippi, but it actually highlights a tension Paul will address in various ways throughout the letter: to belong to the community in union with Jesus Christ means that they are citizens of a kingdom (another kind of empire) and subjects of a Lord (another kind of emperor) at odds in many ways with the empire and emperor of the Roman colony in which they live.[2]

1:2     The greeting—**grace to you and peace from God our Father and the Lord Jesus Christ**—is virtually identical with the greeting to Philemon and the church that meets at his home (Philem 3), but here it has a distinctive meaning. Having

---

1. The more common translation, "servants" (NIV, NRSV, and NJB) obscures this connotation.
2. I take this insight from Stephen E. Fowl, *Philippians*, Two Horizons New Testament Commentary (Grand Rapids: Eerdmans, 2005), 19.

just described himself and Timothy as "*slaves* of Christ Jesus," the title "Lord" identifies the one they serve precisely as master. And naming "God" our Father and the "*Lord* Jesus Christ" in the same sentence prepares the attentive listener for the powerful use of those terms in the Christ hymn coming up in chapter 2: Jesus, who took the form of a slave, will be called Lord by God the Father—and everyone else! The key ingredients are already here in the prescript of the letter.

## Thanksgiving (1:3–8)

[3]I give thanks to my God at every remembrance of you, [4]praying always with joy in my every prayer for all of you, [5]because of your partnership for the gospel from the first day until now. [6]I am confident of this, that the one who began a good work in you will continue to complete it until the day of Christ Jesus. [7]It is right that I should think this way about all of you, because I hold you in my heart, you who are all partners with me in grace, both in my imprisonment and in the defense and confirmation of the gospel. [8]For God is my witness, how I long for all of you with the affection of Christ Jesus.

**OT:** Amos 5:18
**NT:** Rom 15:26; 1 Cor 1:8; 5:5; 2 Cor 1:14; 8:3–4; 9:13; 1 Thess 5:2; 2 Thess 2:2
**Catechism:** oath taking, 2154
**Lectionary:** Second Sunday of Advent (Year C)

A thanksgiving section was a common element at the beginning of Greco-Roman letters of this era. As he did in the Letter to Philemon, Paul makes use of this custom as an opportunity for expressing Christian attitudes and for planting the seeds of themes that he will develop in the body of the letter.

For Paul **every remembrance** of the Philippian community is an occasion of gratitude to **God**, for their very existence as a local church is a work of God. And that thanksgiving is always accompanied by **joy**. As the rest of the letter will demonstrate, this joy is no casual matter of simply feeling good about his readers. The letter is saturated with the joy of sharing in the life and mission of Christ, through the verbs "rejoice" (*chairō*, 1:18; 2:17, 18, 28; 3:1; 4:4, 10) and "rejoice *with*" (*synchairō*, 4:17, 18) and the noun "joy" (*chara*, 1:4, 25; 2:2, 29; 4:1). Paul begins to spell that out by naming here one of the sources of his joy: **your partnership for the gospel.** That phrase may seem at first to refer simply to their common faith in the gospel. But for Paul the partnership is more concrete and practical than that. As Paul uses the word,

"†gospel" can sometimes mean the *message* of the good news itself (God has definitely entered into history to save us through the death and resurrection of his Son), but at other times "gospel" means the *project of sharing that good news*.[3] Here the "partnership in the gospel" for which Paul is grateful seems to refer especially to the financial aid that the Philippians have sent to him through Epaphroditus (see 4:10–20).[4] This aid is partnership in the sense that it is a real contribution to the advance of the gospel. As will become clear, Paul's response to their financial generosity is a delicate matter—and is on his mind from the outset of this letter.

1:6        This generosity of the community at Philippi is, at bottom, a sign of something Paul can call **a good work in you** (the "you" is plural). It is, in fact, a work God himself has initiated in them—the work of sanctification that he began in them through faith and baptism, which Paul is confident God **will continue to complete it until the day of Christ Jesus**. The Christian community is a divine work in progress that began on the "first day" they came to believe in the gospel (v. 5) and will be complete on the "day" of the final coming of Christ—another theme Paul develops in the letter (1:10; 2:16; 3:20–21). This statement is an encouraging reminder that their growth in holiness and Christian maturity is not their work but *God's work* with which they cooperate and which Paul fosters—and God himself will see to the completion of this work. Not only the *community* but also each *individual Christian* is a divine work in progress (1:6, 9). Paul will illustrate this progressive growth from his own experience (see 3:12–16). "The day of the Lord" is a phrase from the Old Testament prophets, referring to the day when the Lord God would decisively intervene in history to save the righteous and bring judgment on the unrighteous. Now that "day" is "the day of Christ Jesus" (1:6; see 1:10; 2:16), the time of resurrection of the dead and final judgment.[5]

1:7        **It is right that I should think this way about all of you.** It might seem oddly self-conscious that Paul should defend the way he expresses his joy and gratitude for the Philippian church. But this phrase, too, is a foretaste of things to come. For the whole letter is about one's mind-set or attitude, especially as something over which one is to exercise control. The word for "think" or "manage one's

---

3. The Greek word *euangelion* ("gospel") has this meaning at Phil 2:22 (where NABRE translates it "the cause of the gospel") and 4:15.

4. Ben Witherington III (*Friendship and Finances in Philippi*, The New Testament in Context [Valley Forge, PA: Trinity Press International, 1994], 37) notes that Paul uses the same phrase "partnership in" (*koinōnia . . . eis*) in other places to refer to financial sharing (Rom 15:26; 2 Cor 8:3–4; 9:13).

5. For more applications of the phrase "day of the Lord" to the †parousia of Jesus Christ, see 1 Cor 1:8 ("the day of our Lord Jesus [Christ]"); 5:5 ("the day of the Lord"); 2 Cor 1:14 ("the day of [our] Lord Jesus"); 1 Thess 5:2 ("the day of the Lord"); and 2 Thess 2:2 ("the day of the Lord").

attitude" (*phroneō*) is a favorite of Paul's.[6] It will be at the heart of the exhortation and Christ hymn of chapter 2 (see 2:2, 5). It links the climactic thoughts of chapter 3 (the good attitude of 3:15 and the bad attitude of 3:19). And in chapter 4 the same verb refers to the desired reconciliation of Euodia and Syntyche (5:2) and the community's concern for Paul (5:10).

The NABRE reflects the traditional translation of the phrase **I hold you in my heart**, but the grammar of the Greek text is ambiguous regarding whose heart holds whom. It can equally be translated "you hold me in your heart" (NRSV), which continues to express the reason for Paul's gratitude and affection.[7] Either way, there is deep mutual affection between Paul and the Christians at Philippi. But since the thanksgiving is mainly about what motivates *Paul's* feelings, the NRSV reading seems best.

Paul identifies his addressees as **you who are all partners with me in grace.** "Grace" is the word Paul uses throughout his letters to refer to the free gift of God given to us through the Lord Jesus Christ. But there are reasons for perceiving that here Paul may have in mind a specific dimension of that gift of God. Paul uses a rare word for "partners" here[8] and at 4:14 (in verbal form, "share in"). In the context of the thank-you note of 4:10–20, the point is that the Philippians have not simply shared Paul's distress but also shared financial aid with him in his distress. Writing to the Corinthians, Paul refers to the financial generosity of the "churches of Macedonia," of which the Philippians were the first, as an expression of "the grace of God" (2 Cor 8:1–2). Paul uses the same language here in Phil 1:7. Thus what at first appears a rather general statement about "sharing in grace" turns out, in context, to allude to their generous *financial aid* as a manifestation of God's grace working in them.[9]

Paul emphasizes that Christians share not only the gift of the good news but also the task of furthering it. The word for **defense** of the gospel, *apologia*, is the origin of the word "apologetics," the area of theology devoted to defending the faith. It is sometimes employed as a legal term for a formal defense at a trial, and Paul, if he is writing from Rome, may be referring to his own upcoming trial

6. Of its twenty-five instances in the New Testament, seventeen occur in two of Paul's Letters (eight in Romans and nine in Philippians).

7. The more traditional translation, "I hold you in my heart," seems to me a redundancy. It seems to say, "I think this way about you simply because I think about you this way."

8. The word is *synkoinōnos* (literally, "co-partner"), which emphasizes the "with" aspect of the simpler and more usual word for partner (*koinōnos*) by adding the prefix *syn* ("with").

9. Jerry L. Sumney (*Philippians: A Greek Student's Intermediate Reader* [Peabody, MA: Hendrickson, 2007], 13) notes that *synkoinōnos* is commonly used for business partners and that "this partnership probably has a broad reference to their relationship, but it may also be related to their repeated and now renewed, financial support of his mission."

(see a similar reference in 2 Tim 4:16). The **confirmation of the gospel** probably refers to confirming and strengthening the faith of those who believe. The truth of the good news is manifested by its fruits in the lives of those who embrace it.

1:8     Paul expresses the same warm affection we met in the Letter to Philemon: **For God is my witness, how I long for all of you with the affection of Christ Jesus.** The word for "affection" is *splanchna*, literally the "innards" or "bowels," which in biblical thought are the seat of emotion. This is the word Paul used so skillfully and playfully with Philemon. Here Paul makes sure to assert that this affection is not simply natural fondness but is rooted in their shared experience of Jesus' love for all of them. We might pass over the phrase "God is my witness" simply as Paul's way of lending emphasis and solemnity to his words. However, generations of readers have noticed that in invoking God as witness, Paul seems to violate Jesus' prohibition of oath-taking in the Sermon on the Mount (Matt 5:34–37). The Catechism addresses this problem in its treatment of the Second Commandment (2154): "Following St. Paul (2 Cor 1:23; Gal 1:20), the tradition of the Church has understood Jesus's words as not excluding oaths made for grave and right reasons" (for example, in court).

## Intercession (1:9–11)

⁹**And this is my prayer: that your love may increase ever more and more in knowledge and every kind of perception, ¹⁰to discern what is of value, so that you may be pure and blameless for the day of Christ, ¹¹filled with the fruit of righteousness that comes through Jesus Christ for the glory and praise of God.**

**NT:** Matt 16:27; Rev 20:13
**Catechism:** prayer of petition, 2629–33; prayer of intercession, 2634–36; the Last Judgment, 1038–41
**Lectionary:** Second Sunday of Advent (Year C), Sacred Heart (option for reading II)

1:9–11     As in the letter to Philemon (Philem 6), Paul prays that his addressees may grow in a **love** grounded in **knowledge** and **perception** of **what is of value**. The point is not speculative knowledge but relational and practical knowledge, that is, knowing Christ personally and knowing *how to live in him*, since the goal is to stand blameless at the judgment on the **day of Christ**, a theme already struck in verse 6. One is judged not on what one knows but on what one does.[10] As one

10. For other expressions of Christian belief about judgment at the †parousia regarding deeds, see Matt 16:27 and Rev 20:13.

becomes familiar with the context of the letter as a whole, it becomes obvious that Paul has in mind the master story of the Christ hymn—Jesus' humble obedience even to death and his subsequent exaltation to glory—as the model for Christian life and love.[11] The examples of his own Christ-enlivened life and of Timothy and Epaphroditus will further illustrate **the fruit of righteousness that comes through Jesus Christ**. The latter phrase refers to the holy and selfless conduct of Christians, especially in their service to one another (3:6–9), which is made possible by their union with Christ. As the Philippian community imitates the self-emptying and self-humbling love of Jesus celebrated in the poem of chapter 2, their life, too, will be **for the glory and praise of God** (see 2:11).

### Reflection and Application (1:3–11)

*Prayer for a church.* In the thanksgiving section of this letter (vv. 3–11), Paul does something that is easy for us to neglect: he prays for a local church as a whole. I rarely do this. I pray for the *universal Church* in the Prayers of the Faithful at Mass. I pray for *individuals* both in and outside of the Church. But I rarely think to pray for a local church, say, all the people of St. John's parish, where I often preside at Eucharist, or for my diocese, which is what really constitutes my local church under the leadership of my local bishop. But that is what we see Paul doing at the beginning of this letter. And his prayer provides an instructive model.

Paul has a practical reason to pray for the Philippians as a church, of course: he is addressing a letter to them, and his subject is their life as a community, a life he shares with them as founder and fellow Christian. But we too have good reason to pray for our faith communities. Most of us engaged in the study of this letter belong to a local faith community, most likely a parish. We may also belong to another kind of faith community—maybe a prayer group, Bible study group, or social action committee. Paul's prayer for the Philippians is a reminder that it should be a very natural and spontaneous thing to pray for the unity and growth of the community in which we are living out our Christian life.

*Thanksgiving first.* The *way* Paul prays is instructive. He begins with gratitude. We would do well to make thanksgiving the default setting of our prayer. Doing so puts the focus immediately on God, the One who has initiated our relationship. Paul's gratitude for the Philippians' faith and love acknowledges

---

11. The idea that Phil 2:6–11 is the master story of Paul's theological vision is developed powerfully in Michael J. Gorman, *Inhabiting the Cruciform God: Kenosis, Justification, and Theosis in Paul's Narrative Soteriology* (Grand Rapids: Eerdmans, 2009).

that what makes them a church is "a good work" of God in them. Once we are in touch with God the Father as the source of all that is good in our shared life, we naturally shift our focus to what we still need from him, and the prayer then moves spontaneously to petition (for what I and we need) and intercession (for what others need). So Paul's way of praying is a good reminder to begin our prayer with thanksgiving, to thank before we ask.

*Prayer for wisdom.* How often do we pray for understanding and wisdom? That is Paul's prayer for the Philippians: that they grow in the personal knowledge of God and his ways that leads to right behavior and will make them "pure and blameless for the day of Christ." We too need such understanding in order to live out who we are as a work of God.

*A church is a growing thing.* While Paul does not speak of the church as the body of Christ in this letter, as he does so powerfully in 1 Corinthians, his way of referring to the Philippian community as a work in progress expresses a related truth. God is in the process of completing the faith community; the church (*ekklēsia*, literally, those "called out" by God) is a living organism whose growth and health can be either nurtured or impaired. We generally think of individuals in this way, but Paul's way of praying for the Philippians can also encourage us to think of our various Christian communities in this way. Each community has a level of spiritual health and a stage of growth, originated and sustained by God, which each of us can either contribute to or hinder by our action and prayer—or the lack thereof.

# The Example of Paul in Chains

## Philippians 1:12–26

Paul moves from his prayer of thanksgiving and intercession to a reflection on his situation as a prisoner. But his report is not simply news shared among friends. He speaks of his confinement and its consequences as the first example of the grace they share (v. 7). In fact, as will become evident, his imprisonment exemplifies what it means to share in the sufferings of Christ (3:10). While this section is about Paul's experience, almost every sentence is also about Christ, whose name occurs nine times. For the Apostle, everything is evaluated in the light of the "advance" of "the gospel" (v. 12).

### How Paul's Chains Advance the Gospel (1:12–18a)

[12]I want you to know, brothers, that my situation has turned out rather to advance the gospel, [13]so that my imprisonment has become well known in Christ throughout the whole praetorium and to all the rest, [14]and so that the majority of the brothers, having taken encouragement in the Lord from my imprisonment, dare more than ever to proclaim the word fearlessly. [15]Of course, some preach Christ from envy and rivalry, others from good will. [16]The latter act out of love, aware that I am here for the defense of the gospel; [17]the former proclaim Christ out of selfish ambition, not from pure motives, thinking that they will cause me trouble in my imprisonment. [18]What difference does it make, as long as in every way, whether in pretense or in truth, Christ is being proclaimed? And in that I rejoice.

**NT:** Eph 6:20; 2 Tim 2:9

1:12      It is likely that for some of the early Christians, the fact that the Apostle Paul had run afoul of the government and been thrown into prison (or put under house arrest) was demoralizing, perhaps even scandalizing. To encourage them, Paul shows how the light of faith changes the way we see and experience the situations in which we find ourselves. In this case even apparently bad news can be understood as good news: **my situation has turned out rather to advance the gospel.** We already heard Paul speak of the Philippians' "partnership in the gospel" (1:5) as including not only their shared belief and fellowship but also their contribution to the spread of the †gospel. Now Paul is saying that even his imprisonment is part of that enterprise.

1:13      First, his imprisonment has made the gospel an item of conversation among the pagans. In the NABRE rendering of verse 13—**my imprisonment has become well known in Christ throughout the whole praetorium**—the phrase "known in Christ" implies that the news of Paul's imprisonment is spreading among Roman guards who are Christian believers. But that would hardly "advance the gospel." In my judgment, the NRSV translation better reflects the meaning of the text: "It has become known through the whole imperial guard and to everyone else that my imprisonment is for Christ."[1] What has become known among the whole Praetorian Guard is the fact that Paul is imprisoned precisely because of his message about the Messiah and not because of a political or criminal matter. It is this awareness that is serving to advance the gospel.

If Paul is imprisoned in Rome, then his use of "praetorium" refers to the Praetorian Guard, the emperor's bodyguard, which in Rome consisted of nine thousand men. If Paul's location is elsewhere, such as Caesarea or Ephesus, it refers to those who live in the governor's palace.[2] The phrase **and to all the rest** (a plural word in Greek) would seem to refer to other persons involved in Paul's imprisonment. Paul's boast that the cause of his confinement has become "known . . . throughout the whole praetorium" would not make much sense in the context of the limited space of the administrative quarters of Caesarea; it fits better as applied to the Praetorian Guard of Rome.

1. This point is made cogently in Gordon Fee, *Paul's Letter to the Philippians* (Grand Rapids: Eerdmans, 1995), 114–17.

2. *Praitōrion* is a Greek loanword from Latin (*praetorium*). Originally referring to the praetor's tent in camp, the word came to mean the place where the governor resided or, as in Jerusalem, did business when he was in town (see Matt 27:27; Mark 15:16; John 18:28, 33; 19:9; Acts 23:35). In the context of Rome, the word could also mean the Praetorian Guard; in the provinces, it could mean those who lived in the governor's palace, i.e., his staff. See BDAG 859. Fee (*Philippians*, 34–36) and Ben Witherington III (*Friendship and Finances: The Letter of Paul to the Philippians*, The New Testament in Context [Valley Forge, PA: Trinity Press International, 1994], 45) understand the Praetorian Guard as the best meaning here, therefore supporting Rome as the location of Paul's imprisonment.

It is not simply the publicity of his imprisonment that Paul rejoices in. Para-    1:14
doxically, his chains have emboldened his fellow Christians. The example of his
courageous commitment to Christ has encouraged many to **proclaim the word
fearlessly**. As usual in Paul's Letters, **brothers** is inclusive, referring not just to
men but to all local Christians. And **the majority** of them have been stimulated to
proclaim the word. Yet even among those who are encouraged to preach Christ,
there is an interesting diversity of motives, which he now proceeds to unpack.

Some of those announcing the gospel are motivated by **good will** and are    1:15–18a
seeking **out of love** to continue what Paul was appointed by the Lord to do but
now cannot. Others **preach Christ from envy and rivalry . . . thinking that
they will cause** Paul **trouble** in his **imprisonment**. Who are these rivals? Since
Paul is reporting news to the Philippians, he must be referring to people on his
end—that is, in Rome. Since these people are said to "preach Christ," they are
fellow Christians. And since he can rejoice that Christ is being proclaimed, the
problem must lie in their motivation and not in the basic content of their preaching. Possibly, they envy Paul's personal influence over the Christian community
of Rome (a church that Paul wrote a letter to but did not found) and seek to
deflate that power by exploiting Paul's confinement to gain their own influence.[3]

Their rivalry is so intense that they even take pleasure in thinking that their
success will cause Paul some grief when he hears of it. Though Paul is aware
of these hostile motives, he chooses to respond by accentuating the positive:
**What difference does it make, as long as in every way, whether in pretense
or in truth, Christ is being proclaimed? And in that I rejoice.** Paul's highest
priority is not his own success but that as many people as possible come to
faith in Christ (see 1 Cor 9:21–23; 2 Cor 4:5). In the thanksgiving, we heard
Paul speak of his joy in the good work God was doing in the shared life of the
Philippians; here, he can rejoice in the wonder that Christ is being proclaimed,
even when such proclamation springs from wrongheaded motivation. Once
again, as in the case of his imprisonment itself, God brings good even from
actions with misguided or tainted intentions.

## Reflection and Application (1:12–18a)

*God can write straight with crooked lines.* Even when Paul learns that rival
preachers exploit his absence by making converts in a spirit of competition, Paul

---

3. Scholars sometimes identify these rivals with the adversaries of 1:28 or "the dogs" of 3:2, but
the adversaries of 1:28 are indeed *adversaries*, not rivals, and they are harassing the Philippians, not
Paul. As for the adversaries mentioned in 3:2, they are clearly false teachers, in whose preaching Paul
would not rejoice.

can find reason to rejoice. Is he simply trying to put a good spin on a bad situation? No. He sees some genuine good springing even from mixed motivation, and he chooses to focus on that. This is not a matter of putting on rose-colored glasses. It is a matter of the intensity with which he desires that Christ be more widely known and loved.

As an illustration, we might compare his situation to that of a pastor today who learns that one of his parishioners, feeling that the pastor fails to emphasize Scripture enough in his homilies, has started a Bible study group and is using a fundamentalist guidebook that would not meet his approval. The pastor might not like the implied criticism of his preaching, but he might find reason to rejoice in the fact that some of his people are taking the initiative to read and reflect on Scripture together. Unlike the imprisoned Paul, of course, this pastor is not powerless to respond, and the use of a fundamentalist study guide is something he needs to correct. But inspired by Paul's attitude, instead of scolding the group leader about "going Protestant" by using that particular program, he might praise the individual for taking initiative. Further, he might take the incident as a prompt to offer his own Bible classes. The pastor might even hear the message that he should take Scripture reading more seriously himself and bring more Bible study into his homily preparation, maybe even including some discussion with members of his congregation.

## Facing the Future (1:18b–26)

Indeed I shall continue to rejoice, [19]for I know that this will result in deliverance for me through your prayers and support from the Spirit of Jesus Christ. [20]My eager expectation and hope is that I shall not be put to shame in any way, but that with all boldness, now as always, Christ will be magnified in my body, whether by life or by death. [21]For to me life is Christ, and death is gain. [22]If I go on living in the flesh, that means fruitful labor for me. And I do not know which I shall choose. [23]I am caught between the two. I long to depart this life and be with Christ, [for] that is far better. [24]Yet that I remain [in] the flesh is more necessary for your benefit. [25]And this I know with confidence, that I shall remain and continue in the service of all of you for your progress and joy in the faith, [26]so that your boasting in Christ Jesus may abound on account of me when I come to you again.

OT: Jer 9:23; Job 13:16
NT: Luke 1:46; 1 Cor 1:29–31; 2 Cor 5:8; 10:17; Gal 3:5; 1 Thess 4:13–18
Catechism: Christian death, 1010–14; life in Christ, 1691–98

**Indeed I shall continue to rejoice, for I know that this will result in deliv-**    1:18b–19
**erance for me.** Scholars have noticed that "this will result in deliverance for
me" echoes the †Septuagint version of Job 13:16, where Job expresses his trust
that God will acquit him as innocent despite false accusations. If Paul has that
passage in view, he may well be thinking of acquittal at his own coming trial
by the imperial court. Then again, he may mean that God will vindicate his
faithfulness no matter what his fate at the hands of the Roman judge. The word
translated "deliverance" (*sōtēria*) is literally †salvation. What counts for Paul is
not the imminent imperial judgment but the judgment that God will render
on the last day, "the day of Christ" (vv. 6 and 10).

Part of his confidence rests in his trust that the Philippians are praying for
him, just as he regularly prays for them (see v. 4). In applying the verse from
Job, Paul shows that salvation—which in the Old Testament usually refers to
rescue from physical harm—for him means the ultimate security of eternal life
with God, whatever the earthly outcome.

The expression **support from the Spirit of Jesus Christ** raises several questions. Does "the Spirit of Jesus Christ" refer to Jesus' human spirit, or to the
Holy Spirit as sent by Jesus? And is the "support" something that *derives* from
the Spirit, or does it *consist in* the gift of the Spirit? The word for "support" is
a rare word, used in verbal form for God's *supplying* of gifts in 2 Cor 9:10 and
Gal 3:5. Galatians 3:5 is especially helpful for clarifying our present verse. There
Paul reminds the Galatians that God "supplies the Holy Spirit" to them and
works mighty deeds among them. It is reasonable to hear a similar meaning in
Phil 1:19: the risen Jesus sends the gift of the Holy Spirit in response to prayer.
The Spirit *is* the gift.

In effect, Paul asserts that his imprisonment is not "all about me"; it is all about    1:20–21
Christ. And he expects the world to see it that way. Normally incarceration is
a shameful affair, perhaps even more in the ancient world than today. But Paul
can say, **My eager expectation and hope is that I shall not be put to shame in
any way, but that with all boldness, now as always, Christ will be magnified in
my body, whether by life or by death.** That his physical fate—death or extended
life—should magnify Christ may seem an odd expression, as if Christ could
somehow be made greater by Paul's lot under the Romans. But in biblical Greek,
"magnify" can mean "to cause to be held in greater esteem," as in the opening
verse of Mary's Magnificat: "My soul magnifies the Lord" (Luke 1:46 NRSV).
Thumbs up or thumbs down, Paul is convinced that his personal fate will "advance the gospel" (1:12)—either by his continuing to live and then to carry out
his ministry, or by his martyrdom for the sake of Christ. Paul's faith enables him

to understand the prospects of his imprisonment as a win-win situation that he can summarize with the memorable saying, **For to me life is Christ, and death is gain.** The cryptic phrase "life is Christ" (or "to live is Christ," RSV) indicates that his relationship with Christ has so changed him that his concept of life itself has changed. For him, living means being in relationship with the risen Lord, a relationship that death does not terminate but only changes. Indeed, biological death has become something positive, the door to being "with Christ" (v. 23), that is, more directly in the presence of the risen Lord.

**1:22–26**
In the next five verses Paul proceeds to unpack what he has said so crisply in the preceding passage. In the process, he gives the Philippians (and us) a rare personal glimpse into his inner life. In the twenty-first-century environment of the internet and personal webpages, one can easily think of Paul as a blogger writing these verses.

**If I go on living in the flesh, that means fruitful labor for me. And I do not know which I shall choose.** The upshot of the legal process is, of course, not up to him. Thus a better translation for the word "choose" would be "prefer." Paul's point is that the possibilities of both acquittal and the death penalty are for him so rich that he does not know which prospect to favor. His desire is to **be with Christ,** to enter through death into a more intimate union than is possible in this life (see Luke 23:43). But Paul's life is no longer about Paul. It is about serving Christ by serving the church at Philippi. That thought leads Paul directly to the conviction that the objectively greater good is to continue to live for the sake of their **progress and joy in the faith.** Notice that the last words pick up the sentiments of the letter's thanksgiving prayer (1:3–6). The Philippian community is God's work in progress, and as God's coworker in this project, Paul wants to help bring the work to completion.

If we wonder what Paul means by **boasting in Christ Jesus,** we learn from his Letters to the Corinthians that it is the opposite of self-commendation. Boasting in the Lord is simply recognizing that it is indeed God who is doing a great work. The unity and growth of the Philippian church is God's doing and not the result of their own cleverness and power. Taking a cue from Jer 9:23–24, he says, "Whoever boasts, should boast in the Lord" (1 Cor 1:29–31; 2 Cor 10:17).[4] While Paul mentions boasting only three times in Philippians (1:26; 2:16; 3:3), history and archaeology show that the practice of boasting was a lively art in that town, in which more public inscriptions of self-celebration have surfaced than in any other Roman colony. The Christians of Philippi have learned, instead, to boast in Christ Jesus.

---

4. Paul's word "boast" reflects the Greek version of Jer 9:23–24.

## Reflection and Application (1:18b–26)

*A new map of honor and shame.* In the Mediterranean cultures of the first century, social behavior was governed largely by what counted as honorable or shameful. Material acquisition, power, and a track record of civic roles and accomplishments earned honor and a good name. Poverty and servitude made for shame and social disregard. In the present passage of Philippians we hear Paul use his imprisonment as an opportunity to remind the Philippian Christians that those who are in Christ see things very differently. For those who honor Jesus Christ as Lord (rather than the emperor), it is not the Roman commonwealth and its officials but the Lord God and his incarnate image, the Lord Jesus Christ, who have the last word about what counts as honorable and shameful. As one scholar has put it, "Paul wishes to remap the zone of what amounted to honorable and what amounted to shameful or taboo behavior."[5] Paul dares to present his own experience in chains as an example of this mind-set because his inspiration and source is nothing less than the self-humiliation of Jesus as it will be spelled out in the Christ hymn of the next chapter.

Here we have a powerful reminder that Christian discipleship is always in some sense countercultural. Not that the vision embodied in Christian faith is essentially oriented *against* a given culture. The point is that *any* culture, for all its rich diversity and strength, needs to be purified by the gospel. Our Christian faith draws from its Jewish roots a warm affirmation of the goodness of creation and rejoices in the diversity of human cultures. Yet the moral implications of the gospel—such as the dignity of all persons, reverence for life from conception to natural death, creative nonviolence, the universal destiny of material resources, the truthful use of speech, sexual fidelity—offer a continual challenge to any culture. In our own lifetime, those of us who live in North America have seen the teaching of our Church challenge elements of our culture with respect to abortion, capital punishment, the criteria for the just use of military force, the neglect of the poor, and the privileging of the profit motive. While there is plenty to affirm in our culture—like the ensuring of certain freedoms, public education, economic opportunity, technological creativity, excellence in the fine arts—we recognize that our Christian vision is also, in important ways, countercultural. At the same time, we have been urged to involve ourselves in the culture through what the United States bishops have been calling *faithful citizenship.*

*Life after death before resurrection.* As Paul reflects on death as a possible outcome of his imprisonment, he does not spell out what he expects life after

---

5. Witherington, *Friendship and Finances*, 48.

death to be like. That is not his subject here. But the little he says is a precious contribution to our own expectations regarding life after death. His words are simple: "I long to depart this life and be with Christ" (1:24). For any reader coming to this statement with 1 Thess 4:13–18 in mind, Paul's words may come as a surprise. There, when he takes up the question of the destiny of individual Christians, he assures the Thessalonians that "the dead in Christ," that is, Christians who die before the final coming of Christ, "will rise first." Then those still alive will be caught up together with them to meet the Lord, like a civic population going out to welcome the visiting emperor. Then they "will be with the Lord," implicitly in the risen state. Whereas 1 Thessalonians implies that only at the †parousia will the dead "be with Christ," here, in his later Letter to the Philippians, Paul envisions being with Christ immediately after death.

In Philippians Paul is considering life after death from a new perspective as he faces the possible prospect of execution. Now that he is a candidate to soon be one of the "dead in Christ," the question of postmortem but preparousia existence has become intensely personal. His reflection on his experience of the risen Lord has led him to believe that even before the general resurrection he will somehow "be with Christ" in a fuller way than in earthly life. He also envisions an interim period between death and bodily resurrection in 2 Cor 5:8, where he speaks of his readiness to "leave the body and go home to the Lord." In Phil 3:21, Paul makes it clear that the bodily resurrection at the parousia will be a further stage of being with Christ: "He will change our lowly body to conform with his glorified body by the power that enables him also to bring all things into subjection to himself." The passage of time, new experience, and further reflection have led Paul to a fresh dimension of Christian hope.

At a time when we sometimes speak of deceased loved ones as if they already enjoy the resurrection (perhaps prompted by a misunderstanding of the phrase "Mass of the Resurrection" designating a Catholic funeral), it is important to recall that the line in the creed "I believe in the resurrection of the body" pertains to the raising up of our bodies at the final appearance of the risen Jesus at the end of history; it is not simply a way of referring to life after death. To "be with Christ" after death is indeed something to be desired, but it is not yet the resurrection from the dead.[6]

---

6. N. T. Wright provides an in-depth exploration of this issue in *Surprised by Hope* (San Francisco: HarperOne, 2008).

# A Call to Conduct Worthy of the Gospel

## Philippians 1:27–2:4

At this point Paul moves from reflection on his own situation and his prospects to the main purpose of the letter—persuading this dear community to more deeply commit themselves to living out their new life in Christ. First, he makes his pitch in general terms (1:27–30). Then he spells out what that means in terms of concrete behavior in the community (2:1–4).

### Strive Together to Hold Firm in the Face of Opposition (1:27–30)

> [27]Only, conduct yourselves in a way worthy of the gospel of Christ, so that, whether I come and see you or am absent, I may hear news of you, that you are standing firm in one spirit, with one mind struggling together for the faith of the gospel, [28]not intimidated in any way by your opponents. This is proof to them not of destruction, but of your salvation. And this is God's doing. [29]For to you has been granted, for the sake of Christ, not only to believe in him but also to suffer for him. [30]Yours is the same struggle as you saw in me and now hear about me.

NT: John 17:20–23; Acts 4:32; 23:1; Phil 3:20
Catechism: life in Christ, 1692
Lectionary: Votive Mass for Persecuted Christians

The key verb Paul uses to launch his exhortation, here translated **conduct yourselves**, is a rare word and very carefully chosen: *politeuomai*. The root *polit-*, as in the word "politics," suggests the civic or social dimension of life.

1:27

89

*Politeuomai* can mean "to be a citizen" or "to rule," or it can simply mean "to conduct oneself" (NABRE, NIV; NRSV has "live your life"). The context of this letter suggests that Paul wants his readers to be alert to the dimensions of their citizenship. They reside, after all, in a Roman colony where one's status as a citizen of the empire, or not, is an important issue. Later in this letter Paul will say, "Our citizenship [*politeuma*] is in heaven" (3:20).[1] We will explore the implications of Paul's statement when we come to that passage; here it is sufficient to note that the theme of citizenship pervades the whole letter. Just as many residents of Philippi identify themselves as citizens of Rome even though they live in Philippi, so also the members of the local church, whether Roman citizens or not, find the root of their identity as citizens of heaven. That their conduct here on earth as citizens of the heavenly commonwealth should be **worthy of the gospel of Christ** is to say that their community life should reflect the good news of Christ their risen Lord and savior (see 3:20, where Paul refers to Jesus as the "savior"—an imperial title—whose visitation they await). This call to a way of life that outwardly manifests the presence of Christ in their midst reflects very much the sense of John 17:23, where Jesus prays "that they may be brought to perfection as one, that the world may know that you sent me, and that you loved them even as you loved me."

Such conduct worthy of the gospel entails **standing firm in one spirit** and **with one mind.** This clause parallels Luke's description of the Jerusalem Christian community: "The community of believers was of one heart and mind, and no one claimed that any of his possessions was his own, but they had everything in common" (Acts 4:32). In Philippians the "one spirit" (*pneuma*) refers to human solidarity but also to the supernatural unity brought about by the Holy Spirit, as in Phil 2:1 ("participation in the Spirit")[2] and 1 Cor 12:13.

The phrase **struggling together for the faith of the gospel** continues to draw on the political and military context of Greco-Roman Philippi. Here Paul employs language first used in the world of sports and later applied to military conflict, a crucial element of citizenship. The verb for "struggling together" (*synathleō*) is a good example. We English speakers can hear in *athleō* the root

---

1. Interestingly, the only other place in the New Testament where this verb is used is in Acts 23:1, in which Paul addresses the Sanhedrin: "My brothers, I have conducted myself [*politeuomai*] with a perfectly clear conscience before God to this day." This occurs just after Paul has been discussing his Roman citizenship with a Roman centurion (22:25–29). Luke may well have chosen the verb to suggest that Paul is proclaiming his innocence precisely as a member of the commonwealth of Israel in covenant with God. Thus Luke may be presenting Paul as having a dual citizenship—as a Roman citizen and as a Torah-keeping Jew.

2. Gordon Fee argues convincingly for this meaning (*Paul's Letter to the Philippians* [Grand Rapids: Eerdmans, 1995], 163–66).

of our word "athlete," and indeed it can mean "to compete in the arena" (see 2 Tim 2:5). It can also mean "contend" in military contexts. Paul combines *athleō* with the prefix *syn-* to create a word that means "contend together" or "strive side-by-side." He will later use that word to describe the labor of Euodia and Syntyche in their promotion of the †gospel at Paul's side (4:3). That these are the only two instances of the word in the New Testament shows that Paul's use of it is quite deliberate. Given the imperial context of his audience, it seems that Paul is speaking more as a commander exhorting his troops than as a coach addressing his team at halftime.[3]

It is not immediately obvious to what adversaries Paul is referring when he    1:28
says, **not intimidated in any way by your opponents**. Since this way of speaking does not seem to fit either the rival preachers of 1:15–17 or the "dogs" of 3:2, these opponents seem to be pagan residents of Philippi who find the Christians' behavior and heavenly allegiance a threat to Roman peace and order, as exemplified in the Philippian episode in Acts 16:20–21.

The Christians' standing firm in one spirit is a **proof** (or "sign," NIV; "evidence," NRSV) of their **salvation** in the sense that their unity and fearlessness demonstrates God's presence with and support of them, again as in John 17:20–23. The gift of †salvation is already evident in their earthly experience of empowerment by God. That empowerment to stand firm is also an omen of the opponents' ultimate **destruction**.[4] In this match, the Philippian Christians know that God is on their side: **And this is God's doing**. Despite immediate appearances, the Philippian Christians are the ultimate winners, their opponents the ultimate losers.

Paul continues the athletic imagery with the word "struggle" (*agōn*), mean-    1:29–30
ing a contest, like a wrestling match: **Yours is the same struggle as you saw in me and now hear about me**. Both he and they are suffering the opposition of the pagan power of the Roman Empire. It is a struggle they share, ultimately, with the Messiah himself: **For to you has been granted, for the sake of Christ, not only to believe in him but also to suffer for him**. Paul, and the New Testament generally, often speaks of the suffering that inevitably accompanies being a follower of Jesus. Rejection and shame are side effects of the Christian mission. Yet such suffering is endured with joy and is considered a privilege, giving Christians a way of bearing witness to Christ

---

3. In this discussion of the political and military framework of Paul's imagery, I am particularly indebted to Timothy C. Geoffrion, *The Rhetorical Purpose and the Political and Military Character of Philippians: A Call to Stand Firm* (Lewiston, NY: Edwin Mellen, 1993).

4. See Fee, *Philippians*, 167–70. For other examples of Paul's use of salvation/destruction language, see 1 Cor 1:18 and 2 Cor 2:15–16.

(1 Cor 4:9–13; Phil 1:12–14) and sharing in his redemptive work (3:10; 2 Cor 1:5–7; Col 1:24).

## Qualities Required for a Christian Community (2:1–4)

[1]If there is any encouragement in Christ, any solace in love, any participation in the Spirit, any compassion and mercy, [2]complete my joy by being of the same mind, with the same love, united in heart, thinking one thing. [3]Do nothing out of selfishness or out of vainglory; rather, humbly regard others as more important than yourselves, [4]each looking out not for his own interests, but [also] everyone for those of others.

NT: Rom 12:3, 10; 1 Cor 10:24, 33; Gal 5:26
Catechism: concern for others, 2635–36
Lectionary: Consecration of Virgins and Religious Profession; Pastoral and Spiritual Meetings

2:1      The four if-clauses in verse 1 ("if" is used four times in the Greek) may make Paul sound as though he is doubtful that the Christian community at Philippi has the five attributes mentioned. But Paul has made it clear in the thanksgiving that he recognizes both the "good work" God has begun in them and their "partnership" in grace with him (1:5–6). They already have a lot going for them, and we do well to be attentive to the qualities he ascribes to their shared life.

Paul has already spelled out how the Philippians have provided **encouragement** for him in his imprisonment, especially in their "prayers and support from the Spirit of Jesus Christ" (1:19). He in turn encourages them in the very act of writing this letter. That encouragement (*paraklēsis*) is not just a sentiment but an inner strengthening of faith and steadfastness.[5] And it derives from their being **in Christ**, Paul's shorthand for a profound personal union with Christ and a participation in the shared life of the Christian community, whose source is Jesus and the Father. Another form of that encouragement is their experience of **solace** (or "consolation," NRSV) in their mutual **love**, a balm that heals the pain of their social rejection. **Participation** (or "communion," "fellowship") **in the Spirit** is the brotherly-sisterly unity that is a gift of the Spirit. Since love is a characteristic gift of God the Father (see Rom 5:5; Eph 2:4), Paul is pointing to the trinitarian foundation of their shared life: *Christ*, God's *love*, and *the Spirit*. Not just human sentiment or common interests but also participation in divine life enables the church to be what it is called to be.

---

5. Encouragement (*paraklēsis*) is related to *paraklētos* ("consoler," "comforter," "counselor," or "advocate"), a title for the Holy Spirit in the Gospel of John (John 14:16, 26; 15:26; 16:7).

**Compassion** (*splanchna*) translates again that favorite "innards" word applied to Christ in the thanksgiving prayer (1:8). And **mercy** is a quality usually attributed to the Lord God in the Old Testament. Here, it implies that the church is to imitate the compassion of God, as in Jesus' saying in the Gospel of Luke about imitating the Father: where Matthew's version says, "So be perfect, just as your heavenly Father is perfect" (5:48), Luke has, "Be merciful, just as your Father is merciful" (Luke 6:36).

Their progress thus far has been a source of **joy** for Paul; now he tells them how they can **complete** that joy. Paul has four ways of expressing the desired state of the community:

    being of the same mind,

    with the same love,

    united in heart,

    thinking one thing.

In the first and fourth phrases, Paul uses a verb that is especially important in this letter, *phroneō*. It is a rich word, meaning to "think, form/hold an opinion, judge," "set one's mind on, be intent on," "be minded/disposed."[6] He employs it ten times in Philippians. "Being of the same mind" could sound like a call to think the same thoughts or hold the same opinions. Paul does indeed regard doctrinal unity as essential (see Rom 16:17; Gal 1:8–9; Eph 4:13–14), but the sameness he has in mind here has more to do with unity of spirit than with similarity of ideas (see his use of the same phrase in Rom 12:16; 15:5–6). Those whose whole aim is to honor the Lord Jesus and further the spread of his gospel cannot be in disunity—even where there may be sharp differences of personality, opinion, interest, and background. Indeed, the two middle phrases—"with the same love, united in heart"—also point in the direction of unity of spirit.

Having urged unity, Paul clarifies his meaning by pointing out attitudes and behaviors that damage unity: **Do nothing out of selfishness or out of vainglory.** The word for "selfishness" describes the motive of some of the rival preachers mentioned in 1:17. Paul suspects that this selfish ambition and contentious spirit also threatens the unity of the Philippian community.

**Rather, humbly regard others as more important than yourselves, each looking out not for his own interests, but [also] everyone for those of others.** "Humbly" (*tapeinophrosynē*) describes an attitude strikingly counter to

2:2

2:3–4

---

6. BDAG 1065–66.

## Habits of the Heart in Paul

**BIBLICAL BACKGROUND**

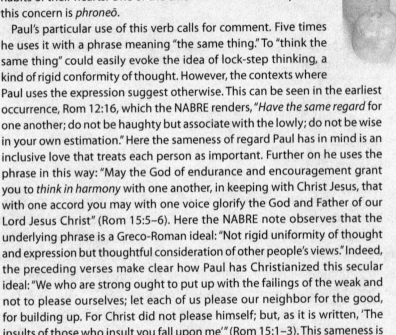

In two of his letters, Romans and Philippians, Paul spends a good bit of ink urging his addressees to focus their thinking in a certain way, to manage their minds in a Christian manner, to attend to the habits of their hearts. One of the chief words he uses to speak of this concern is *phroneō*.

Paul's particular use of this verb calls for comment. Five times he uses it with a phrase meaning "the same thing." To "think the same thing" could easily evoke the idea of lock-step thinking, a kind of rigid conformity of thought. However, the contexts where Paul uses the expression suggest otherwise. This can be seen in the earliest occurrence, Rom 12:16, which the NABRE renders, "*Have the same regard* for one another; do not be haughty but associate with the lowly; do not be wise in your own estimation." Here the sameness of regard Paul has in mind is an inclusive love that treats each person as important. Further on he uses the phrase in this way: "May the God of endurance and encouragement grant you to *think in harmony* with one another, in keeping with Christ Jesus, that with one accord you may with one voice glorify the God and Father of our Lord Jesus Christ" (Rom 15:5–6). Here the NABRE note observes that the underlying phrase is a Greco-Roman ideal: "Not rigid uniformity of thought and expression but thoughtful consideration of other people's views." Indeed, the preceding verses make clear how Paul has Christianized this secular ideal: "We who are strong ought to put up with the failings of the weak and not to please ourselves; let each of us please our neighbor for the good, for building up. For Christ did not please himself; but, as it is written, 'The insults of those who insult you fall upon me'" (Rom 15:1–3). This sameness is really profound human solidarity. The phrase expresses a similar solidarity in the conclusion of 2 Corinthians: "Finally, brothers, rejoice. Mend your ways, encourage one another, *agree with one another*, live in peace, and the God of love and peace will be with you" (2 Cor 13:11). Here in Philippians Paul uses the same phrase to urge Euodia and Syntyche to "*come to a mutual understanding* in the Lord" (4:2).

Paul uses *phroneō* in a variety of other ways to describe the Christian mind-set or attitude. An illuminating example is in Rom 12:3: "I tell everyone among you not *to think* of himself more highly than one ought to think, but *to think* soberly, each according to the measure of faith that God has apportioned."

the Roman culture of Philippi, where one's place in the imperial pecking order was a matter of great concern and where upper-class men were expected to ambitiously pursue honor. Its verbal form (*tapeinaō*) will describe Jesus' self-humbling in verse 8 (see also 4:12).[7] "Regard" (*hēgeomai*) is another crucial word in Paul's discussion of Christian habits of the heart.[8] Here it means "think, consider, regard" in a way that is synonymous with *phroneō*. Its appearance here prepares the way for verse 6, where Christ does not "regard" his divine status as something to be clung to or exploited, and 3:7–8, where Paul "regards" all his previous privileges as nothing in comparison with knowing Christ. Christians are to do what is humanly unheard of: to regard everyone else as more important than themselves and to put everyone else's interests ahead of their own.

**Have among yourselves the same attitude that is also yours in Christ Jesus.**    **2:5**
Since this sentence introduces the Christ hymn of the next six verses, we will examine it carefully in the next section. I also include it here because it not only introduces the Christ hymn but also, as a bridge, completes the exhortation begun at 1:27. The qualities and behavior urged on Christians are precisely those expressed in the incarnation, life, and death of Jesus, whom Paul will celebrate as the best example of all.

## Reflection and Application (1:27–2:4)

When Christians today talk about growth in holiness, they typically talk about it in terms of one's personal journey. Our interest in the individual spiritual journey would not have been alien to Paul. Indeed, in Phil 3:1–16 he reflects on his own process of spiritual growth in Christ. But his emphasis in this letter is really on a Christian *community's* growth in the Spirit. The passage we have just finished studying is a rich example of his thought on the subject.

We would do well to apply this passage to our own attitudes about the various cells of Christian community to which we belong—family, parish, diocese, and the Church universal. Each of these bodies—including such subgroups as prayer groups, reading groups, youth groups, Christian Life Communities—are called to mature as a body, to travel a communal journey. We can help our faith community flourish to the extent that we act according to the vision Paul communicates in this letter.

---

7. Even though I do not presume that the readers of this commentary know Greek, I include key Greek words to highlight the fact that, when Paul exhorts the Philippian Christians to ways of thinking and acting that foster unity, he is deliberately choosing language that occurs in the Christ hymn. The point: the mind-set he is urging them to adopt is illustrated by the "mind of Christ Jesus" as described in the hymn.

8. BDAG 434. Six of Paul's seven uses are here in Philippians (2:3, 6, 25; 3:7, 8 [twice]).

1. "This is God's doing" (1:28). That is, a local church is an *ekklēsia*, a group that exists only because people have literally been "called out" by God and have responded in faith to something God is doing among them.
2. The group experiences the gift of the Spirit of God as he empowers them to relate to one another in love and compassion (2:1–2).
3. God's calling has made the faith community a kind of alternative homeland or commonwealth (3:20).
4. Citizenship in this commonwealth means relating to others in the way of Jesus, which differs from the way of the world in that one looks out for others' interests more than one's own (2:3–4).

In the life of a parish, we nurture these realities especially in the celebration of the Sunday Eucharist, in which we leave behind all worldly markers of status and act simply as the body of Christ, thanking God the Father for what he has done in creation, in his covenant with Israel, in the incarnation of his Word in Jesus of Nazareth, and in his presence with us now through the Spirit. We respond to these divine initiatives by joining in Jesus' self-offering to the Father in the power of the Spirit. Then, having been nourished at the table of Word and sacrament, we move back into our ordinary life to carry into the world the divine love and grace we have experienced in the liturgy. This entails concrete acts of friendship, forgiveness, mediation, reconciliation, visiting the sick, offering hospitality, lending a hand to disabled neighbors, contributing to committee work, and the like. In these ways, we grow as a community that reflects the supernatural vision of the Church in Paul's teaching.

# The Best Example of All: Christ's Self-Emptying Love and Service

## Philippians 2:5–11

We come now to the Christ hymn, the famous †*Carmen Christi* that has nurtured the prayer and the theology of the Church in a special way for two millennia. As we will see, whatever history this poem might have had as a freestanding composition prior to the writing of the letter, this celebration of Jesus' incarnation, life, death, and exaltation to glory is for Paul very much part of his communication to the Philippian Christians. Indeed, a good case can be made that Paul himself composed it. Here Jesus is presented as the primary model of the behavior Paul has been advocating.

### The Christ Hymn (2:5–11)

⁵Have among yourselves the same attitude that is also yours in Christ Jesus,

> ⁶Who, though he was in the form of God,
> did not regard equality with God something to be grasped.
> ⁷Rather, he emptied himself,
> taking the form of a slave,
> coming in human likeness;
> and found human in appearance,
> ⁸he humbled himself,
> becoming obedient to death, even death on a cross.

⁹Because of this, God greatly exalted him
and bestowed on him the name that is above every name,
¹⁰that at the name of Jesus
every knee should bend,
of those in heaven and on earth and under the earth,
¹¹and every tongue confess that
Jesus Christ is Lord,
to the glory of God the Father.

OT: Isa 45:23

NT: John 1:1–2; 1 Cor 8:6

Catechism: prayer, 2641, 2667; the Word become flesh, 461; Jesus as our model, 520; Jesus the Lord, 201, 449; life in Christ, 1694, 2842; Christ is God and man, 472, 602, 705, 713, 1224, 2812; Docetism, 465

Lectionary: Passion (Palm) Sunday; For Unity of Christians; Triumph of the Cross; Votive Mass for the Holy Name (during Easter season)

2:5     **Have among yourselves the same attitude** refers to the attitude described in the previous four verses. The second half of the verse, which points ahead to the Christ story that Paul is about to unfold, is more clearly rendered, "that was" **also in Christ Jesus.** The verb for having an attitude (*phroneō*) is the same one used twice in 2:2. Christians are to not only imitate but also assimilate into themselves Jesus' way of thinking.

2:6     Paul begins the story of Christ by describing him as the one **who, though he was in the form of God, did not regard equality with God something to be grasped.**

This verse, along with the following one, has been interpreted in two very different ways: (a) as a reference to the eternal Son choosing to become incarnate, or (b) as a reference to Jesus in his human existence refusing to yield to the temptation of Adam and Eve to be godlike (Gen 3:6). The solution to this dilemma hangs mainly on the meaning of two words—*harpagmon*, rendered by the NAB as "something to be grasped," and *morphē*, which the NABRE renders as "form."

*Harpagmon* is the most challenging word to translate since it can mean two quite different things. On the one hand, it can mean something *not yet possessed* but viewed as something to be stolen, seized, or claimed; on the other hand, it can mean something *already possessed*, as something to be taken advantage of. Since the English word "grasp" can mean "seize" as well as "hold on to," the NABRE translation "something to be grasped" is open to either interpretation. However, recent scholarship has revealed that the ancient Greek usage of the phrase "to consider something as *harpagmon*" means to consider the thing already

Fig. 7. This painting of Christ crucified by Diego Velázquez (1599–1660) catches the utter dereliction and denigration of a victim of this form of Roman capital punishment.

possessed as something to be used to one's advantage. This meaning is expressed in the NRSV: "did not regard equality with God as something to be exploited."[1] This understanding supports the traditional interpretation of verses 6–7 as referring to Christ's incarnation. In this interpretation the eternal Son, who eternally possesses equality with God the Father, empties himself by becoming man. But precisely *what* the eternal Son emptied himself of depends on that other difficult word, *morphē* ("form").

The ordinary meaning of *morphē* is "outward appearance" or what we usually mean by "form" in English.[2] "God," as is usual in the New Testament, means God the Father. Since Scripture asserts that God is invisible ("No one has ever seen God," John 1:18; see also Exod 33:20), "the form of God" is a puzzling concept. God's form, then, must mean the visible *manifestation* of his holiness and power through his mighty deeds, or what the Old Testament means by God's "glory."[3] By becoming man the Son emptied himself of the glory, majesty, and privilege that belong to him as divine.

---

1. The same interpretation is reflected in the Jerusalem Bible paraphrase: "yet he did not cling to his equality with God."

2. *Morphē* means "external appearance" in the only other place it appears in the New Testament, Mark 16:12, where the risen Jesus "appeared in another *form* to two of them walking along on their way to the country" (apparently referring to the Emmaus episode of Luke 24:13–32). We find the same meaning of *morphē* in the Septuagint: for example, in Job 4:16 ("there was no form before my eyes"), Isa 44:13 (a wooden idol is carved "in the form of a man"), and Dan 5:6, 9, 10; 7:28 ("countenance").

3. One recent interpretation takes *morphē* as an allusion to the "image" of Gen 1:26–27 and reads "emptied himself" as a reference to the earthly life of Jesus. That is, in his incarnation the Son took on the image of God by assuming human nature, but he refused to succumb to the temptation of Adam and Eve, to grasp for equality with God ("You will be like gods," Gen 3:5). That understanding may resonate with the idea of Jesus as the New Adam, which appears in other letters of Paul (e.g., Rom 5:12–21), but it does not really fit the language of this poem. If the Christ hymn had intended an allusion to Gen 1:26–27, it would have used *eikōn*, the Septuagint's word for the "image" of God in Gen 1:26–27, not

# The Fathers Ponder the Hymn

Like many Christians after them, the patristic writers found much to ponder in this passage. Eusebius of Vercelli found in it an expression of the atonement.

> How then did he *empty himself?* When the *form of God accepted the form of a slave*, when he who is preeminently the Lord deigned to take on himself what belongs to a slave. The Word was made flesh by bearing and doing what was beneath him in his indulgence and compassion toward us. All that he possessed by nature is emptied into this his person. Having been made obedient as a man in the true *fashion of humanity*, he has restored to our nature by his own humility and obedience what had perished through disobedience in Adam.[a]

The Fathers had no trouble understanding that the self-emptying of the eternal Son was a model to be imitated by mere humans. For example, here is Ambrosiaster.

> *Taking the form of a slave.* He indeed was taken captive, bound and driven with blows. His obedience to the Father took him even as far as the cross. Yet throughout he knew himself to be the Father's Son, equal in divine dignity. Yet he did not make a display of this equality. Rather he willingly subjected himself. This patience and humility he teaches us to imitate. We are to refrain from making a display of our claims to equal dignity, but even more so we are called to lower ourselves into service as we follow the example of our Maker.[b]

For Eusebius of Caesarea, the hymn celebrates the Son's solidarity with humanity as a whole.

> Read the record of his compassion. It pleased him, being the Word of God, to *take the form of a slave*. So he willed to be joined to our common human condition. He took to himself the toils of the members who suffer. He made our human maladies his own. He suffered and toiled on our behalf. This is in accord with his great love of humankind.[c]

*continued on next page*

The phrase "equality with God" clarifies Paul's meaning. Translated more literally, it is "*the* equality with God"; "the" signals that the phrase picks up what has already been said. In other words, "equality with God" is synonymous with "being in the form of God." A similar phrase appears in the Gospel of John, where the Jewish leaders accuse Jesus of "making himself equal to God" (John 5:18).

**2:7–8**   **Rather, he emptied himself.** Paul's assertion here mirrors the prologue of the Gospel of John: "The Word became flesh" (John 1:14). The next lines, especially

---

*morphē* ("form"). Moreover, the tempter in Eden promises Eve that the couple will be "*like gods*," not that they will be "equal to God."

With his special sensitivity to language, John Chrysostom focuses on the doctrinal implications.

> He was not only human, which is what he appeared to be, but also God. . . . We are soul and body, but he is God, soul, and body. For this reason Paul says *in the form*—and so that when you hear of his emptying you may not suppose that he underwent change, degradation and some sort of annihilation of his divinity. Rather remaining what he was he assumed what he was not. Becoming flesh, he remained the Word of God. So it is in this respect that he is *in the likeness of men*, and for this reason he says *and in form*. His nature was not degraded, nor was there any confusion [of the two natures], but he entered a *form*.[d]

If "in human likeness" seems to compromise Christ's full humanity, Theodoret has a clarification.

> He says of the divine Word that, being God, he was not seen to be God but wore a human appearance. Yet the words *in the likeness of men* are appropriate to him, for the nature that he assumed was truly human, and yet he was not [merely] a man, though he at first glance appeared to be only a man.[e]

a. *On the Trinity*, quoted in ACCS 8:245.
b. *Epistle to the Philippians* 2.8.1–2, quoted in ACCS 8:246.
c. *Demonstrations of the Gospel* 10.1.22, quoted in ACCS 8:246–47.
d. *Homily on the Philippians* 8.2.5–11, quoted in ACCS 8:248.
e. *Epistle to the Philippians* 2.6–7, quoted in ACCS 8:248.

"coming in human likeness," make clear that Paul has in mind the †incarnation, rather than Jesus' deportment during his earthly life. This way of speaking about the eternal Son's incarnation also parallels Rom 8:3, where Paul writes of God "sending his own Son in the likeness of sinful flesh."

**Taking the form of a slave** may seem an unlikely denigration of human nature, but the point is not the lowliness of human nature in itself. Rather, the hymn contrasts the vast difference between divinity and humanity. In the cultural context of the Roman colony of Philippi, social pecking order was a matter of great interest. If Paul is promoting the countercultural Christian virtue of humility, as he surely is in verses 1–4, and if he is now presenting Jesus as the supreme model of humility, then his point is the stunning contrast between being "in the form of God" (a status Roman citizens ascribed to the emperor) and being "in the form of a slave" (the very bottom of the social status scale). In this context "form," "likeness," and "appearance" allude to the realm of social status, not metaphysics—although the implications regarding Christ's preexistence and divinity are metaphysical indeed.

If the phrase **in human likeness** seems to dilute the full humanity of Jesus, it may help to consider again the parallel with Rom 8:3, "sending his own Son in the likeness of sinful flesh." There "flesh" (*sarx*) refers to the humanity of Jesus, just as in John 1:14, "the Word became flesh." "Likeness" allows for the fact that the Son's enfleshment did not include sinfulness (see 2 Cor 5:21). Similarly, "coming in human likeness"—literally "born in the likeness of human beings"—asserts that Christ is fully human but also allows that he is different, in that he is also divine. Paul is not slipping into an early †docetism![4]

**And found human in appearance,** or "being in every way like a human being" (NJB), or still more literally, "in appearance found to be like a human being"—is virtually a paraphrase of the previous phrase, "coming in human likeness." As the Letter to the Hebrews puts it, Christ "had to become like his brothers in every way" (Heb 2:17)—he ate, drank, worked, laughed, wept, and suffered like all human beings. At this point, Paul moves from focusing on what the preexistent Christ has done as God (becoming human) to how he lived out his human life.[5] The Son, who had already emptied himself of divinity, **humbled himself, becoming obedient to death.** Since "obedient to death" could seem to describe death as Christ's master, a clearer translation is that of the NRSV: "obedient *to the point of* death." This obedience to the Father as a humble servant characterizes the whole earthly life of Jesus (see Mark 10:45).

**Even death on a cross** is not an addendum but the very climax of the statement. In Paul's world, death on a cross was the ultimate extreme not only of pain but also, and especially, of humiliation.[6] Paul is, after all, expanding on the self-abasement of Jesus. First came his self-emptying in the incarnation; then came his self-humbling in his human life, which culminated in the most humiliating death of all, the gruesome form of Roman execution reserved for criminals who were noncitizens of the empire, especially slaves. If the city of Philippi was filled with inscriptions posted by citizens boasting of their accomplishments in the Roman honors race, Paul counters this mind-set with his acclamation of Jesus Christ's self-emptying humility—to which God the Father responded by bestowing the supreme honor that is about to be described.

---

4. Docetism is the heresy of holding that Jesus Christ only *appeared to be* human.

5. The word for "appearance," *schēma*, is quite rare in the Bible, occurring only once in the Greek Old Testament (Isa 3:17, meaning outward form or shape) and one other time in the New Testament (1 Cor 7:31, "The world in its present form is passing away"). It seems reasonable to take it as synonymous with "form" as we are understanding *morphē* in this passage.

6. The New Testament writers focus more on the *shame* than on the pain involved in Jesus' crucifixion. The author of Hebrews writes, "For the sake of the joy that lay before him he endured the cross, *despising its shame*" (12:2). In Acts, when the Sanhedrin has the apostles flogged and orders them to stop speaking in the name of Jesus, again it is the shaming that Luke highlights: "So they left the presence of the Sanhedrin, rejoicing that they had been found worthy to *suffer dishonor* for the sake of the name" (Acts 5:40–41).

At verse 9 there is suddenly a complete reversal. **Because of this, God greatly**        2:9–11
**exalted him.** The Greek verb for "greatly exalt" (*hyperypsoō*) means in effect
to "*hyper*-exalt."[7] Though the hymn surely alludes to Jesus' resurrection, the
emphasis here is on the lofty status to which he has been raised.[8] Jesus' exaltation is not a matter of being raised from the human to the divine, since he
already possessed "the form of God" and "equality with God." Rather, it was
the Father's public vindication of the supremely honorable human life of the
Son. Christ is now, *in his human nature*, exalted to divine glory and enthroned
as Lord of the universe. This reversal from humiliation to exaltation evokes
Isaiah's fourth servant song, where God foretells that his suffering servant
shall "be exalted and glorified exceedingly" (Isa 52:13 LXX). The humiliated
one is glorified!

God **bestowed on him the name that is above every name.**[9] Obviously, this
clause calls for clarification: what name? Given that Jews even today sometimes
refer to †YHWH or the Lord God simply as "the Name" (*hashem* in Hebrew),
the phrase points to the name of God. The next phrase, however, **at the name**
**of Jesus,** raises the possibility that "Jesus" is the name in question; but the incarnate Son has already had that name since infancy. Rather, Paul's assertion is
that the proper name of Jesus is "†Lord," in its full sense of divinity.[10] The hymn
carefully builds toward this proclamation.

The Father's exaltation of Jesus is such that at the very mention of his name,
**every knee should bend . . . and every tongue confess that Jesus Christ is Lord.**
"Lord," then, is the name or title "that is above every other name." The wording
alludes to a rich text from Isaiah that teaches how we are to hear that name.
Isaiah 45:18–25 is one of the fullest expressions of Israelite monotheism, as the
following partial quotation demonstrates:

> [18]I am the LORD, and there is no other. . . .
> [22]Turn to me and be safe,
>> all you ends of the earth,
>> for I am God; there is no other!
> [23]By myself I swear,
>> uttering my just decree,
>> a word that will not return:

---

7. The term appears only here in the New Testament, although "exalt," or "raise up" (*hypsoō*) occurs
with some regularity, often as the opposite of "to humble," as in 2 Cor 11:7: "I humbled myself so that
you may be exalted."

8. Indeed, the entry for the word in BDAG is "to raise to a high point of honor" (1034).

9. The superiority of Jesus' name to all others is similarly emphasized in Eph 1:21; Heb 1:4.

10. In biblical languages "name" can refer to a title as well as a proper name.

> To me every knee shall bend;
>> by me every tongue shall swear,
> [24]Saying, "Only in the LORD
>> are just deeds and power.
> Before him in shame shall come
>> all who vent their anger against him.
> [25]In the LORD all the descendants of Israel
>> shall have vindication and glory."

Paul's words echo verse 23 of this passage. Listeners who heard the echo would have recalled that the passage is an oracle of the Lord God speaking as the sole creator of the universe and the savior of Israel, asserting his absolute uniqueness over against the idols of the nations. The passage foretells that one day all nations will assemble and "every knee will bend and every tongue confess" that the God of Israel is the one God and Lord of all. That Paul can take this absolute declaration of monotheism and apply it to Jesus of Nazareth would have been astounding in the context of the Judaism of his day. But for Paul, as for the rest of the New Testament writers, the proclamation of Christ's divinity is in no way contrary to the biblical revelation that God is one, as we will see below.

From Paul's quotation of Isa 45 both here and in Romans we know how important this prophetic passage was to him. In Rom 14:10–12 he uses it to evoke Isaiah's image of God gathering the Gentiles as a prelude to the final judgment: "Come and assemble, gather together, you fugitives from among the gentiles!" (Isa 45:20). Here too, in writing to the mainly Gentile church at Philippi, Paul would surely have been attentive to the end-time implications of his writing. God's gathering of the Gentiles—that is, gathering them to faith in Christ—is a sign that the final judgment is near. Paul is keenly aware that with the resurrection of Jesus the expected age to come has already dawned, and the gathering of the Gentiles in response to the gospel is a sign that humanity is now moving toward the final judgment, no matter how far in the future it may yet be.

Paul's listing of **those in heaven and on earth and under the earth** ensures that "every knee" and "every tongue" refers to every personal entity in the cosmos—angels and demons, living human beings, and dead people yet to be raised.[11] The sovereignty of Jesus embraces the full extent of creation, as described in Isa 45, over which the Lord God is sovereign. This way of referring to all creation also

---

11. "Those in heaven and on earth and under the earth" reflects the three-level cosmos of Gen 1 and Exod 20:4 ("You shall not carve idols for yourselves in the shape of anything in the sky above or on the earth below or in the waters beneath the earth").

occurs in the commandment against idolatrous images in Exod 20:4 and Deut 5:8: "You shall not carve idols for yourselves in the shape of anything in the sky above or on the earth below or in the waters beneath the earth."

In the NABRE (and all English translations known to me), Paul's next words are translated **that Jesus Christ is Lord**. But the Greek particle "that" often functions simply as a quotation mark, so the sentence could also be rendered, "and every tongue confess, 'Jesus Christ is Lord.'" This acclamation is the simplest and most basic confession of Christian faith: He is Lord! In the Greek Old Testament, the title "the Lord" (*kyrios*) is used in place of YHWH, the unspeakable name of God. Those who do not hear the echo of Isaiah 45 will still get the point, but those who do catch the echo will hear more powerfully and clearly that the final verses of the poem proclaim nothing less than the divinity of Jesus Christ: "Jesus Christ is Lord!" Now it is out. The name given to Jesus is "Lord" (*kyrios*)—the very name of God.

Is this proclamation of Jesus' divinity then an expression of bitheism (two gods)? To prevent such a misunderstanding, which would be contrary to biblical revelation, Paul completes the statement with the ringing phrase: **to the glory of God the Father**. Jesus' lordship is in no way that of another god in competition with the God of Israel. Rather, God freely shares his glory with the Son, who is equal to him from all eternity. The Gospel of John expresses a similar idea: God glorifies the Son so that the Son may in turn glorify the Father (see John 17:1).

Even a reader who knows no Greek can appreciate the power of expression in the final two phrases (a rhyming pair of three-beat verses) when read aloud (accented syllables italicized).

*Ký*rios Iē*sous* christ*os*
eis *dox*an the*ou* pat*ros*.

This expression matches the careful phrasing of the credo of 1 Cor 8:6.

> Yet for us there is one God, the Father,
>     from whom all things are and for whom we exist,
> and one Lord, Jesus Christ,
>     through whom all things are and through whom we exist.

## Reflection and Application (2:5–11)

*The passage as example.* The first and best application of this passage is the one Paul himself makes in the Letter to the Philippians. The Christ hymn illustrates the mind-set he exhorts Christians to take on in the preceding verses (1:27–2:4). Then in the verses that follow (2:12–18) he will apply the example of Christ in concrete ways to the life of the community.

*The passage as a prayer of the Church.* The passage has such beauty and wholeness that it lends itself to being lifted from its epistolary context and used as a freestanding text for prayer, meditation, liturgical reading, and song. Indeed, it is likely that more Christians have experienced the text in these contexts than in the context of the letter itself. In that way, it is like the three canticles drawn from the infancy narrative of the Gospel of Luke—the Magnificat (1:46–55), the Benedictus (1:68–79), and the Nunc Dimittis (2:29–32).

*The passage as a source of doctrine.* Paul speaks of Christ as being "in the form of God" and not considering "equality with God" as something to be taken advantage of. In all this, he refers to the preexistent, eternally divine Son of God in a way that parallels the thought of Heb 1:1–14, the prologue of John (1:1–4), the affirmation of 1 Cor 8:6, and the hymn of Col 1:15–20. It is important to notice that Paul is not teaching the preexistence of the Son as something new. He *presumes* that this is common knowledge among Christians as he moves to present first Christ's self-emptying in his †incarnation and then the self-humiliation of his earthly life and shameful death as the pattern and standard for the life of a Christian.

While Paul is not explicitly spelling out the doctrine of Jesus as Second Person of the Trinity, his text provided some of the raw material that the Church, some three centuries later, would use to formulate the doctrine of Jesus as the eternal Son "consubstantial" with the Father.

# Paul Applies the Example to Christian Living

## Philippians 2:12–18

Having presented the Christ story as the ultimate paradigm for Christian living, Paul now proceeds to apply that model more explicitly to the Philippians' lives, and also to his. He makes it clear that the "working out" of salvation is both a gift of God and a communal task—one that entails sacrifice. Addressing people who live in the midst of a culture of "boasting," Paul celebrates that the Philippian Christians' "boasting in the Lord" is his own greatest boast as their mentor.

### Living the Hymn (2:12–18)

[12]So then, my beloved, obedient as you have always been, not only when I am present but all the more now when I am absent, work out your salvation with fear and trembling. [13]For God is the one who, for his good purpose, works in you both to desire and to work. [14]Do everything without grumbling or questioning, [15]that you may be blameless and innocent, children of God without blemish in the midst of a crooked and perverse generation, among whom you shine like lights in the world, [16]as you hold on to the word of life, so that my boast for the day of Christ may be that I did not run in vain or labor in vain. [17]But, even if I am poured out as a libation upon the sacrificial service of your faith, I rejoice and share my joy with all of you. [18]In the same way you also should rejoice and share your joy with me.

OT: Exod 29:38–42; Num 28:1–10; Ps 2:11
NT: Rom 8:15–17; 9:4; 12:1; 1 Cor 2:3

2:12         **So then** is not simply a signal that Paul is resuming his exhortation to the community. The Christ hymn, in other words, was not an interruption, but was the very heart of his exhortation. "So then" signals that what he is about to urge *flows from* the Christ story he has just celebrated. Putting on the mind of Jesus has practical implications.

The Philippian Christians are **beloved** in several ways: beloved of God the Father and the Lord Jesus, beloved of one another (1:9; 2:1, 2), and the objects of Paul's affection, "*my* beloved."

When Paul acknowledges that the Philippians have been **obedient**, he echoes what he has just said of the self-humbling life of Jesus (v. 8). Obedience to whom? Obedience to God, one would think. But here it refers to their obedience to Paul, given that he says **not only when I am present but all the more now when I am absent**. Since Paul was their apostolic founder, obedience to him *is* their way of being obedient to God.

The sentence concludes with Paul's famous mandate: **work out your salvation with fear and trembling**. As an isolated statement, this might sound like a grim instruction. That, however, would be to hear it apart from its biblical context. First, as in 1:28, the "your" is plural. Paul is still addressing the Philippian church as a whole. They are to work out their salvation together. Further, as in 1:28, "salvation" is the divine rescue that they *have already begun to experience* in God's enabling them to be steadfast in the face of opposition. Finally, "fear and trembling" does not mean high anxiety. Rather, it is a scriptural expression for awe and profound reverence in the presence of the holy God, as in Ps 2:11 (to the Gentile kings, "Serve the Lord with fear; / exult with trembling"). Jeremiah 33:9 even promises that people will react with "fear and trembling" to all the good God will do to Jerusalem! Paul already referred to the Philippians' experience of God's support in their "struggling together" in the face of their opponents as proof of their "salvation" (1:28). Here again, with words that remind them they are working in the holy presence of God, he encourages them to keep up that struggle.[1]

2:13         Lest anyone think Paul is saying that salvation is something people can accomplish on their own power, he adds, **For God is the one who, for his good purpose, works in you** (plural) **both to desire and to work**. Notice how Paul

---

1. It is telling that Paul combines the same notions of obedience to community leadership and "fear and trembling" in 2 Cor 7:15, referring to Titus's ministry with the Corinthian community: "And his heart goes out to you all the more, as he remembers the *obedience* of all of you, when you received him with *fear and trembling*." Further, Paul applies the "fear and trembling" phrase to himself in 1 Cor 2:3, and in Eph 6:5 it is applied to Christian slaves, who are urged to attend more to the presence of the risen Christ and the will of God than to the oversight of their earthly masters.

plays with the root word for "work" (*erga*, which shows up in such English words as "energy," "erg," and "ergonomics"). Having exhorted the community to "work out" (*katergazomai*) their common salvation in a spirit of awe, aware of God's presence among them, he hastens to remind them that in reality it is "God" who is working (*energeō*) among them. God both moves them from within to "desire" his will and empowers them to "work" (*energeō*) at carrying it out. This language helps us see that when Paul refers to his fellow missioners, for example Epaphroditus or Clement (2:25; 4:3), as coworkers (*synergos*) he means collaborators in the work of God.

Paul's use of "fear and trembling" to evoke an Old Testament resonance is    2:14
only the beginning of an amazing cascade of biblical allusions in the next five verses. When Paul dares to name what is lacking in the Philippians' community life, he chooses his words carefully: **Do everything without grumbling**. The word for "grumbling" carries a distinct biblical echo, especially referring to the murmuring of the Israelites in the wilderness (see Exod 16:7–8). This implies that such complaining is resistance to the will of God and the liberating work that God is trying to do in their midst. Paul clearly has the Exodus context in mind when he uses the word in 1 Cor 10:10, exhorting the Corinthian community and citing the bad example of the Israelites in the desert: "Do not grumble as some of them did, and suffered death by the destroyer." That the Philippian Christians should live their community life without **questioning** could seem to suggest an unreflective, rigid conformity. A better translation is "arguing" (NIV, NRSV, JB) or "complaining" (NJB). It is not questioning but contentiousness that Paul objects to.

Christians are to be **blameless**—a quality to which God calls Abram as he    2:15–16
renews his covenant with him: "Walk in my presence and be blameless" (Gen 17:1). In referring to Christians as **children of God**, Paul applies to them an Old Testament term used for the chosen people. While all human beings are made in the *image* of God, the people of Israel are singled out as *children* of God. Sometimes Israel as a nation is called "son of God"; see Hosea 11:1 ("Out of Egypt I called my son") and Exod 4:22 ("Thus says the LORD: Israel is my son, my firstborn"). In Romans especially, Paul is explicit in applying this privileged status to believers in Jesus: they have received "a spirit of adoption" and are "children of God" (Rom 8:15–16). Even for Jewish Christians, being baptized into the body of Christ is a step into a new kind of relationship with the God of the covenant.

Paul calls the Philippians to be **without blemish**, using an Old Testament term reserved for the flawless animals to be used in temple sacrifices. He thereby anticipates an image from the realm of temple worship that he will develop at the end of this passage (v. 17). For Paul, the baptized person becomes "without blemish" by becoming progressively free from sin and from tarnished motives, enabled to love and serve with a pure heart.

When Paul says the Philippian Christians live **in the midst of a crooked and perverse generation,** he applies to the surrounding pagan society language that the Song of Moses applied to Israelites as God's rebellious children (Deut 32:5; see Ps 78:8). Christians are to be the reverse—obedient children of God. Alluding to the end-time scenario of Dan 12:3, Paul calls the members of the church—now living in the end times inaugurated by the life, death, and resurrection of Christ—to **shine like lights in the world.** "Lights" is perhaps better translated in the biblical sense as "luminaries" or "stars" (NIV, NRSV), as in the creation narrative (Gen 1:16). The image works both as a contrast to darkness (the church versus the pagan world) and as a source of illumination (Christians as bearers of the light of Christ). Both aspects find expression in the next clause: **as you hold on to the word of life.** The word for "hold on to" also means "hold out" in the sense of "offer." Scholars argue for one or the other meaning—either holding the gospel firm against persecution, or holding the gospel out to those who have not yet heard it. The ambiguity may well be deliberate, as with "lights": Christians hold fast to the gospel life in contrast to their neighbors, and in doing so they are a light for the world.

As he did earlier in this letter (1:3–18), Paul takes personal joy in the prospect of their eventual flowering in Christ: **so that my boast for the day of Christ may be that I did not run in vain or labor in vain.** Paul echoes Isaiah's description of the servant of God who fears having "labored in vain" (Isa 49:4), but who is triumphantly vindicated by God. The phrase also evokes the blessed state of the faithful in end-time Jerusalem: "They shall not toil in vain, / nor beget children for sudden destruction; / For they shall be a people blessed by the LORD / and their descendants with them" (Isa 65:23). Paul is hopeful that in the final judgment, the spiritual maturity of the Philippian community will demonstrate that his ministry was fruitful.

**2:17–18**     Verses 17–18 conclude the exhortation that began all the way back at 1:27. In fact, as will become clear, these two verses form a kind of †*inclusio* with the passage on the community's struggle for the sake of Christ (1:27–30), framing this whole exhortation, which is at the heart of the letter. Both the Philippians' struggle and Paul's are a participation in the self-emptying love of Christ celebrated in the Christ hymn.

The world of temple sacrifice that Paul hinted at in the phrase "without blemish" (v. 15) now comes to full expression. Both his own life and that of the

## Salvation: A Process of God's Rescue, Beginning Now

**BIBLICAL BACKGROUND**

These days, it is common to think and speak of salvation mainly in the ultimate sense of being fully united with God in heaven. But the biblical sense of salvation is richer and more present than that. In the Old Testament, "salvation" usually refers to rescue in a this-worldly sense—rescue from slavery, from enemies, from sickness, from foreign occupation, from exile. The New Testament writers often speak of God's salvation of his people as a process that begins in this life with Christian faith and baptism and will culminate in the resurrection of the dead and eternal union with God.

For example, Paul speaks of salvation as already begun, in the sense that believers have been rescued from bondage to sin and Satan: "by grace you have been saved" (Eph 2:5; see Rom 8:24). Salvation is a continuing process in this life: "The message of the cross is foolishness to those who are perishing, but to *us who are being saved* it is the power of God" (1 Cor 1:18; see 2 Cor 2:15). And Luke can say of the Jerusalem Christian community that was formed after Pentecost, "Every day the Lord added to their number *those who were being saved*" (Acts 2:47). Paul speaks of salvation in a similar way when he tells the Philippians that their ability to stand firm in the face of opposition is "proof . . . of your salvation. And this is God's doing" (1:28). But salvation will only be complete at the final coming of Christ and the resurrection of the dead (see Rom 13:11).

---

Philippian church are a kind of sacrifice: **even if I am poured out as a libation upon the sacrificial service of your faith**. Paul is referring to the prospect of his eventual execution, a possibility he entertains even though he expects to be released from his chains this time (1:19, 25–26). His wording evokes the twice-daily sacrifice in the Jerusalem temple, which included a "libation"—the pouring out of wine—along with the "sacrificial" offering of a lamb (Exod 29:38–42; Num 28:1–10). To lay down his life in imitation of Christ, then, would be the highest form of worship (see 2 Tim 4:6). Since pagan worship also included the pouring out of wine, oil, or some other liquid as an offering to the deity, Paul's Gentile audience would have readily understood his meaning even if they missed the scriptural allusion.

When Paul describes the libation as poured "upon the sacrificial service of your faith,"[2] he implies that Christians' self-emptying service to one another is

---

2. The word translated "service" is *leitourgia*, the Greek term for public worship and the origin of our word "liturgy."

## US Bishops on the Dignity of the Human Person Realized in Community

Paul's vision of the salvation of the human person in the community of the Church has informed magisterial teaching: the dignity of the human person requires participation in the secular dimensions of human community as well. This understanding is foundational in the United States Catholic bishops' teaching regarding economic justice:

> The basis for all that the Church believes about the moral dimensions of economic life is its vision of the transcendent worth—the sacredness—of human beings. *The dignity of the human person, realized in community with others, is the criterion against which all aspects of economic life must be measured.* All human beings, therefore, are ends to be served by the institutions that make up the economy, not means to be exploited for more narrowly defined goals. Human personhood must be respected with a reverence that is religious. When we deal with each other, we should do so with the sense of awe that arises in the presence of something holy and sacred. For that is what human beings are: we are created in the image of God (Gen 1:27). Similarly, all economic institutions must support the bonds of community and solidarity that are essential to the dignity of persons.[a]

a. National Conference of Catholic Bishops, *Economic Justice for All: Pastoral Letter on Catholic Social Teaching and the U.S. Economy* (Washington, DC: 1986), 28.

also true worship of God, much as he says in Rom 12:1, "Offer your bodies as a living sacrifice, holy and pleasing to God, your spiritual worship," and then interprets that sacrifice as loving service to one another (Rom 12:3–21).[3] This paralleling of sacrifices, theirs and his, harmonizes nicely with the passage that began this section, 1:27–30, which speaks of the Philippians' suffering as a share in Paul's—and both are a participation in the self-offering of Christ.

### Reflection and Application (2:12–18)

As a Christian motto, "Work out your salvation with fear and trembling" (Phil 2:12) can easily be heard as a mandate addressed to a struggling individual. But in fact "your" is plural here in the Greek, as is the verb "work out." Similarly plural are all the personal references in the first half of the sentence: "beloved . . . obedient . . . you have always been."

3. See also Rom 15:15–16, where Paul compares his ministry to the Gentiles to the offering of a temple priest in worship.

Besides the accident of language—that the plural is not always perceptible in English—another reason we tend to miss Paul's tone is that North American culture tends to focus on individual striving more than communal sharing. Fortunately, Paul provides us with an immediate corrective in the next verse: "For *God* is the one who, for his good purpose, works in you [or "among you"] both to desire and to work." Thus this passage is not only a call to a common task but also a plea to see this task as a *collaboration* with God in something he is already doing among us and even giving us the desire to do. It is God's intimate presence in our very desires and efforts that warrants the biblical phrase "with fear and trembling," that is, with awe that springs from the awareness of God's presence. When we savor the full context, this mandate, which could seem to appeal to individualism and independent striving, is really an antidote to those very tendencies. This biblical insight is reflected in Catholic social teaching, for instance in the United States Catholic bishops' pastoral letter *Economic Justice for All* (1986), which stresses that human dignity and fulfillment always entails participation in community. It is for this reason that the assembly of the Christian community at worship is not a matter of convenience but an essential expression of our identity as one in the body of Christ.

# Two More Examples:
# Timothy and Epaphroditus

## Philippians 2:19–3:1a

Paul has some practical plans to share: the Philippians should prepare to receive visitors. He plans to send Timothy soon, as soon as he finds out how the court will rule in his case. And he himself hopes to return shortly after that. More immediately, he is sending back to the Philippians their own emissary, Epaphroditus, weakened from a recent illness, with a commendation and a request for a well-deserved welcome. One might expect such travel plans to come at the end of the letter, but Paul chooses to speak of these good men at this point, apparently because they provide further examples of the very mentality that he has been advocating. His choice of language, harking back to the prime example of Christ in the hymn of 2:5–11, suggests that he wants his readers to see the connection.

### The Incomparable Timothy (2:19–24)

[19]I hope, in the Lord Jesus, to send Timothy to you soon, so that I too may be heartened by hearing news of you. [20]For I have no one comparable to him for genuine interest in whatever concerns you. [21]For they all seek their own interests, not those of Jesus Christ. [22]But you know his worth, how as a child with a father he served along with me in the cause of the gospel. [23]He it is, then, whom I hope to send as soon as I see how things go with me, [24]but I am confident in the Lord that I myself will also come soon.

**Soon** Paul hopes **to send Timothy**, and then to come himself. He is careful to    2:19
say that his hopes are **in the Lord Jesus**, in the spirit of James's advice to speak
of one's plans conditionally, with a reverent nod to divine providence: "You
have no idea what your life will be like tomorrow. You are a puff of smoke that
appears briefly and then disappears. Instead you should say, 'If the Lord wills
it, we shall live to do this or that'" (James 4:14–15). Paul expresses this trust
explicitly in the Lord *Jesus*. He will reiterate this expression of trust in verse 24.

Paul desires news of the Philippians like a lover desiring news of his be-    2:20–21
loved. He is confident the news will be encouraging to Timothy, and he wants
to be encouraged himself. Paul cannot mention Timothy without singing his
praises. The NABRE translation, **I have no one comparable to him**, does not
quite catch the tone of a special word Paul uses here—*isopsychos*, "of like soul
or mind"—a word he may well have chosen to echo a quality he advocated for
the community in 2:2, "being of the same mind" [*sympsychos*]. Paul continues
to describe Timothy in language that connects with his earlier exhortations.
He commends Timothy's **genuine interest in whatever concerns you**, the very
quality Paul urged in 2:4. Then, still echoing 2:4, he describes the contrasting
attitude of others, apparently Christians, who are around him in his present
situation: **For they all seek their own interests, not those of Jesus Christ**. Paul
is implying that the mind-set he advocated in 2:3–4, seeking the interests of
fellow Christians, is precisely to seek the interests of Jesus Christ!

When Paul reminds the Philippians, **you know his worth**, he may be refer-    2:22
ring to Timothy's presence with him during his first visit to Philippi (see Acts
16). Paul employs a verb that powerfully echoes the mind-set of Christ in the
hymn of chapter 2: **he served along with me in the cause of the gospel**. The
Greek verb "serve" (*douleuō*) is built on the word for "slave" (*doulos*). Indeed,
the lexicon defines the verb as "to perform the duties of the slave, serve, obey."
Paul began this letter by identifying himself and Timothy as "slaves [*douloi*] of
Jesus Christ," and he portrayed the incarnation as Christ's taking "the form of
a slave." (It is important to recall that in first-century Philippi, servants were
slaves.) So Paul no doubt chose the verb describing Timothy's service because it
embodied the spirit of humble obedience exemplified by Christ. That Timothy's
collaboration with Paul was like **a child with a father** may refer to a kind of
apprenticeship relationship, but also to a deeper filial bond. Paul uses similar
language about Timothy in 1 Cor 4:17: "I am sending you Timothy, who is my
beloved and faithful son in the Lord; he will remind you of my ways in Christ."

**How things go with me** appears to refer to the upshot of Paul's upcoming    2:23–24
trial. He is **confident in the Lord** that he himself **will also come soon**, echoing

his earlier "hope in the Lord Jesus" to send Timothy soon (v. 19). In six verses, Paul's hope has become confidence.

## Epaphroditus, Faithful unto Death (2:25–3:1a)

[25]With regard to Epaphroditus, my brother and co-worker and fellow soldier, your messenger and minister in my need, I consider it necessary to send him to you. [26]For he has been longing for all of you and was distressed because you heard that he was ill. [27]He was indeed ill, close to death; but God had mercy on him, not just on him but also on me, so that I might not have sorrow upon sorrow. [28]I send him therefore with the greater eagerness, so that, on seeing him, you may rejoice again, and I may have less anxiety. [29]Welcome him then in the Lord with all joy and hold such people in esteem, [30]because for the sake of the work of Christ he came close to death, risking his life to make up for those services to me that you could not perform.

[3:1]Finally, my brothers, rejoice in the Lord.

**NT:** 1 Cor 16:17

2:25–29     The mission of Epaphroditus is quite different from that of Timothy. Whereas Paul will send Timothy as his agent to fetch fresh news, in the case of Epaphroditus, Paul is returning an emissary of the Philippian church. This is a delicate matter. As the later thank-you passage (4:10–20) makes clear, the Philippians sent Epaphroditus to bring financial aid to Paul, and perhaps also to stay on and help him in his imprisonment. Verse 30 indicates that he fell sick on the way. He has since recovered somewhat, but not enough to continue working for the Apostle. So now Paul has decided to return him to the Philippians—no doubt earlier than they had expected. Since Epaphroditus may be embarrassed at returning early and will possibly be considered to have partially failed in providing the service that the Philippians intended, Paul seeks to ensure he is welcomed back warmly.

Beyond consideration for Epaphroditus's health, there may be another motive behind Paul's returning him at this time. Given that the Philippian church chose Epaphroditus to bring their gift, he may be a respected leader in that church. If Paul is concerned about the division between Euodia and Syntyche (and their respective followers?—see 4:2–3), he may be hoping that Epaphroditus can help resolve the conflict in the Philippian community.

As soon as Paul mentions **Epaphroditus** he hastens to characterize him very positively—first as regards himself, **my brother and co-worker and fellow**

116

**soldier,** and then from the Philippians' perspective, **your messenger and minister in my need.** And in describing the man's relationship to his home community Paul reaches for some elegant words, "messenger" (*apostolos*) and "minister" (*leitourgos*). In its root sense *apostolos*, from which we get the word "apostle," means "one who has been sent." The common meaning of *apostolos* was an ordinary messenger, delegate, or envoy; but it could also mean a messenger with extraordinary status, even an envoy of God.[1] *Leitourgos* has a similar range. In the wider Greco-Roman world it could simply mean "one who performs a public service," but it also had the special meaning of "one engaged in priestly service in the temple." It is possible that Paul has the civic overtones in mind here, in the sense of "public servant" of the heavenly commonwealth (1:27; 3:20), but there is also an allusion to temple service, as we will see in verse 30 below.

Paul has decided that it is **necessary** to send Epaphroditus back both for his sake (Epaphroditus misses them) and for their sake (they have heard about his near-death sickness and are concerned about him).[2] Sending him home will also relieve Paul of his own concern for Epaphroditus. He speaks of the man's sickness as **sorrow upon sorrow;** sending the good man home, Paul will "have less anxiety"—literally, he will be less beset by sorrow.

Paul's charge to **hold such people in esteem** seems at first an odd generalization to insert here. But when we recall the environment of competitive striving for worldly honor in the Roman colony of Philippi, Paul's statement comes as a pertinent reminder that the Christian community lives by a different honor code, one supremely exemplified by Jesus and also illustrated in the ministries of Timothy and Epaphroditus.

To persuade the Philippians to receive Epaphroditus back warmly, Paul chooses language that links Epaphroditus's personal sacrifice with that of Christ. Far from being a failed emissary who turned out not to have the right stuff, the man actually imitated Christ—**because for the sake of the work of Christ he came close to death.** Paul here uses the very phrase that describes

2:29

2:30

1. Given the usually elevated meaning of this term in the New Testament, as applied to prominent leaders, one cannot help but hear it as a special compliment in this context. The NABRE joins the NIV and the NRSV in the translation "messenger," though the Douay-Rheims has "apostle" and the NRSV includes "apostle" here as a footnote.

2. The fact that the Philippians have learned of Epaphroditus's illness does not necessarily imply a special round-trip journey of another messenger. Paul's description of the circumstances—Epaphroditus's risking his life for them in carrying out his mission—implies that he fell sick on the way to Paul. A plausible scenario is that a traveler who was part of the Christian network, perhaps a courier from the "household of Caesar" (4:22) heading east on the Egnatian Way, brought news of their emissary's illness. This scenario is suggested by Ben Witherington III, *Friendship and Finances: The Letter of Paul to the Philippians,* The New Testament in Context (Valley Forge, PA: Trinity Press International, 1994), 79–80.

## Epaphroditus and Epaphras, One Person or Two?

**BIBLICAL BACKGROUND**

Paul speaks of one Epaphras (usually pronounced EP-ah-frass) in three places—Philem 23; Col 1:7; 4:12. He also mentions the Epaphroditus (e-pah-fro-DI-tus) we encounter in Phil 2:25 and 4:18. Apparently Epaphras is a shortened form of Epaphroditus, as Tom is short for Thomas, leading some to assume that the two versions of the name refer to the same person. The contexts, however, suggest that we are dealing with two persons. Writing to the Colossians, Paul says,

> Epaphras sends you greetings; he is one of you, a slave of Christ [Jesus], always striving for you in his prayers so that you may be perfect and fully assured in all the will of God. For I can testify that he works very hard for you and for those in Laodicea and those in Hierapolis (Col 4:12–13).

Earlier in the same letter he reminds the Colossians that they had first learned "the word of truth," the gospel, from Epaphras, "a trustworthy minister of Christ on your behalf" (1:5–7). These two references to Epaphras make it clear that he is both the founder of the Colossian Christian community and a leader in the nearby churches of Laodicea and Hierapolis.

Epaphroditus, however, is a prominent member of the Philippian church in Macedonia, some four hundred miles to the northwest of Colossae. It is unlikely that the same person would have a prominent role in two distant churches. Moreover, evidence from ancient inscriptions indicates that Epaphroditus/Epaphras was a common name in the first-century eastern Mediterranean.

Since the meaning of the name Epaphroditus is "favored by or dedicated to the goddess Aphrodite," the goddess of beauty and love—and, some hold, of gambling—a person so named is obviously a Gentile.

Jesus' obedience to the point of death in the Christ hymn (2:8). Further, he says Epaphroditus was **risking his life to make up for those services** (*leitourgias*) **to me that you could not perform**. The Greek word *leitourgia* can simply mean "service," but here there is reason to hear a cultic or liturgical resonance (as with *leitourgos* in v. 25). For in the other two places where Paul employs this word he alludes to the temple liturgy. In verse 17 above he referred to his suffering as a libation poured out on the Philippians' *leitourgia* of faith. And in 2 Cor 9:12 he speaks of the Corinthians' financial contribution to the Jerusalem fund as a *leitourgia* that produces thanksgiving to God. Perhaps even more pertinently, when Paul later thanks the Philippians for the gift that Epaphroditus brought, he calls it " 'a fragrant aroma,' an acceptable sacrifice, pleasing to God" (4:18).[3]

**Finally, my brothers, rejoice in the Lord.** In the traditional chapter-and-verse    3:1a
numbering this sentence is separated from what came before, but it forms a nice conclusion to the passage. The phrase translated "finally" need not signal a closing of a document. It can be a segue that concludes one section and leads to another, as in 1 Thess 4:1. "And so" might be a more appropriate translation than "finally." If Epaphroditus's return due to sickness seems like bad news, his Christlike example of giving his all and his return from death's door are really cause for joy.

## Reflection and Application (2:19–3:1a)

Ancient analysts of human speech, like Aristotle in his *Rhetoric,* note that discourse can be divided into explanation, persuasion, praise, and blame. Regarding the last two types, anecdotal evidence—especially from online blogging, radio talk shows, and political discourse—reveals that we typically do more blaming than praising. In contrast to this contemporary experience, it is fascinating to see how much ink Paul spends on *praising.* He praises his addressees in the thanksgiving part of his letters, to affirm and encourage them. He commends the carriers of his correspondence, to ensure their positive reception. He praises coworkers like Timothy and Epaphroditus, to highlight them as models of Christian living. In this positive use of speech, Paul himself becomes a model of what we might call the ministry of commendation. In our culture, where blaming, scapegoating, and back-biting pollute both domestic and public discourse, we do well to take Paul as a model of edifying (building-up or constructive) speech. As we watch Paul write his letter to build up the Christian community at Philippi, we note that he has a place for confrontation, constructive criticism, lament, regret, and even blame. But he is also alert to the power of praise for encouragement, for commendation, for reconciliation, and especially for spotlighting as models for imitation people who embody the mind of Christ in their behavior. Pondering Paul's ministry of commendation can help us become alert to opportunities to encourage others face-to-face and to build them up (behind their back) in the minds of others. We all have daily opportunities for this kind of community-building.

---

3. In Eph 5:1–2 the same phrase is applied to the sacrifice of Christ, presented as a model for Christian imitation: "So be imitators of God, as beloved children, and live in love, as Christ loved us and handed himself over for us as a sacrificial offering to God for a fragrant aroma." See also Rom 12:2.

# The Example of Paul's Faithful Citizenship in Christ

## Philippians 3:1b–4:1

This whole letter is an exhortation to stand fast as a community united in Christ, a work-in-progress of God the Father. Paul has encouraged them by presenting examples of faithfulness to the Father and love of others—primarily the example of Christ himself, and then the examples of Timothy and Epaphroditus. Aware that a leader teaches by modeling the behavior he desires in his disciples, Paul now makes bold to present *himself* as an example—not of his personal achievements but of what God has done in him through Jesus. Paul has already made an example of himself through the grace of his serenity in dealing with imprisonment and imminent Roman judgment (1:12–26). Now, to encourage the Philippians in their struggle, he shares what it has meant for him to be conformed to the mind of Christ in his own conversion. He transitions to this testimony by revisiting what seems to have been a persistent issue: a faction in the Philippian church sought to convince Gentile Christians that they needed to take up all the practices of the Mosaic law, including circumcision for the men, if they were to be proper followers of the Messiah of Israel.

## "Beware of the Dogs!"
### Rehearsing a Familiar Issue to Make a Personal Point (3:1b–7)

3:1b Writing the same things to you is no burden for me but is a safeguard for you. ²Beware of the dogs! Beware of the evil workers! Beware of the mutilation! ³For we are the circumcision, we who worship through the Spirit of God, who boast in Christ Jesus and do not put our confidence in flesh, ⁴although I myself have grounds for confidence even in the flesh. If anyone else thinks he can be confident in flesh, all the more can I. ⁵Circumcised on the eighth day, of the race of Israel, of the tribe of Benjamin, a Hebrew of Hebrew parentage, in observance of the law a Pharisee, ⁶in zeal I persecuted the church, in righteousness based on the law I was blameless. ⁷[But] whatever gains I had, these I have come to consider a loss because of Christ.

---

**OT:** Gen 17:1–14; Deut 10:16; 30:6; Jer 4:4; 9:25
**NT:** Rom 2:25–29; Col 2:11
**Catechism:** Jesus and Pharisees, 575

---

**Writing the same things to you is no burden** points to what Paul is about    3:1b
to say, not to what he has just concluded. His talk about the imminent travels of Timothy and Epaphroditus is, after all, not old business but new. "The same things" must therefore refer to the issue he is about to bring up. As will become clear, Paul uses his response to a familiar problem in the early Church as a springboard to further elaborate on his experience as a disciple of the Lord Jesus—what he earlier summarized in a sentence, "To me life is Christ" (1:21). What he is about to say is **a safeguard for you.** In the context of the letter, that means his message will help the Philippians stand fast in the struggle they share, first described in 1:27–31.

**Beware of the dogs.** Like most cultures, first-century Jews had derogatory    3:2
terms for outsiders. Jews sometimes referred to Gentiles as "dogs," a practice that comes into play in the witty exchange between Jesus and the Syrophoenician woman in Mark 7:27–28. The identity of the "dogs" becomes clear in what follows. They are called, in turn, **evil workers** and **the mutilation.** The word for "mutilation" (*katatomē*) could also be translated "incision" and is obviously chosen as wordplay on "circumcision" (*peritomē*). "The circumcision"—short for "those of the circumcision"—is a term Paul sometimes uses to refer to Jews collectively (Rom 3:30; 4:9; Gal 2:7–9). Paul coins the term "the *in*cision" to refer to those who would misguidedly impose circumcision, and the full ethnic lifestyle it represents, on Gentile Christians. Thus in calling these adversaries "dogs," Paul ironically applies a term usually reserved for outsiders to refer to insiders, Christians who have in effect become outsiders by adopting this policy of trying to turn Gentile Christians into Jews. Paul declares the extreme gravity of this †Judaizing error in Gal 5:4, where he tells those who have succumbed to

## Who Are the Judaizers?

The term "Judaizers" is not found in the Bible. It is a label used by scholars to describe those early Christians, presumably Jewish Christians, who were convinced that Gentile believers in Christ needed to follow the Mosaic law completely, including having the males circumcised. For twenty-first-century readers, this may seem an odd position, but among some early Christians it seemed a reasonable approach to incorporating Gentiles into church. After all, God himself had given the people of Israel the Sinai covenant as the privileged way to relate to him, and the covenant included all the stipulations of the law. It was difficult to conceive that God had now overcome the distinction he himself had established between the Jews as his chosen people and all other peoples of the world.

It helps to remember that the first disciples of Jesus were all Jews. In the Acts of the Apostles Luke describes the early Christian community in Jerusalem as composed entirely of Jews and converts to Judaism (Acts 1–9). Later, when Gentiles begin to join the growing church, some felt that these Gentiles should be asked to do what was always expected of Gentiles who joined the Jewish people, namely, to practice the full Mosaic law.

Luke devotes an episode to the issue in Acts 15. Some Jerusalem Christians visit the mixed community of Jews and Gentiles in Syrian Antioch and tell them, "Unless you are circumcised according to the Mosaic practice, you cannot be saved" (Acts 15:1). After testimony from Peter, Paul, and Barnabas regarding the influx of Gentiles into the church, James (who was by then the leader of the Jerusalem church), proposes that Gentile converts should simply be required to keep the minimal rules required of "resident aliens" in Lev 17–18: "to avoid pollution from idols, unlawful marriage, the meat of strangled animals, and blood" (Acts 15:20). These rules ensure that they break from idolatrous practice and avoid food that is abhorrent to Jews, thereby facilitating table fellowship.

The evidence of Paul's Letter to the Galatians, however, suggests that the issue was not settled all that simply or quickly, for some Jewish Christians were still promoting the policy of full compliance with Mosaic law for Gentile converts, a policy that Paul utterly rejects as compromising the very essence of the gospel and putting false reliance on human works (Gal 5:3–8). These promoters are the people whom scholars have come to call "Judaizers."

---

it, "You are separated from Christ, you who are trying to be justified by †law; you have fallen from grace."

3:3     Paul quickly adds, **for we are the circumcision,** drawing on the biblical theme of circumcision of the heart (Deut 10:16; 30:6; Jer 4:4; 9:25), the whole-hearted dedication that God desires as contrasted with mere external observance. Paul applies this idea in Rom 2:28–29: "True circumcision is not outward, in the flesh. Rather, one is a Jew inwardly, and circumcision is of the heart, in the spirit, not the letter; his praise is not from human beings but from God." Here in Phil 3:3, "we are the circumcision" is a way of claiming that Christians live the vocation of Israel: **who worship through the Spirit of God** and **boast in Christ Jesus and do not put our confidence in flesh**. Paul is contrasting here not merely flesh and the *human* spirit, but flesh and *the Spirit of God*, the same contrast he makes in Galatians between walking "in the Spirit" and following the desires of "the flesh" (Gal 5:16–25). As he says in Rom 12:1, for the Christian, all of life is now a kind of *worship*.

To "boast in Christ" is a way of saying that Christians, Jew and Gentile alike, make no claim to righteousness based on their own actions but rather rejoice in being made righteous only by their union with Christ.

By saying he is "writing the same things to you," Paul implies that they have been through all this before—no doubt in language similar to his treatment of the issue in Gal 5 and Rom 2–4. Paul brings up the issue again to remind the Philippians that they need to continue to stand firmly against this challenge. And doing so provides him with an occasion for sharing how his own experience of transformation in Christ provides a model of resistance.

Paul still has a keen sense of his Jewish identity—he does not think of himself as engaged in a new religion but rather as a Jew who has found the long-awaited Messiah. He has revisited the issue of the Judaizers to emphasize that, in Christ, he shares a common identity with his beloved Gentile Christians. To underscore this fact, he first highlights his Jewish pedigree, his reasons for having been **confident in flesh**—mainly, his physical kinship with the people of the covenant.     3:4

He begins with his own physical circumcision: **circumcised on the eighth day**, the customary time of circumcision as instructed by God in Gen 17:1–14.[1]     3:5

He is **of the race of Israel**, that is, an Israelite by birth, which entitles him to all the privileges of the chosen people (Rom 9:1–5).

That he is **of the tribe of Benjamin** is a point of pride since Benjamin had within its borders the city of Jerusalem and the temple (Judg 1:21) and had given Israel its first king, Saul, after whom Paul (Saul) was named.

**A Hebrew of Hebrew parentage** refers to the Hebrew language and underscores that Paul was *raised* Jewish; he was not simply biologically rooted in the people of Israel.

---

1. In Genesis 17 circumcision is mandated as the outward sign of the covenant already established through God's promise of descendants and land to Abram and Abram's response of faith (Gen 15:1–6).

## Circumcision

**BIBLICAL**
**BACKGROUND**

Circumcision is mentioned briefly but prominently in this letter (3:3–5), and some background is called for to make sense of its place in the argument of chapter 3. The word "circumcision" is from the Latin translation of the Greek noun *peritomē*, derived from a verb meaning "to cut off, cut around." In the Bible the verb usually means to cut off the foreskin of the male genital organ.

While the custom of circumcising males was present in various regions of the ancient Near East before Abraham's time, it became an important identity marker for the ancient Hebrews, distinguishing them as a people from the noncircumcising Philistines and Babylonians. The meaning of circumcision is given in Genesis 17, where God instructs Abraham to circumcise himself and all his male descendants as a sign of the everlasting covenant between himself and his people.

The Hebrew Scriptures often speak metaphorically of a circumcision of the heart (Lev 26:41; Deut 10:16; 30:6; Jer 4:4; 9:25), the lips (Exod 6:12, 30), the ears (Jer 6:10), and even fruit trees (Lev 19:23). For example, before the Israelites enter the Promised Land Moses calls them to a renewed dedication to the Lord by saying, "Circumcise your hearts, therefore, and be no longer stiff-necked" (Deut 10:16).

Circumcision of the heart refers to the fervent dedication to God signified by circumcision of the flesh. The imperative, "Circumcise your hearts," then, means something like, "Let your interior disposition, your mind and your will, mirror the meaning of your fleshly circumcision. And let that circumcision of the heart manifest itself in your living of the covenant relationship with God." Likewise, just as cutting off the foreskin may be understood as the removal of a barrier, so a renewed attentiveness and devotion to God's Word is a "circumcision" of ears and lips, that is, the removal of a barrier to hearing and speaking the word of God. The first Christian martyr, Stephen, stands in the tradition of Deuteronomy and Jeremiah when he challenges his adversaries with these words: "You stiff-necked people, uncircumcised in heart and ears, you always oppose the holy Spirit; you are just like your ancestors" (Acts 7:51).

When Paul states that **in observance of the law** he is **a Pharisee**, he means he is a professional when it comes to keeping the †Torah; that is, he taught and modeled for others how to do it. Readers familiar with the Gospels may find it hard to hear the word "Pharisee" in a positive sense, for the Gospel writers present the Pharisees mainly as adversaries of Jesus. (Luke 16:14 calls them, literally, "money-lovers.") But like priests, ministers, and rabbis today, most Pharisees were intent on helping people put their faith into practice. Pharisees were generally devout laymen

## Comments on Paul's Boast from One Close to the Scene

Because he grew up and later ministered in Antioch of Syria, where there was a robust Jewish community, St. John Chrysostom was sensitive to issues of Jewish and Christian identity. That enabled him to make some telling commentary on Paul's famous boast about his own identity:

Paul first mentions the very point that was [the Judaizers'] chief boast, the ritual of circumcision. He was, he says, *circumcised on the eighth day*. So he makes it clear that he comes *of the stock of Israel*. By this language he shows that he is not a proselyte (hence the eighth day), nor was he born of a proselyte background (for he comes of the stock of Israel). And so that no one may suppose that *of the stock of Israel* means from one of the ten ["lost"] tribes, he further specified that he is *of the tribe of Benjamin*. This is a highly respected Jewish identity. . . .

It was possible to be *of Israel* but not a *Hebrew of the Hebrews*. For there were many who had already misplaced their Hebrew heritage. Long residing among Gentiles, they had become ignorant of their Hebrew tongue. Not so with Paul.[a]

Chrysostom also knows that Paul's subsequent boast of his treasured identity as a Christian (Phil 3:7–9) is not a denigration of his Jewish tradition but rather a way of celebrating that tradition's fulfillment in Jesus. He makes that point in the following paraphrase of Paul:

"If then it was because of my good breeding and my zeal and my way of life, and I had all the things that belong to life, why," he says, "did I let go those lofty things, unless I found that those of Christ were greater, and greater by far?"[b]

a. *Homily on Philippians* 11.3–5
b. Ibid., 11.3.6

---

devoted to teaching ordinary folks how to practice the laws of Moses in daily life. As a teacher of the law, Paul was especially competent in keeping the law himself.

**In zeal I persecuted the church.** Prior to his conversion, Paul identified the Jesus movement as a threat to Judaism as he understood it, perhaps because the "Jesus people" made Jesus more authoritative than Moses and because their honoring Jesus as †Lord seemed blasphemous and provoked Roman suspicions regarding possible revolt. This aroused Paul's passion for the integrity of Jewish life and worship. His "zeal" was such that he tried violently to halt the spread of the Jesus movement (Acts 9:1–2; 26:9–11).

3:6

**In righteousness based on the law I was blameless.** Paul caps the list of seven credentials and also generalizes it in a way that includes all 613 laws of the Torah (the number counted in later rabbinic tradition). To top it off, "blameless" happens to be the quality that God asks of Abram in the passage where circumcision is established as a sign of the covenant: "I am God the Almighty. Walk in my presence and be blameless" (Gen 17:1).

3:7     **[But] whatever gains I had, these I have come to consider as loss because of Christ.** Here Paul makes a stunning rhetorical turn. For as much as he prized these Jewish credentials, they fade into insignificance in the light of the radical overturning of values he experienced in encountering the risen Christ. The verb for "consider" is the same one he used for a Christian mind-set ("*regard* others as more important," 2:3), which imitates the mind-set of Christ ("he did not *regard* equality with God something to be grasped," 2:6). Now, in 3:7–8, he uses this same word three more times to show how, by the grace of God, he has come to that same new way of seeing, the same mind-set, in his own life. He draws on the commercial language of gains and losses to elaborate on the new value system that has governed his life since meeting the risen Christ on the road to Damascus (Acts 9:1–9).

## Reflection and Application (3:1b–7)

In this passage, Paul reviews his Jewish credentials, of which he is rightly proud. Some features were simply given by nature and nurture—his Jewish parentage, Hebrew culture, and circumcision. Others are the fruit of his commitment—his legal expertise as a Pharisee, his religious zeal in persecuting the church (which he now in retrospect sees as misguided), and righteousness based on fidelity to the laws of the Torah. As we will see from what follows, he mentions these points of pride to show how they are utterly transcended by Jesus the †Messiah and Lord. Nothing in his writing suggests that Pharisee Paul ever thought of himself as leaving his Judaism behind. Rather, he has come to know Jesus as the *fulfillment* of Judaism. The old covenant and its rituals, precious as they were, were powerless to bring salvation. His identity is now rooted in Christ, who alone bestows "the righteousness that comes from God" and, ultimately, resurrection from the dead (Phil 3:7–8).

As Christian readers, we can take this list of credentials in two ways. First, we can hear in Paul's list a reminder that we, too, owe much of our understanding of God to the people of Israel, whose Messiah we are privileged to have embraced. Second, we can contemplate Paul's list as a reminder that, like him, each of us is blessed with a heritage (biological and ethnic) and signs of accomplishment (degrees, skills, honors) that, to a great extent, tell us who we are. Yet, knowing where Paul is going in this letter, we can each gratefully ponder our own list of credentials and ask: At the end of the day, do I place my sense of worth in my heritage and accomplishments? Or can I join Paul and "boast in Christ Jesus" with a joyful and free heart and acknowledge him as the One in whom I have become a child of God?

## Paul's Righteousness Comes from God (3:8–11)

⁸More than that, I even consider everything as a loss because of the supreme good of knowing Christ Jesus my Lord. For his sake I have accepted the loss of all things and I consider them so much rubbish, that I may gain Christ ⁹and be found in him, not having any righteousness of my own based on the law but that which comes through faith in Christ, the righteousness from God, depending on faith ¹⁰to know him and the power of his resurrection and [the] sharing of his sufferings by being conformed to his death, ¹¹if somehow I may attain the resurrection from the dead.

**NT:** Rom 3:22, 26; 8:16–18; Gal 2:16; 3:22
**Lectionary:** Fifth Sunday of Lent (Year C); Common of the Saints (during Easter season); Consecration of a Virgin and Religious Profession; For Vocations of Priests and Religious; Triumph of the Holy Cross (during Easter season)

With these verses we come to the real point of Paul's strong contrast between the value of **knowing Christ** and what he had held dear in his Jewish heritage. His prizing of **Jesus my Lord** as his **supreme good** makes *everything else* **loss** in comparison. This verse makes it clear that his point is not a denigration of his status as a Jew, a member of the covenant people; he is emphasizing his discovery of the fulfillment of that covenant in Jesus his Messiah and Lord, precisely as expressed in the Christ hymn of chapter 2.

That he can speak of "knowing" Jesus as *his* Lord shows that his experience of the risen Lord is far more than a mere belief in what was revealed to him on the road to Damascus. That encounter marked the difference between *knowing about* Jesus and beginning to *know* Jesus directly—as the Messiah who fulfilled the Scriptures and as the Lord of all. Paul's experience of the risen Lord has led to a heartfelt love of Jesus that now transcends even the passionate engagement with God that he knew in his service of the people of Israel as a Pharisee.

Paul proceeds to emphasize the relative disvalue of everything else with even stronger language: **For his sake I have accepted the loss of all things and**

3:8–9

**I consider them so much rubbish.** "Rubbish" is an acceptable translation, but it does not quite catch the earthiness of the Greek word, which earlier English versions (e.g., KJV and Douay-Rheims) render "dung."[2]

It is not simply that Paul sees things differently. His reevaluation is purposeful; he deliberately considers things

Fig. 8. Image of an ancient latrine, to make concrete the background metaphor euphemistically translated "rubbish" (for human waste).

in this way *so that* he may **gain Christ and be found in him.** When does he envision this being "found" in Christ to occur? Given his stated readiness to die and his confidence that, after death, he will "be with Christ" (1:20–23), it will apparently be either at the moment of his death or at the †parousia of the Lord, whichever comes first. Yet he often speaks of life "in Christ" as simply being a baptized Christian, as at the beginning and end of this letter (1:1; 4:21). As Christ is "found" human in appearance in the incarnation (2:7), Paul, like any Christian, is "found" in Christ Jesus at baptism; but that *already* status looks forward to the *not yet* of finally being conformed with Christ's risen body (3:21). He has begun to experience "the supreme good of knowing Christ Jesus my Lord" (3:8). Now he proceeds to elaborate regarding how that knowledge comes about.

The NABRE translation, **not having any righteousness of my own based on the law but that which comes through faith in Christ,** offers one solution to an ambiguous Greek phrase. Scholars have debated whether the Greek phrase *pistis Christou* should be rendered "faith in Christ" (as in the NABRE) or "the faithfulness of Christ."[3]

Several things lead us to understand the phrase as a reference to the faithfulness of Jesus:

2. BDAG lists various senses of this word, *skybala*, as "excrement, manure, garbage, kitchen scraps" (932). We get the point.

3. Greek *pistis* can mean either "faith," that is, the act of believing or trusting, or "faithfulness, fidelity." The grammar leaves open whether Christ is the *object* of our faith or the *subject* who possesses faith or faithfulness. Similar phrasing that joins faith and Jesus Christ occurs in six other places in Paul: Rom 3:22, 26; Gal 2:16 (twice), 20; 3:22. Interestingly, the KJV (early seventeenth century) renders the phrases as *faith of* Jesus/Christ in all of these instances except Rom 3:26.

1. Understanding *pistis* as a quality of Jesus fits Paul's emphasis on the "mind of Christ," especially his obedience, in the hymn of chapter 2;
2. "the faithfulness of Jesus" more obviously fits the contrast between "†righteousness of my own" and "righteousness from God";
3. taking *pistis* as Jesus' quality here makes sense of the phrase **depending on faith** at the end of verse 9, which seems redundant if the previous phrase is rendered "through faith in Christ."

Thus Paul's focus is primarily on *Jesus' faithfulness* as shown in his obedience to the Father, especially in his self-emptying humility celebrated in the hymn. Only secondarily does Paul focus on his own *faith in Christ*, mentioned in the final phrase "depending on faith." This interpretation fits with Paul's earlier reference to the "righteousness that comes through Jesus Christ" (1:11).[4] On this understanding, the faith of Paul, and any Christian, is a participation in Jesus' own fidelity and trust in God the Father.[5] Through faith we have access to **the righteousness from God**, the right relationship with the Father that is a divine gift, not the product of our own observance of the law.[6]

With this new way of being in right relationship with God—righteousness based not on law but on faith—comes a new way of knowing Jesus. It comes by knowing **the power of his resurrection and [the] sharing of his sufferings**. At first glance "the power of his resurrection" might seem to refer to Paul's own hope of one day being raised from the dead, which will find expression in verse 11. But knowing "the power of Jesus' resurrection" is parallel with "sharing of his sufferings," and Paul has already intimated that his sharing of Christ's sufferings is a matter of present experience—specifically, his imprisonment. He has already described both his own suffering and that of the Philippian Christians in language that echoes the self-emptying of Christ (2:17 echoing

**3:10**

---

4. Romans 3:3 offers helpful support for this translation. Contrasting the infidelity of Israel with the fidelity of God, Paul writes to the Romans, "What if some were unfaithful? Will their infidelity nullify the fidelity of God?" Here "the fidelity of God" translates the same grammatical construction that appears in Phil 3:9, which we are rendering "the faithfulness of Christ." See, too, "the faith of Abraham" at Rom 4:16.

5. That same relationship between the faithfulness of Jesus and the responsive faith of the Christian is reflected in Gal 3:16 as rendered in the Douay-Rheims version: "Knowing that a man is not justified by the works of the law, but by *the faith of Jesus Christ*, we also *believe in Christ Jesus*, that we may be justified by the *faith of Christ*." Here, as in the KJV and the notes of the NRSV, the same construction we met in Phil 3:9 is rendered as a quality of Christ ("the faith of Christ") and stands on either side of a reference to Christians' believing *in* Christ.

6. Gordon Fee (*Paul's Letter to the Philippians* [Grand Rapids: Eerdmans, 1995], 325–26) represents well the arguments in support of the traditional translation "through faith in Christ." The fact that a strong case can be made for both the "objective" and the "subjective" interpretations raises the possibility that Paul may well have embraced the ambiguity of the phrase; both renderings express aspects of the relationship between Christians and Christ.

2:7–8), and he has reminded them: "To you has been granted, for the sake of Christ, not only to believe in him but also to suffer for him. Yours is the same struggle as you saw in me and now hear about me" (1:29–30). For both him and them, present suffering is an imitation of Christ as modeled in the hymn. At the same time, the *empowerment* they experience, enabling them to stand firm in the face of opposition (1:28), is the power of Jesus' resurrection, that is, the power of the risen Lord working in their midst. For Paul, as for the Philippian Christians, their suffering can be described, again echoing the Christ hymn, as **being conformed to his death**. The English word "conformed" (Greek *symmor-phizomenos*) catches Paul's wordplay exactly, since it echoes "form" (*morphē*) in the hymn—"form of God" and "form of a slave" (2:6–7). Being "conformed to his death" does not refer to how we will breathe our last breath but rather to the ongoing process of imitating Christ's self-emptying love.[7]

3:11      With the final clause, **if somehow I may attain the resurrection from the dead**, Paul looks ahead to the hoped-for outcome of this process of becoming conformed to Christ, his own resurrection from the dead. The tentative tone of "if somehow" could be heard as an expression of doubt. More likely, it acknowledges that joining Jesus in the glory of his resurrection is not the product of Paul's effort but the enjoyment of a gift of God that comes from his cooperation with God's initiative. This clause confirms that "to know the power of his resurrection" in verse 10 is not a reference to Paul's future resurrection. The power of *Jesus'* resurrection already sustains him in his ministry; he *looks forward* to his own resurrection.

Paul's thoughts in verses 10–11—his current share in both the power of Jesus' resurrection and in suffering that imitates Jesus' past suffering, leading to his own resurrection on the last day—echo his language in Rom 8:16–17: "The Spirit itself bears witness with our spirit that we are children of God, and if children, then heirs, heirs of God and joint heirs with Christ, if only we suffer with him so that we may also be glorified with him."

Paul's basic insight—that the life of a Christian, with its suffering and joys, replicates and manifests the death and resurrection of Jesus—is reflected powerfully in his famous "earthen vessels" passage: We are "always carrying about in the body the dying of Jesus, so that the life of Jesus may also be manifested in our body. For we who live are constantly being given up to death for the sake of Jesus, so that the life of Jesus may be manifested in our mortal flesh" (2 Cor 4:10–11). The Christian life is a process of imitating the self-emptying love of Christ and experiencing the "power of his resurrection."

---

7. The REB catches this meaning nicely: "in growing conformity with his death."

# Apostolic Suffering in the New Testament

Neither Jesus nor the writers of the New Testament treat the topic of suffering in a general sense—what philosophers call "the problem of pain." The New Testament deals with suffering that is specifically apostolic—that is, the suffering that accompanies the following of Christ and the pursuit of the Christian mission: rejection, shaming, vilification, and persecution. It is the suffering that Jesus promises in the last beatitude (Matt 5:10–11; Luke 6:22–23). Jesus' statement about taking up one's cross also appears to refer to apostolic suffering (Matt 16:24; Mark 8:34), for it refers to the Roman practice of requiring a person sentenced to crucifixion to carry the crosspiece through the streets to the site of execution, to be humiliated and vilified by the crowds along the way. Jesus' implication is this: follow me and you will be similarly rejected and shamed.

The Acts of the Apostles tells us that during the first mission into Asia Minor, Paul and Barnabas suffer persecution and even stoning at Iconium and Lystra. Even so, they retrace their steps to strengthen the new Christians there, and they preach, "It is necessary for us to *undergo many hardships* to enter the kingdom of God" (Acts 14:22). In 2 Tim 3:10–12, Paul can generalize that experience of affliction as typical of Christian life: "You have followed my teaching, way of life, purpose, faith, patience, love, endurance, persecutions, and sufferings. . . . Yet from all these things the Lord delivered me. *In fact, all who want to live religiously in Christ Jesus will be persecuted.*" And writing to the Thessalonians, encouraging them not to be disturbed by persecution, Paul says, "For you yourselves know that *we are destined for this.* For even when we were among you, we used to warn you in advance that we would undergo affliction, just as happened, as you know" (1 Thess 3:3–4). Christian tradition has rightly understood "carry your cross" as extending to other kinds of suffering beyond specifically apostolic afflictions—for instance, illness, the death of loved ones, natural disasters, and other tragedies—but it is important to recognize that the New Testament writers focus especially on the suffering that comes from bearing witness to Christ.

If all this seems a grim invitation, recall that most of these New Testament passages about apostolic suffering speak of the joy that accompanies these experiences. In Matthew's version of the Beatitudes, Jesus promises his disciples, "Rejoice and be glad, for your reward will be great in heaven," and he reminds us that, in bearing insult and persecution because of him, we join the prophets who were before us (Matt 5:11–12). In Luke's version Jesus' expression is even more exuberant: if we suffer hatred, exclusion, and insults on account of him, "Rejoice and leap for joy on that day! For their ancestors treated the prophets in the same way" (Luke 6:23). Luke illustrates this attitude in the apostles' joyful response to being flogged by agents of the Sanhedrin in Acts 5:40–41. Such joy that cannot be explained by psychology is a constant aspect of discipleship as portrayed throughout the Christian Scriptures.

## Reflection and Application (3:8–11)

Paul describes the transformation of his heart and mind as an *example* to encourage his fellow Christians, not simply as a revelation of his thoughts to friends. This implies that the Philippians—and we, too—can experience such a transformation if we yield to God's gift. Simply knowing that others have suffered loss for the sake of Christ can bring encouragement to those enduring a similar loss. An episode from the life of the recently beatified Austrian martyr of conscience Franz Jägerstätter illustrates this dramatically. Drafted to serve in the Nazi army, Jägerstätter, who was not a pacifist but a conscientious objector to Hitler's wars, refused to serve. Awaiting his execution in Berlin (by beheading, on August 9, 1943), Jägerstätter was informed by the Catholic chaplain there at that time that a Pallotine priest, Franz Reinisch, had died in that same cell for the same reason. The chaplain wrote to Jägerstätter's widow, "I have never seen a more fortunate man in prison than your husband after my few words about Franz Reinisch."[8]

## The Fullness of this Knowledge Is Still to Come (3:12–16)

¹²It is not that I have already taken hold of it or have already attained perfect maturity, but I continue my pursuit in hope that I may possess it, since I have indeed been taken possession of by Christ [Jesus]. ¹³Brothers, I for my part do not consider myself to have taken possession. Just one thing: forgetting what lies behind but straining forward to what lies ahead, ¹⁴I continue my pursuit toward the goal, the prize of God's upward calling, in Christ Jesus. ¹⁵Let us, then, who are "perfectly mature" adopt this attitude. And if you have a different attitude, this too God will reveal to you. ¹⁶Only, with regard to what we have attained, continue on the same course.

**NT:** Eph 2:4–10
**Catechism:** on presumption, 2092

3:12–14    Having described the radical overturning of his values and the incomparable gift of his relationship with Christ (vv. 7–11), Paul is now moved to elaborate on his current situation: he is in the middle of things in a double sense. First, in his life story as briefly reviewed in verses 4–11, he is already blessed with

8. Quoted in an unpublished study by Roger Bergman, "Toward a Sociology of Conscience: The Example of Franz Jägerstätter and the Legacy of Gordon Zahn." Jägerstätter was beatified as a martyr by Benedict XVI on October 23, 2007.

empowerment by the risen Lord but is still looking forward to joining Jesus in his risen state. Second, in terms of God's initiative and his own free response, he is in the middle of grace and free will. In other words, he grapples with the mystery that his life is not only unfinished business, but it is not entirely *his* business. He is cooperating with something God is doing in him. God has taken the initiative. Now Paul is responding with all his strength.

To try to capture this mystery of the *already* and *not yet* of God's initiative and his own collaboration, Paul engages in some wordplay: he uses forms of the same word (*lambanō*, "to take, receive," and *katalambanō*, "to make something one's own, grasp") four times in two verses (these two words here in italics): **It is not that I have already *taken hold of* it or have already attained perfect maturity, but I continue my pursuit in hope that I may *possess* it, since I have indeed *been taken possession of* by Christ [Jesus]. Brothers, I for my part do not consider myself *to have taken possession*.** The wordplay highlights both the incompleteness of Paul's journey and the interaction between himself and God. You could call it the dance of discipleship.

Describing his life as a process headed toward a goal readily evokes the image of running a race, which Paul now develops. **Just one thing: forgetting what lies behind but straining forward to what lies ahead, I continue my pursuit toward the goal, the prize of God's upward calling, in Christ Jesus.** The phrase "just one thing" means something like, "I *focus on* one thing." The word "goal" suggests something that one looks at, attends to, concentrates on. The "prize" for completing the race is to arrive at what God the Father has been calling him to all along, nothing less than to be glorified with Christ Jesus, which will be described in the climax of this passage in verses 20–21.

**Let us, then, who are "perfectly mature" adopt this attitude.** The NABRE translators put quotation marks around "perfectly mature" possibly to imply that Paul is here using language employed by some Philippians as a self-description, language he does not himself embrace, judging from his earlier refusal to claim full maturity for himself ("not that I have already attained perfect maturity," v. 12). In other words, those who think of themselves as already spiritually mature need to adopt Paul's sense of being God's unfinished business. Indeed, the next verse, addressing the Philippians directly, drives that point home: **And if you have a different attitude, this too God will reveal to you.** The word for having an attitude (*phroneō*) recalls his exhortation to put on the attitude of Christ (2:5) as manifested in his self-emptying obedience to the Father (2:6–11). Those who think of themselves as already fully mature need to learn that putting on the mind of Christ is a matter of lifelong learning.

The next verse nuances the point: **Only, with regard to what we have attained, continue on the same course.** Paul does not deny their progress, already acknowledged in the thanksgiving part of the letter (1:6), just as he acknowledged the "supreme good" that he already has in Christ Jesus. But Paul's point is that the Philippians avoid complacency and move ahead. The meaning of the word for "continue on the same course" (*stoicheō*) is particularly appropriate to this letter: "to be in line with a person or thing considered as standard for one's conduct."[9] That standard is Christ, who emptied himself and was exalted by God (2:5–11).

## Our Identity, Our Citizenship, Our Goal: Conformation to Our Lord and Savior (3:17–4:1)

[17]**Join with others in being imitators of me, brothers, and observe those who thus conduct themselves according to the model you have in us. [18]For many, as I have often told you and now tell you even in tears, conduct themselves as enemies of the cross of Christ. [19]Their end is destruction. Their God is their stomach; their glory is in their "shame." Their minds are occupied with earthly things. [20]But our citizenship is in heaven, and from it we also await a savior, the Lord Jesus Christ. [21]He will change our lowly body to conform with his glorified body by the power that enables him also to bring all things into subjection to himself.**

[4:1]**Therefore, my brothers, whom I love and long for, my joy and crown, in this way stand firm in the Lord, beloved.**

**NT:** 1 Cor 15:20–28, 42–53; Gal 5:11; Eph 1:19–23; Phil 1:27; Col 3:1–5
**Catechism:** church and state, civil authority and conscience, 2234–46
**Lectionary:** Second Sunday of Lent (Year C); Masses for the Dead

3:17    Paul's exhortation to be **imitators of me** may sound strange to our ears. We are reluctant to present ourselves as moral or religious examples. But in the ancient Greco-Roman world it was a common and acceptable practice for teachers to point to themselves as examples. It is human nature to look for examples to imitate; and teachers know that their role inevitably makes them examples, for better or for worse. Moreover, we acknowledge this fact in plenty of ways in our own culture: consider the recovering alcoholics who tell their stories to other alcoholics to encourage them, or excercise enthusiasts who speak of the new energy they have gained from an exercise program in order to prompt sluggish friends to join them in the gym.

9. BDAG 946.

Paul describes the imitation in a careful way: **join with others in being imitators of me**, literally, "be co-imitators of me." Since this word appears nowhere else in the New Testament, nor in Greek literature generally, it seems that Paul has coined it to emphasize imitation as a communal enterprise; they are to collaborate as a church in emulating Paul's way of life. Indeed, he develops that idea: **observe those who thus conduct themselves according to the model you have in us**. They are to imitate *one another* as they follow Paul's way of imitating Christ himself. The plural "us" underscores the fact that Paul is not the only model. For example, his cosender Timothy and the Philippians' emissary Epaphroditus are also to be viewed as models (2:19–30).

Having reminded the Philippian Christians whom they should take as models, Paul now reminds them of those they should *not* imitate—those who **conduct themselves as enemies of the cross of Christ**. Some scholars take this to be another reference to the †Judaizers mentioned earlier (the "dogs" of 3:2). But Paul's further description of this group suggests otherwise. That they are **many** and that he has **often told** the Philippians about them, and **now** tells them **in tears** suggests that (1) they are not part of the Philippian church, for then the Philippians would not need to hear about them from Paul, especially if they are "many"; and (2) they are nonetheless fellow Christians, for we would hardly expect Paul to be reduced to tears by the normal behavior of pagans. That they are "enemies of the cross" implies that they *know* both what the crucifixion of Christ means and its implications for disciples. Thus Paul seems to be referring to slackers who identify as Christians but fail to live the self-emptying way of life modeled by Paul, Timothy, and the other co-imitators of verse 17.[10] Since Philippi was situated at a crossroads, on the major road from Rome to Asia Minor and with access to a nearby port, the Philippians would have had occasion to meet travelers who were nominally Christian but whose worldly behavior was quite the opposite of true Christian conduct.

**3:18**

**Their end is destruction** because a human life ends either as salvation or destruction (see 1:28; 1 Cor 1:18). In other words, these are pagan converts for whom the message of the cross never quite took. They are backsliders who have returned to the pagan ways of indulging their appetites shamefully. And so he can say of them, **Their God is their stomach; their glory is in their "shame."** One is reminded of the Corinthian libertines whose theme song Paul quotes in 1 Cor 6:13: "Food for the stomach and the stomach for food."

**3:19**

When Paul says **their minds are occupied with earthly things**, he once again employs the verb *phroneō*, which he used for the mind-set that should

---

10. My interpretation of these enemies of the cross draws heavily on that of Fee, *Philippians*, 362–75.

characterize the Christian community (2:2, 5), namely, the self-emptying mind of Christ exemplified in the hymn. These "enemies of the cross" live with a mind-set precisely opposite of the mind of Christ. In the next two verses, Paul puts into words how the Christian life will also imitate the second half of the Christ hymn—not only self-emptying but also exaltation by God.

**3:20**   **But our citizenship is in heaven, and from it we also await a savior, the Lord Jesus Christ.** Paul chooses his language wonderfully, bringing to a climax the line of thought he has been developing since 1:27–30. Everything connects with both the Roman culture surrounding the Philippians and the Christ hymn of chapter 2. To the attitude of wayward Christians, fixed on earthly matters, Paul contrasts an authentic Christian mentality looking toward heaven. The rare word "citizenship" (*politeuma*) here echoes the verb for "conduct yourselves" (*politeuomai*) in 1:27, which conveys the idea of being a good citizen. Now, two chapters later, Paul harvests the seed planted in 1:27. The residents of Philippi were exquisitely aware that some of them were Roman citizens, protected by the laws of Rome, whereas others were mere Greeks and did not enjoy the security of Roman citizenship. The Roman citizens who lived in Philippi looked to Rome as the source of their sense of identity, allegiance, and security. Indeed, they even worshiped the emperor as "Lord" and "Savior." The Christian community, too, included both citizens and noncitizens. Therefore, when Paul asserts that the citizenship of Christians truly is[11] in heaven, he is not saying they do not have a life in Philippi, but rather that the source of their security and identity is the risen Messiah, whom *they* worship as Lord and Savior. If Jesus is Lord and Savior in the most absolute sense, then Caesar is not. So the point is not that the Philippian Christians are in exile but that, as members of the church, they live as a colony of *heaven*, not of the Roman Empire; their ultimate allegiance is to the Lord Christ, not to Lord Caesar.[12] And they await a visitation not from the Roman savior but from the Savior Christ.[13]

**3:21**   The expected coming of the Messiah as Savior and Lord of the universe—what Paul elsewhere calls the †parousia (the Greek word for a visit by the emperor)—will be the time of the resurrection from the dead. **He will change our lowly body to conform with his glorified body by the power that enables him also to bring all things into subjection to himself.** Once again Paul echoes the

---

11. I use the expression "truly is" here because Paul uses an especially heavy word for "is" in this verse, *hyparchō*, for which BDAG gives as the essential meaning "to really be there" (1029). Paul uses it at only one other place in this letter, to say Christ "was [*hyparchō*] in the form of God" (2:6).

12. This primary allegiance to Christ does not relieve Christians of legitimate obligations to civil authority. See Paul's famous consideration of that aspect of Christian life in Rom 13:1–7.

13. Although "savior" comes easily to the lips of contemporary Christians, it is a relatively rare title for Paul to use of Jesus, appearing only here, once in Ephesians, and ten times in the Pastoral Letters.

## The Risen Body

While we would love to know more about the nature of the risen body, Paul is quite clear on several aspects. First, resurrection is not resuscitation, that is, a mere return to biological existence, as in the case of Lazarus. Rather, resurrection is *a transformation*. Second, our bodies will be glorified by their share in divine life, like that of the risen Jesus. Paul addresses this matter at greater length in 1 Cor 15. To free up the imaginations of his largely Gentile audience, he has them first reflect on the apparent dying of a seed sown in the ground and the emergence of something that looks quite different (1 Cor 15:36–38). Then he has them ponder the diversity of flesh in the natural world (hairy, scaly, feathery, pale, luminous) and draws the analogy that the human body is "sown corruptible" and "raised incorruptible," "sown a natural body . . . raised a spiritual body" (1 Cor 15:42–44). We would love to know the details, but it is enough that Paul precludes our thinking of the resurrection as the return of a warmed-over corpse, teaching us instead to think of a profound transformation, much as the Gospel authors portray the bodily presence of the risen Jesus in his appearances to his disciples (see Luke 24:16, 36–43; John 20:14).

Christ hymn. A more literal rendering of this verse is, "He will *transform* the body of our *humiliation* that it may be *conformed* to the body of his glory, by the *power* that also enables him to make all things subject to himself" (NRSV). I have bolded the elements that echo the vocabulary of the Christ hymn in chapter 2.[14] By using words that resonate with the hymn, Paul underscores the theme of Christian life as a replication of the obedience and exaltation of Jesus, Messiah and Lord.

**Therefore, my brothers, whom I love and long for, my joy and crown, in this way stand firm in the Lord, beloved.** This burst of affectionate language    4:1
shows that Paul's challenging exhortation is motivated by a tender affection. He addresses these "brothers [and sisters]" as "beloved" and "longed for" (echoing 1:8), "my joy" (echoing 1:4), and "crown"—even repeating "beloved" at the end of the sentence. Although the traditional chapter division sets this verse apart from 3:21, it follows quite naturally as the conclusion of the previous passage.

---

14. "Conformed" (*symmorphon*) echoes "form" (*morphē*) in 2:6–7. "Transform" (*metaschēmatizō*) picks up "appearance" (*schema*) in 2:7, "humiliation" (*tapeinōsis*) echoes "humbled himself" (*tapeinoō*) in 2:8, and "power" (*energeia*) recalls "work" (*energeō*) in 2:13. Moreover, the risen Lord subjecting "all things" to himself mirrors the image of every knee bending and every tongue confessing that Jesus Christ is Lord (2:10–11).

The charge to "stand firm" echoes the same charge in 1:27, forming an †*inclusio*, or bracket, signaling that 1:27–4:1 is a coherent unit—indeed, the core of this letter. It is all about standing firm in the Lord, with Paul, Timothy, and Epaphroditus exemplifying the imitation of the primary model, Christ Jesus.

## Reflection and Application (3:12–4:1)

*Faithful citizenship: Paul's metaphor and our reality.* We have noted how Paul draws on this colony's preoccupation with Roman citizenship and reminds the Philippian Christians that, whether or not they possess citizenship in the Roman Empire, they can rejoice in another, greater kind of citizenship—their membership in the "empire of God," whose Lord and Savior, King Jesus, will someday come again to be present with them. This reality is true for us as well. It is also a reminder that those of us Christians who are citizens of contemporary democracies are called to exercise our political citizenship in a way that implements our Christian social vision, that is, our pursuit of the universal common good. In our voting and our communication with elected officials, the "upward call of God in Christ" calls us not simply to protect our vested interests but also to support candidates and policies that promote genuine justice and peace, with special attention to the poor, the neglected, the suffering, and the unborn.[15]

*Imitation of Christ by way of imitation of other Christians.* Paul's readiness to promote himself as a model to be imitated is really not self-promotion at all. Like Augustine in his *Confessions*, Paul speaks of his graced experience to encourage other believers that the same God who works in and through him can work in and through us. Paul is not celebrating his accomplishments but pointing to the gift of God. This is exactly the point of pondering the lives of the saints. Imitation of Christ quite often takes the form of emulating friends and family members whose faithful lives inspire us. So Paul's boasting in the Lord is not a quirky way of speaking but a reminder of a basic Christian reality. Like a bad example, a good example is contagious.

---

15. For a comprehensive account of Catholic social teaching, see the *Compendium of the Social Doctrine of the Church* by the Pontifical Council for Justice and Peace (Washington, DC: United States Conference of Catholic Bishops, 2004).

# A Final Call to Unity and Joy

## Philippians 4:2–9

Having reminded his audience of their call to grow in their new life in Christ, Paul turns again to some practical implications of living that life in community. In this section he rounds out his exhortation by moving from a quite particular issue—a call for two leaders to reconcile—to a summons to rejoice and affirm whatever is worthy and true as a sure way to the peace of God (v. 7), which will open them to the presence of the God of peace (v. 9).

### Reconcile! Rejoice! Pray! Focus on Whatever Is Good, True, and Beautiful! (4:2–9)

[2]I urge Euodia and I urge Syntyche to come to a mutual understanding in the Lord. [3]Yes, and I ask you also, my true yokemate, to help them, for they have struggled at my side in promoting the gospel, along with Clement and my other co-workers, whose names are in the book of life.

[4]Rejoice in the Lord always. I shall say it again: rejoice! [5]Your kindness should be known to all. The Lord is near. [6]Have no anxiety at all, but in everything, by prayer and petition, with thanksgiving, make your requests known to God. [7]Then the peace of God that surpasses all understanding will guard your hearts and minds in Christ Jesus.

[8]Finally, brothers, whatever is true, whatever is honorable, whatever is just, whatever is pure, whatever is lovely, whatever is gracious, if there is any excellence and if there is anything worthy of praise, think about these

things. ⁹**Keep on doing what you have learned and received and heard and seen in me. Then the God of peace will be with you.**

---

OT: Ps 145:18
NT: Matt 6:25–34
Lectionary: Third Sunday of Advent (Year C); Votive Mass for Civil Needs for Peace and Justice

4:2–3    **I urge Euodia and I urge Syntyche to come to a mutual understanding in the Lord.** Paul's singling out by name two women in a letter addressed to a community is striking. It seems unlikely that Paul would refer to a private disagreement between these two women. Since Paul does not address them directly ("Euodia and Syntyche, I urge you") it seems that their disagreement is a community concern, which suggests they hold positions of leadership among the Philippian Christians. Indeed, the language Paul uses to describe them in the next verse supports that impression. He says that these women **have struggled at my side in promoting the gospel**, using the very verb he used in exhorting the whole community to "stand firm . . . *struggling together* for the faith of the gospel" (1:27). Further, they are included **along with Clement and** Paul's **other co-workers, whose names are in the book of life** (v. 3). Paul thus regards them among worthy Christian leaders, certainly not among his adversaries. Recall that Paul reserves the descriptive term "co-worker" for fellow evangelists and community leaders, like Epaphroditus (Phil 2:25), Philemon, Mark, Aristarchus, Demas, and Luke (Philem 1, 24). The women's disagreement may well be one of the challenges to unity in the community, for in urging their reconciliation he uses the same phrase he used in exhorting the community as a whole in the introduction to the Christ hymn. "Come to a mutual understanding" translates the same Greek phrase as "be of the same mind" (*to auto phroneō*) in 2:2. Paul's concern with their disagreement is at the heart of this letter. Yet their conflict must not entail any malice on their part, for Paul includes them among those "whose names are in the book of life," a biblical metaphor for salvation.[1]

We don't know the identity of Paul's **true yokemate.** The fact that "yokemate" (*syzygos*) sometimes means "spouse" has led some scholars to speculate that Paul was married and is referring to his wife. As it would be the only such reference in the New Testament, however, that interpretation seems unlikely (see 1 Cor 7:7; 9:5). The conjecture that it is a personal name, Syzygos, is surely possible, but it is not supported by the appearance of that word as a proper name in any known first-century source. It could be Paul's nickname for a particular

---

1. See Exod 32:32–33; Ps 69:29; Dan 12:1; Rev 3:5; 13:8; 20:12, 15. It occurs only here in Paul's writings.

## The Quality of These Women

LIVING
TRADITION

John Chrysostom, who was just as alert as contemporary scholars to the importance of women in leadership roles in the early Church, saw fit to comment on the implications of Paul's reference to Euodia and Syntyche:

> Do you see how great is the virtue of these women, according to his testimony? As great as that which Christ told his apostles . . . *your names are written in the book of life* [Luke 10:20; Rev 3:5]. . . . Did they toil with him? Yes, he says. They contributed in no small part. Even though there were many fellow workers, yet in many affairs they also took a hand. Great therefore was the cohesion of the church at that time when the most respected, whether men or women, enjoyed such honor from the rest. There were many good consequences.[a]

a. *Homily on Philippians* 14.4.2–3, in ACCS 8:280.

individual. We may simply have to admit that we distant and late readers simply do not have the information to know to whom "yokemate" refers.

Whoever "yokemate" is, when Paul urges this comrade to **help them**, he implies helping in an active way. Luke uses the same word to express the help Peter and companions call for when their nets are tearing from the weight of the miraculous draft of fish (Luke 5:7). Clearly, the reconciliation of Euodia and Syntyche is an urgent community matter. About Clement we know nothing except what is stated here, that he was an honorable coworker of Paul's.

**Rejoice in the Lord always. I shall say it again: rejoice!** This letter is saturated with references to joy and rejoicing. Paul rejoices in the Philippians and they in him. This is not simply the joy of human fellowship; it is joy "in the Lord." Several times Paul's enthusiasm takes him from the indicative to the imperative, as here: "Rejoice!" When speaking of his sacrificial service for the Philippians' faith he says, "You also should rejoice and share your joy with me"; he concludes his commendation of Epaphroditus with "Finally, my brothers, rejoice in the Lord" (3:1). But how can one *exhort* others to rejoice? Is this the organized elation of the cruise-ship events director? No. Paul knows from experience that, no matter what the circumstances, being mindful of their union with the risen Lord will evoke a deep, mysterious joy. He can *mandate* that frame of mind because he and they know that Christian joy is not simply a feeling; it is a choice. This comes right after his call for reconciliation between Euodia and Syntyche, to remind them that their common ground lies not simply in good will but also in attending to the joy of being "in the Lord."

4:4

**4:5**      **Your kindness should be known to all.** The "kindness" (*epieikes*) Paul calls for here is a special kind, which the lexicon describes as "not insisting on every right or letter of law or custom; yielding, gentle, kind, courteous, tolerant."[2] He may have chosen this rare word as a necessary virtue for the two women leaders mentioned above, as well as for those dealing with them.

In this context, Paul's statement **The Lord is near** is not a general truism. In Ps 145:18, a psalm that praises God's goodness as creator and redeemer, the phrase "You, Lord, are near" expresses confidence that God is responsive to those who call upon him. Here in Philippians the short assertion that the Lord is near carries the psalm's resonance but applies it to the one who is specifically honored as Lord in this letter—Jesus the risen Messiah. Since the context of this passage is a call for prayer of petition (v. 6), "near" seems best understood as immediate presence, as in Psalm 145, rather than the temporal imminence of the †parousia.

**4:6–7**    The phrase **Have no anxiety at all** could provoke the anxious person to respond, "Easy for *you* to say." But this is not wishful thinking. Paul reminds his addressees that they have a God whom they can trust to respond to their anxiety and provide for their needs. There is a practical way to address anxiety: **in everything, by prayer and petition, with thanksgiving, make your requests known to God.** "In everything" means *in every circumstance*—imprisonment, community conflict, harassment from external adversaries. Help is at hand, for the asking. In urging prayer of petition, Paul insists that it be made with "thanksgiving" (*eucharistia*)—a reminder that their confidence in God rests on the ways they have already known his power that "began a good work" in them (1:6). The result? **The peace of God that surpasses all understanding will guard your hearts and minds in Christ Jesus.** It takes something that transcends human understanding to guard human hearts and minds. And this happens precisely "in Christ Jesus," that is, in the risen Lord and the messianic community joined to him. Note that Paul is putting in other language Jesus's teaching at the heart of the Sermon on the Mount (Matt 6:25–34): the remedy for anxiety is not simply emptying the mind of worry but seeking first the kingdom of God and his righteousness (Matt 6:33). Trusting in God, expressed in prayer within the believing community, leads to peace of mind.

**4:8**      People writing and speaking these days about successful living sometimes speak of "getting your head straight," "getting clear," or being "purpose-driven." These phrases name a common human quest, a quest Paul, in his role as pastor and fellow Christian, is addressing in this letter. Up to this point he has been

2. BDAG 371.

writing much about attitude, learning to consider or think about everything in a new, Christian way—to put on the mind of Christ, especially as illustrated in the Christ hymn and exemplified by Timothy, Epaphroditus, and Paul.

The final verses of this section provide a summary of that theme. Having stressed the importance of Christlike self-donation, he now broadens the horizon of what is worthy of Christian attention by including whatever is good and positive in Greco-Roman culture. He uses language familiar to any Philippian, Christian or not. **Finally, brothers, whatever is true, whatever is honorable, whatever is just, whatever is pure, whatever is lovely, whatever is gracious, if there is any excellence and if there is anything worthy of praise, think about these things.**

But when it comes to *behavior*, not simply thinking, Paul returns to the specifics of their life as a faith community: **Keep on doing what you have learned and received and heard and seen in me.** That is, let your behavior be governed by the tradition that we share, which I have taught you and have been graced to model for you.

4:9

## Reflection and Application (4:2–9)

*The perennial need for reconciliation.* Although we are in the dark regarding the nature of Euodia and Syntyche's disagreement, the mere fact that Paul, at the heart of this letter to a church, calls them by name to come to a mutual understanding powerfully indicates that the need for reconciliation has been a pastoral issue from the beginning of the life of the Church. It reminds us that people of good will and dedication can find themselves in disagreement in ways that challenge the unity and peace of the community on any level: diocesan, parish, or family. And Paul's response to this rift shows that such conflicts, humanly predictable as they may be, are nevertheless not "of the Lord." The differences must be addressed, directly and lovingly. Christian leadership, in other words, entails the ministry of reconciliation. Paul devotes a whole letter, the one we call 2 Corinthians, to the theme of reconciliation—first reconciliation between himself and the Corinthian Christians and, second, reconciliation as the Church's ministry to the world—that is, sharing in God's work of "reconciling the world to himself in Christ" (2 Cor 5:18–21).

*The duty of rejoicing and letting go of anxiety.* It may seem odd that Paul should *exhort* his addressees to rejoice and not to be anxious, as if people can change their mood simply by willing it. But Paul is not simply cajoling them, as if he were telling them to lighten up! By urging them to acts of kindness he reminds them that genuine joy comes from right relationships. In effect, he is saying, "Looking for joy? Then rejoice in the Lord. That is, be filled with praise and gratitude for what we have, for what God has done for us in Christ. That will free you to let go of self-preoccupation and attend to the needs of others." This is precisely what he says in the introduction to the Christ hymn in 2:1–4. And his remedy for anxiety is eminently practical: in effect, "The Lord is near. Acknowledge his nearness by praying in thanksgiving and in confidence for your needs and the needs of others. When you have done what you can do, leave the rest to the Lord and express that trust in prayer."

*Forming good habits of the heart.* Paul spends a good bit of papyrus advising his readers to monitor their interior dispositions, to form what some nowadays call "habits of the heart."[3] It is instructive that, toward the end of a letter emphasizing how Christians are to live in a countercultural way ("without blemish in the midst of a crooked and perverse generation," 2:15), he rounds off his exhortation with the robust call to affirm whatever is good or true or beautiful. True to his Jewish heritage, he celebrates whatever in nature and in human culture manifests the goodness of the Creator.

The teaching of 4:8 can help when we encounter church policies and styles of religious expression that do not fit our taste and we are tempted to dismiss them with ready labels like "liberal" or "conservative," "pious" or "trendy," "orthodox" or not. Paul would say to us, "Forget about the knee-jerk responses of your circle; affirm the good and the true and the beautiful wherever you find it. Then your critique of what may be bad, false, or ugly can be heard." Our first instinct should be to look for and affirm the evidence of grace wherever we find it.

---

3. This phrase came into prominence as the title of a book by Robert N. Bellah and others in 1985—*Habits of the Heart: Individualism and Commitment in American Life* (Berkeley: University of California Press).

# Thanks and Final Greetings

## Philippians 4:10–23

As Paul moves toward the closing of his letter, he returns to the expressions of affection for the Philippian Christians with which he began. The theme of equanimity that he modeled in chapter 1, as he considered possible outcomes of his imprisonment ("Christ will be magnified in my body, whether by life or by death," 1:20), is echoed here as he reflects on his God-given ability to live either in humble circumstances or in abundance (4:12–13).

### A Delicate Thank You (4:10–14)

<sup></sup>¹⁰I rejoice greatly in the Lord that now at last you revived your concern for me. You were, of course, concerned about me but lacked an opportunity. ¹¹Not that I say this because of need, for I have learned, in whatever situation I find myself, to be self-sufficient. ¹²I know indeed how to live in humble circumstances; I know also how to live with abundance. In every circumstance and in all things I have learned the secret of being well fed and of going hungry, of living in abundance and of being in need. ¹³I have the strength for everything through him who empowers me. ¹⁴Still, it was kind of you to share in my distress.

OT: Ps 49:1–21; 52:9; Isa 5:8–13
NT: John 15:5; 2 Cor 12:9; 1 Tim 6:2–10, 17–19

Paul now turns to the business of thanking the Philippians for the gift they sent through Epaphroditus. As we will see, it was financial aid: the kind of

4:10

support Paul alluded to at the beginning of the letter (1:5). Paul intimates that Epaphroditus's arrival occurred well into the period of his imprisonment: **I rejoice greatly in the Lord that now at last you revived your concern for me.** Since that remark could sound like a sarcastic expression of self-pity (as in, "Finally, you remember your old friend Paul, languishing in prison"), he hastens to add, **You were, of course, concerned about me but lacked an opportunity.** Paul does not disclose what delayed the opportunity; Paul may in fact be making a courteous assumption, a way to let them save face for not coming to his aid sooner.

4:11     Having addressed the question of their tardy help, Paul is moved to comment on the topic of his need. He has already spilled a good bit of ink describing his experience as a kind of model for their own coping with the struggles of being Christian. Now he hastens to add that, actually, he has learned to cope with any circumstance, for the Lord has sustained him throughout: **Not that I say this because of need, for I have learned, in whatever situation I find myself, to be self-sufficient.**[1] But he has already implied that *his* self-sufficiency, or contentment, is the result of his trusting in divine providence (4:6–7) and is the fruit of the community's intercessory prayer for him (1:19). Perhaps the translators should have put quotation marks around "self-sufficient" here, given that Paul seems to be using this Stoic term ironically; in fact, his peace comes from acknowledging that he is utterly *dependent* on God.

4:12     In spelling out what he means by self-sufficiency, he reaches for language that recalls, once again, the mind of Christ expressed in the hymn of chapter 2: **I know indeed how to live in humble circumstances.** The last six words translate a single Greek verb (*tapeinoō*), whose more literal translation would be "to humble oneself, to be humbled." Our NABRE rendering catches the meaning well enough, but the word pointedly echoes its last use, in the Christ hymn: "found in human form, he *humbled* himself" (2:8). It simultaneously recalls the noun "humility" in 2:3b: "In *humility* regard others as better than yourselves" (NRSV). The link to 3:21 is equally significant: "He will transform the body of our *humiliation* to conform to the body of his glory" (NRSV). Consequently, the verb here might be more accurately and elegantly rendered by the RSV's translation: "I know how *to be abased* and I know how to abound." Paul here refers not only to his poverty but also to his suffering in the cause of the gospel. While the power of Christ has enabled him to be

---

1. "Self-sufficient" translates *autarchēs*, which appears only here in the New Testament; it comes from the vocabulary of the Stoics (see BDAG 152 on *autarkeia* and *autarkēs*). NIV and NRSV have "content." Stoicism was a school of Greek philosophy that taught that happiness was achieved through virtue.

peaceful in good times and in bad, the darker moments more closely unite him with Christ crucified.

To show that he is fine with either circumstance, he expands: **I know also how to live with abundance. In every circumstance and in all things I have learned the secret of being well fed and of going hungry, of living in abundance and of being in need.** To "learn the secret" means to learn something privy to the insiders of a group. Paul uses it to remind the Philippians that this ability to be content in every circumstance is available to all the baptized who have put on the mind of Christ.

Paul summarizes what he has just said with a general statement: **I have the strength for everything through him who empowers me.** Contemporary readers may be more familiar with the RSV translation, often used as a kind of maxim: "I can do all things in him who strengthens me." As to the identity of the one who strengthens (the Father, or Christ?), the prevalence in this letter of the phrase "in Christ" suggests that Paul means Christ.[2] He applies this principle to his empowerment for mission in Col 1:29: "For this I labor and struggle, in accord with the exercise of his power working within me." 4:13

Lest Paul's "sidebar" on his ability, in Christ, to cope with any circumstance (vv. 12–13) seem to make him unappreciative of their gift, he returns to the note of gratitude: **Still, it was kind of you to share in my distress.** Here Paul uses a weighty word for "share": *synkoinōneō*, which means that they have *shared jointly*—as a community—in his troubles. Paul seems to realize that they deserve even more acknowledgment than that. And so he will proceed to spend the next five verses expanding on their beneficence—no matter how much he may insist that he didn't really need it. 4:14

## Reflection and Application (4:10–14)

*Balanced "self-sufficiency."* Always conscious that he is a model of Christian attitude and behavior for his converts, Paul labors to make sure his beloved Philippians understand both his relationship to material goods and his relationship to them as fellow Christians. He is most grateful for their gift. But he wants to remind them that, as a Christian, his ultimate security lies in Christ. He is as content as any good Stoic aims to be; yet his ability to deal both with famine and feast, suffering and comfort, lies not in philosophical independence but in proper *dependence* on the Lord. Paul's attitude is a healthy challenge to our

2. Indeed, the presence of *Christō* at this point in some manuscripts points to this as the obvious meaning.

North American culture. Like the Roman Philippians, we too prize and admire self-sufficiency and deem it a kind of dishonor to be dependent on others.

Consider the following example of our cultural fear of dependence. An acquaintance told me how hard it was for him to face being seen using the food stamps that his family was given by the federal government as part of disaster relief in the wake of a tornado that damaged his neighborhood. For a long time the food stamps just sat there, unused. He did not want to be seen in a grocery store spending the stamps and therefore viewed as needing that kind of help. Finally, disguising himself in a cap and dark glasses, he spent the food stamps in another neighborhood, where he was less likely to be recognized.

Paul's example reminds us that any true independence we have is ultimately rooted in profound dependence on the Lord, and that kind of dependence calls us to look after one another's needs, especially within the community of faith.

*Detachment from material goods.* While Paul can "live in humble circumstances," he also knows how to "live with abundance." We should not take that lightly, as if to say, "Who has a problem with living in abundance?" In fact, a good many of us in North America live in abundance, but we are unmindful of what that abundant lifestyle is doing to others and to ourselves. To touch on just one aspect, our way of eating and the industrial mode of farming that supports it has led to a national diet that is high in fat, sugar, and salt; such a diet has made us susceptible to a variety of diseases, favors the production of animal feed over grain for humans, and relies on a pattern of land use that some argue is unsustainable. These issues were not on Paul's mind, of course, but his knowing how to live in abundance can challenge us to examine how *we* live with *our* abundance. Regarding the possession of wealth, Jesus challenged rich people in a uniquely personal way. The rich man of Mark 10:17–22 needed to be called to sell all and give to the poor to follow Jesus. Zacchaeus simply had to restore fourfold to his former victims of extortion and give half his possessions to the poor (Luke 19:1–10).

Both Testaments remind us that wealth and prosperity can delude us into thinking we do not need to depend on the God who has created us and sustains us.[3]

## Further Thanks, Greetings, and a Blessing (4:15–23)

[15]You Philippians indeed know that at the beginning of the gospel, when I left Macedonia, not a single church shared with me in an account of giving

3. E.g., Isa 5:8–13; Pss 49:1–21; 52:9; 1 Tim 6:2–10, 17–19; James 4:13–16.

and receiving, except you alone. [16]For even when I was at Thessalonica you sent me something for my needs, not only once but more than once. [17]It is not that I am eager for the gift; rather, I am eager for the profit that accrues to your account. [18]I have received full payment and I abound. I am very well supplied because of what I received from you through Epaphroditus, "a fragrant aroma," an acceptable sacrifice, pleasing to God. [19]My God will fully supply whatever you need, in accord with his glorious riches in Christ Jesus. [20]To our God and Father, glory forever and ever. Amen. [21]Give my greetings to every holy one in Christ Jesus. The brothers who are with me send you their greetings; [22]all the holy ones send you their greetings, especially those of Caesar's household. [23]The grace of the Lord Jesus Christ be with your spirit.

**OT:** Gen 8:21; Exod 29:18; Ezek 20:41
**NT:** Acts 16:11–17:15; Rom 12:1
**Catechism:** sacrifice, external and internal, 2099–2100

The topic of the Philippians' recent financial aid recalls for Paul their similar    **4:15** generosity to him when he moved on from Macedonia to Achaia.[4] The phrase **beginning of the gospel** refers to his first visit to Philippi, where for the first time he preached the good news on the continent we now call Europe (Acts 16:11–17:15). After preaching in Philippi, Thessalonica, and Beroea, which all lie in **Macedonia,** Paul moved on to Athens and Corinth (Acts 17:16–18:17). At that time the Philippian community was unique in the matter of **giving and receiving,** that is, the spontaneous financial support that accompanies genuine friendship. This implies that the churches of Thessalonica and Beroea did no such thing, at least not at that time. However, his reference to the generosity of "the churches of Macedonia" in 2 Cor 8:1–5 indicates that these other churches eventually did aid the mission generously.

Paul then recalls an earlier time when, as he was working down the road from    **4:16–17** Philippi in **Thessalonica,** the Philippians more than once sent him financial aid—**something for my needs.** "Needs" here is the same word used for Epaphroditus's mission to Paul (2:25). That said, Paul hastens to emphasize, once again, that his concern is not for his needs—**not that I am eager for the gift**—but for the Philippians' growth in Christian generosity. This sentiment is expressed in a clever metaphor drawing on the vocabulary of accountancy, nicely rendered by the NABRE: **rather, I am eager for the profit that accrues to your account.**

---

4. The Roman province of Macedonia includes much more than the area of the modern country of the same name. It included much of what now constitutes the north of modern Greece. Philippi sat in the eastern corner of the province, some eighty miles east of Thessalonica.

4:18        When Paul says, **I have received full payment**, he continues the financial
metaphor. With **I abound** he picks up on his earlier statement about living
in contentment with either need or abundance (v. 12). In effect, he is saying,
"Thanks for giving me the occasion to live in abundance, which I welcome as
happily as a time of need."

Finally, Paul indicates precisely what gift he is talking about: **what I received
from you through Epaphroditus**—that is, bringing the Philippians' financial
aid package to the imprisoned Paul—which was the main reason for their emissary's ill-fated journey. Paul finishes this rhapsody of gratitude by shifting the
metaphor from the arena of commerce to that of temple sacrifice (as in 2:17):
their gift to him was **"a fragrant aroma," an acceptable sacrifice, pleasing to
God**.[5] This is the same imagery he uses so strategically to describe Christian
community life in Rom 12:1: "I urge you, therefore, brothers, by the mercies of
God, to offer your bodies as a living sacrifice, holy and pleasing to God, your
spiritual worship." Paul's phrasing is no mere rhetorical flourish. In reaching out
to him and aiding his mission, the Philippians are living in a way that mirrors
the mind of Christ and participates in his sacrifice as celebrated in the hymn
of chapter 2. In this way, they are honoring the ultimate Benefactor.[6]

4:19–20        Finally, Paul acknowledges that the supplier behind their mutual service is
God, now called **My God**, as in the prayer with which he began the letter ("I give
thanks to my God," 1:3). He assures them that this grace will come **in accord
with his glorious riches in Christ Jesus**, which the NRSV renders more literally,
"according to his riches in glory in Christ Jesus." We need to take "glory" back
to its biblical roots to unpack this dense phrase. In the Old Testament, "glory"
often refers to the perceptible manifestation of God's presence, particularly in
the temple liturgy. Given that "in Christ" is a shorthand expression for being in
the church, the body of the risen Christ, God's "riches in glory in Christ Jesus"
would seem to be the Philippians' lived experience of being empowered by the
Father in the shared life of their community, founded on the lordship of Christ.

"Glory" can also mean "honor," and it is in this sense that Paul uses it in the
next verse: **To our God and Father, glory forever and ever. Amen.** The "*my*
God" of verse 19 is also "*our* God and Father." This doxology echoes not only
the letter's greeting (1:2) but also the climax of the Christ hymn ("Jesus Christ
is Lord, / to the glory of God the Father," 2:11). The title "Father" invokes the
early Church's practice of addressing God as *Abba* (Gal 4:6; see Rom 8:15),

---

5. These expressions draw on biblical texts like Gen 8:21; Exod 29:18; Ezek 20:41.
6. Ben Witherington III, *Friendship and Finances: The Letter of Paul to the Philippians*, The New
Testament in Context (Valley Forge, PA: Trinity Press International, 1994), 132–33.

thus consciously sharing in Jesus' own filial relationship. Moreover, given the Roman colonial context of the Philippian church, Paul may intend the Christian term "*our* God and Father" to contrast similar titles used in emperor worship.

We might be tempted to pay little attention to the final greetings and bene-       **4:21–23**
diction, taking them to be customary farewell greetings. Yet they prove to be as carefully worded as the rest of the letter. Whereas in 1:1 he addressed the letter to "*all* the holy ones in Christ Jesus," he now asks that his greetings be extended to **every holy one in Christ Jesus**. That may seem a distinction without a difference, but the careful distributive phrase may well convey Paul's emphasis on a unified community that includes respect for each and every individual.

**The brothers who are with me** are apparently fellow Christians confined with Paul, given that they are distinguished from **all the holy ones** in the following verse, which includes every Christian in the neighborhood of his imprisonment. When Paul highlights **those of Caesar's household**, he is still talking about Christians, in this case slaves, freedmen, and soldiers who are part of the emperor's household. Together with the earlier reference to "the whole praetorium" (1:13), this verse provides a clue to the location of Paul's imprisonment, most probably Rome. Since greetings from strangers are less meaningful, perhaps these members of "Caesar's household" are those who have actually become familiar to some of the Philippian Christians, possibly couriers who frequented the Egnatian Way carrying messages between Rome and its colony Philippi.

Though virtually identical to the benedictions with which Paul closes other letters (1 Cor 16:23; Gal 6:18; 1 Thess 5:28; 2 Tim 4:21; Philem 25), **The grace of the Lord Jesus Christ be with your spirit** carries a special resonance in this letter, as it echoes the resounding confession that ends the Christ hymn (2:11). The thought might be paraphrased this way: May the one who emptied himself, becoming obedient unto death on a cross, and whom God greatly exalted above every name, *the Lord* Jesus Christ—may he extend grace and favor to your inmost self. "Your" is plural here, so Paul is referring distributively to the inner spirit of each individual.

## Reflection and Application (4:15–23)

Paul often uses the language of temple sacrifice to speak of the ordinary activities of the Christian community. This follows from the basic notion that the Church, the community of faith, is the new temple that was expected in the end times (see Ezek 40–48). What goes on in a temple is primarily the worship of God. Since worship of God is at the heart of Christian life, Paul readily describes his ministry and that of other Christians as sacrifices offered to God (2:17; 4:18; and see Rom 12:1 as elaborated by Rom 12:2–21). By speaking of ordinary activity, especially mutual service, in this way, he reflects the way the Torah mixes rules for worship with laws regarding human relations. (Leviticus 19 is a ready example of such a blending of liturgical and moral matters.) For people living the Sinai covenant, the whole fabric of communal life was bound up with their relationship to God. Jesus expresses that same tradition when he delivers the Sermon on the Mount, "If you bring your gift to the altar, and there recall that your brother has anything against you, leave your gift there at the altar, go first and be reconciled with your brother, and then come and offer your gift" (Matt 5:23–24). Our relationship with God is as good as the quality of our relationship with other human beings (see 1 John 4:20). Jesus, of course, renews the covenant by the giving of his own body and blood, and we Christians join in that covenant renewal by participating in the eucharistic sacrifice.

Paul says the same thing in his own way. This, of course, does not mean that fostering good human relationships can *replace* liturgical worship of God. Paul's temple talk works in two directions. On the one hand, it reminds us that, given the proper disposition—like that expressed by the Morning Offering in devotion to the Sacred Heart—everything we do (homework, housework, commuting, socializing, what have you) can be offered to our God as a way of honoring and praising him.[7] On the other hand, it reminds us that our daily life is in fact a living out of the offering we make and the mission we receive in our participation in eucharistic worship. Paul is saying that all of Christian life, in union with Christ, is a sacrificial offering to God (Rom 12:1). Life becomes liturgy; our smallest activities of work or service become an act of worship.

---

7. This is the text of the Morning Offering: "O Jesus, through the Immaculate Heart of Mary, I offer you my prayers, works, joys, and sufferings of this day in union with the holy sacrifice of the Mass throughout the world. I offer them for all the intentions of your Sacred Heart: the salvation of souls, reparation for sin, the reunion of all Christians. I offer them for the intentions of our bishops and of all the apostles of prayer, and in particular for those recommended by our Holy Father this month."

# Paul's Letter to the Christians in Colossae

Paul and Timothy send this letter from prison to a Christian community in the Lycus River Valley, some 120 miles east of Ephesus. Although Paul knows some of the Christians who meet at Philemon's house in Colossae (see Philem 1–2), he is not acquainted with most of the Christians in the area, especially those downriver in the larger communities of Laodicea and Hierapolis, and wherever Nympha hosts another community at her place (see Col 4:13–15). These people were evangelized by Paul's delegate Epaphras, who is imprisoned with Paul and Timothy at the time of this writing. The occasion of the writing appears to be Epaphras's report about the churches in the Lycus Valley area. The life of the Christian communities is robust, but it is threatened somewhat by the emergence in the neighborhood of a so-called †philosophy (2:8)—a worldview and set of practices—that appears to be a mix of Jewish tradition, pagan folk religion, and Christianity. As in the case of the †Judaizers Paul faces in the Letter to the Galatians, this philosophy purports to offer greater protection against evil cosmic powers than the gospel they had learned from Epaphras. Although some Colossian Christians have been attracted to this deceptive, "new and improved" brand of Christianity, it seems at the time of the writing to be mainly an external distraction and a *possible* threat.

Paul, in his response, reminds his addressees that they have all they need in the gospel of Christ to which they were converted. Therefore, the letter stresses the universal—indeed, cosmic—sovereignty of Jesus Christ (1:15–20). If they desire something more in their spiritual life, that greater dimension can be found in knowing Christ and dedicating themselves to the life of the body of Christ into which they were baptized—the way of compassion, kindness, humility, gentleness, and patience, of bearing with one another and forgiving one another

(3:12–13), as well as extending the mission by relating to outsiders with grace and wit (4:5–6). While the precise nature of the rival philosophy remains obscure, the letter's response has stood through the centuries as a persuasive reminder that deepening our faith in the risen Jesus as Lord of all and maturing in the basics of the Christian way of life are all we need for true spiritual fulfillment and purpose amid the changing tides of history. Along with the later Letter to the Ephesians, Colossians has done much to foster among Christians the sense that we are part of a *worldwide* Church under the lordship of Jesus Christ, even as we live out our daily lives in the local faith communities of diocese and parish.

Like Philippians, Colossians is brief (four chapters), and features a poetic celebration of the preeminence of Jesus so beautifully crafted that it has taken on a life of its own as a free-standing hymn in the prayer and worship of the Church (1:15–20). Like the self-emptying Christ hymn of Philippians (Phil 2:6–11), the Colossians poem is so thoroughly integrated into the fabric of the letter that it can be plausibly thought of as the work of Paul himself.

### Who Really Wrote This Letter?

The vocabulary and †eschatological perspective of Colossians, very close to that of the Gospel of John in its emphasis on salvation as already realized in the present, are so distinctive that some scholars have disputed Paul's authorship. My own study of the letter has persuaded me to join the growing number of scholars who hold that the primary author of this letter is indeed the same as the author of Philemon and Philippians—Paul. The reasons for this conviction will emerge in the course of the commentary, but it will help to address some basic issues here in the introduction.

Careful readers of Paul's Letters cannot miss the striking similarities between Colossians and Ephesians. Both letters celebrate Jesus Christ as head of the universal Church, described as his "body" in language that has a poetic and hymnic quality. Both speak of God's plan entailing the "†mystery" of God's revelation to the Gentiles. Both explain how life in the body of Christ transforms all the relationships of the household—husband and wife, parent and child, master and slave. Both letters appear to be addressed to several communities. And both speak of Tychicus (in virtually identical words!) as the bearer of the letter (Col 4:7–8; Eph 6:21–22). The relationship of Colossians to Ephesians is analogous to the relationship between Galatians and Romans. In each case the earlier letter addresses an urgent problem (the Judaizers in Galatians and the exponents of the philosophy in Colossians), and in each case the second letter elaborates on the themes of the first in a calmer, more orderly way. It has been said that Galatians reads like a rough draft of Romans, and Colossians like a (not so rough) draft of Ephesians.

Indeed, it is plausible that, after overseeing the composition of Colossians, Paul recognized that its basic message—regarding the transcendent lordship of Christ as the source of unity for the church and the absolute sufficiency of Christ for salvation—was worth sharing with all the churches in the province of Asia and its environs. And so he commissioned a more general version of the letter, which we know as the Letter to the Ephesians. Ephesians is actually an encyclical or circular letter, and Paul had copies made with a blank space for the different addressees. (In Eph 1:1 the majority of surviving manuscripts have "in Ephesus" where the blank space would have been.)[1] Paul then sent Tychicus off, accompanied by the slave Onesimus, with three letters—the one to Philemon; the one to the Colossian community, to be shared with the Christians in Laodicea and perhaps in Hierapolis; and the more generic version of the latter to be delivered to the Ephesians. This scenario accounts for the striking similarities between Colossians and Ephesians as well as the shift in emphasis between the two, with Ephesians focusing on the more general, less locally particular issue of the union of Jews and Gentiles in the one body of Christ.[2]

The greeting (1:1) of the Letter to the Colossians identifies Paul and Timothy as its authors. Further, at the end of the letter, we read, "The greeting is in my own hand, Paul's." Curiously, this greeting seems both to testify to the Apostle's personal authorization and to distance him slightly from the letter. It suggests that the physical writing of the letter was the work of a scribe (possibly Timothy); for why would Paul emphasize that the final greeting comes "in my own hand" unless someone else's hand was involved in writing the letter? This is a helpful reminder that the authorization of a text is not the same as the physical application of pen to parchment. This fact also leaves room for distinguishing the essential content from the style of expression.

Those who question Paul's authorship point mainly to two features of the letter that they feel go beyond what might be attributable to the work of a scribe authorized by Paul: (a) the use of diction that is quite different from the †undisputed letters of Paul, and (b) an emphasis on a †realized eschatology, focusing

---

1. For a discussion of the manuscript evidence for understanding Ephesians as an encyclical, see Bruce M. Metzger, *A Textual Commentary on the Greek New Testament*, 2nd ed. (New York: American Bible Societies, 1971), 532.

2. Notice that this scenario also allows for the hypothesis that the city of Ephesus was the location of Paul's imprisonment at the time of the writing of these letters. Just as Martin Luther King Jr. addressed the clergy of Birmingham, Alabama, from the Birmingham jail, it is plausible that Paul issued his letter to the Ephesian Christians from an Ephesian jail, and that Tychicus served as messenger to both Colossae, some one hundred miles away, and to the church(es) in Ephesus and possibly beyond.

on the blessings of salvation that Christians *already* enjoy, which appears to be at variance with the end-time vision we know from the other Pauline Letters. It can be argued, however, that the author's word choice in this letter is largely determined by the nature of the particular challenge he faces in the Colossian church; that is, people tempted to believe that they need other spiritual powers than Christ for security and salvation. Thus Paul may be using some of the catchwords of his adversaries to refute their philosophy. And the emphasis on realized eschatology may derive from the author's need to underscore what the Colossian Christians already know and experience in their life with the risen Lord Jesus, thus rendering unnecessary any borrowing of ideas and practices from Judaism or neighboring folk religions.

Given that the authenticity of Paul's Letters was regarded as of great importance (see Col 4:18, "The greeting is in my own hand, Paul's. Remember my chains"[3]), and given that this letter was unanimously attributed to Paul in the early Church, I join those who are not convinced that this letter is †pseudonymous. The reader may judge whether the details of this commentary support Pauline authorship.

## Who Were the Colossians and Why Did Paul and Timothy Write to Them?

The town of Colossae was part of a cluster of three towns—Laodicea, Hierapolis, and Colossae—in the Phrygian region of the Roman province of Asia, which was in the southwestern corner of what we today call Turkey. These towns are nestled in the Lycus Valley, the Lycus being a tributary to the Meander River, which meanders (yes, the verb comes from the name of the river) westward till it empties into the Aegean Sea near Miletus. Laodicea, ten miles down the river from Colossae and one of the seven cities addressed in the book of Revelation (Rev 1:11; 3:14–22), was the major city of the region, and the church there was also an intended recipient of this letter, as 4:16 indicates.[4] Paul is writing to communities that he did not found and apparently has yet to meet (2:1). His coworker and fellow prisoner Epaphras (to be distinguished from Epaphroditus of Philippi) is the one who brought the gospel to the Lycus Valley (1:7; 4:12),

---

3. See also 1 Cor 16:21; Gal 6:11; 2 Thess 2:2; 3:17.

4. It is worth noting that the superscript of the message to the Laodiceans in Revelation gives, as one of the titles of the risen Christ, "the source of God's creation [*hē archē tēs ktiseōs tou theou*]" (Rev 3:14), a phrase that echoes the hymn of Colossians (1:16, 18). The author of Revelation appears to know that the church at Laodicea would appreciate a reference to the kind of cosmic Christology expressed in the letter to the Christian communities of the Lycus Valley.

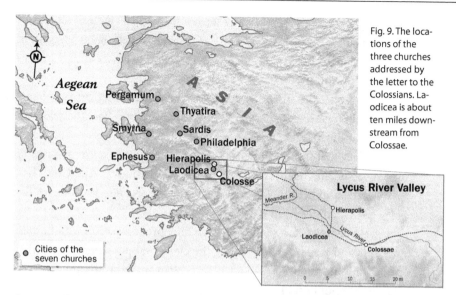

Fig. 9. The locations of the three churches addressed by the letter to the Colossians. Laodicea is about ten miles downstream from Colossae.

forming this young Christian community of Gentiles (the majority) and some Jews (1:5–7; 4:12).

Since Paul appears not to have met all the Christians of the Lycus Valley—given the phrase "for you and for those in Laodicea and all who have not seen me face to face" (2:1)—he seems to be responding to what he has learned of the life of the Colossian church from their founder, Epaphras (1:3–8). What he has learned includes the presence in their neighborhood, perhaps even in their community, of thinking and practice that threatens the integrity of their Christian faith—what Paul calls "an empty, seductive philosophy" (2:8). Determining the nature of this "philosophy" is a matter of guesswork, since all we know about it derives from Paul's response to it. Though the Colossians of course knew what he was talking about, we can only guess. What we do know comes from Paul's warnings in chapter 2 of the letter—especially in verses 16–23.

The givens supplied by the letter are the following.

1. The proponents of the "philosophy" appear to be erring Christians rather than outsiders such as unconverted pagans or members of neighboring synagogues, for Paul describes them as "not holding closely to the head," that is, Christ (2:19), a phrase that would be meaningless with regard to people who did not have *some* place for Christ in their religious worldview. Moreover, Paul's question, "Why do you submit to regulations as if you were still living in the world" (v. 20), implies that at least some of his Christian addressees have been drawn to the practices of the "philosophy."

2. The proponents of the "philosophy" have apparently set themselves against the majority of the Colossian Christians, dismissing the latter as ignorant and perhaps irreligious "in matters of food and drink or with regard to a festival or new moon or Sabbath" (2:16).

3. They also fault fellow Christians for lacking in physical asceticism and being ignorant in regard to the "worship of angels," and they base their convictions regarding proper Christian practice on personal "visions" (2:18).

4. Paul judges that these enthusiasts misunderstand the supreme priority of Christ as "the head, from whom the whole body"—the Church—"supported and held together by its ligaments and bonds, achieves the growth that comes from God" (2:19).

5. These elements of the "philosophy" entail a preoccupation with human precepts and teachings regarding "the elemental powers of the world" and prohibitions about contact with certain material things: "Do not handle! Do not taste! Do not touch!" (2:20–21).

6. The mention of "Sabbath" in conjunction with "new moon" and "festival" (2:16) implies that aspects of Jewish practice are part of the mix.

All of this invites the formation of a hypothesis that makes sense of these facets of the letter. In my judgment, the most plausible scenario comes from recent research on the Jewish and pagan folk practices known to be operative in first-century Phrygia, Lydia, and Caria—the geographical context of the Lycus Valley, east of Ephesus and Miletus.[5] Study of inscriptions, amulets, and magical texts, both pagan and Jewish, from this region reveals the presence of a variety of popular beliefs and practices that have in common a concern for relating properly to cosmic powers, some benevolent and some hostile. According to this evidence, while not worshiped as divine, these entities can be called upon for protection and addressed with names like "elements of the world" or "principalities and powers" or "angels, messengers" (*angeloi*). A group close to and perhaps within the Colossian church appears to have espoused a version of this religious mix, or syncretism. They appear to have been somewhat similar to Paul's Judaizing opponents in Galatia in that they argue that a Christian can only qualify as complete if he or she takes on this particular set of beliefs and practices, which involve fasting, severe physical discipline, the experience of visions, and the appeasing of various spiritual go-betweens called "principalities and powers" or "elements of the universe." This group's preoccupation with

5. See Clinton E. Arnold, *The Colossian Syncretism: The Interface between Christianity and Folk Religion at Colossae* (Tübingen: J. C. B. Mohr [Paul Siebeck], 1995).

other mediators leads Paul to emphasize the fullness that Christians already possess through baptism into the risen Lord Jesus Christ, the One through whom everything was created and who is the reconciler of all that is in the universe.

## From Where Did the Authors Write?

As in the cases of Philemon and Philippians, Paul informs us in Colossians that he is imprisoned (4:3, 18) but is not specific about the location. Scholarly hypotheses regarding the location have usually focused on geographical distances. Ephesus has emerged as a popular candidate because of its proximity to Colossae, roughly 120 miles away, and because other New Testament references to Ephesus suggest sufficient trouble to make imprisonment there plausible.[6] Paul learned from his fellow prisoner Epaphras (Philem 23) of that minister's successful foundation of a Christian community in Colossae; he also heard about the challenge that this mainly Gentile church faces from the faction who hold the "philosophy." Paul, with Timothy, writes to assure these new Christians that they already have all the protection and saving power they need in the Lord Jesus Christ.

## A Letter to Christians Today

Like all the books of the Bible, Colossians is not only a letter written to people long ago in a land far away but also a letter from God to Christians today. "In the sacred books, the Father who is in heaven comes lovingly to meet his children, and talks with them."[7] Colossians is particularly relevant as a response to the perennial temptation to spiritual novelties—doctrines and practices that purport to bring special knowledge, power, or fulfillment but in reality can lead people into spiritual bondage. Such pseudospirituality can appear in the form of occultism, the teaching of self-appointed spiritual gurus, and private revelations that draw people's focus away from the core of Christian faith and into what is secondary. In the face of these grave dangers to faith, Paul powerfully exalts the all-sufficiency of Christ. For the spiritually hungry, there is no need to go looking elsewhere. Jesus himself inaugurated all the "new age" elements we need (see Matt 19:28). The fullness of wisdom, fulfillment, and life come sfrom entering more deeply into "the riches of the glory of this mystery," which is "Christ in you, the hope for glory" (Col 1:27).

6. For more details on the place or places of Paul's writing of the Prison Letters, see the general introduction to this book.
7. Catechism, 104.

# Outline of the Letter to the Colossians

The most satisfying outline of Colossians I have found is that of John Paul Heil in his recent commentary.[1] He divides the letter into ten elements, which are based on the †chiastic structure he has discerned as governing the movement of this document from beginning to end. A chiasm is a pattern of writing in which phrases are arranged in parallel such that the order of elements in the first part is mirrored in reverse in the second part. Within the framework of this overall *macro*chiasm, Heil also finds that each of the ten units is itself a *mini*-chiasm. While my commentary will not refer in detail to all of the parallelisms he has found, I will advert to some of them when they illuminate the meaning of a given passage in a substantial way. I will, however, use most of his major divisions to mark the text divisions of the commentary. Note that Heil's titles for the ten major units are carefully worded both to summarize the content of each unit and to underscore its parallelism with the corresponding unit in the chiastic structure. I will sometimes provide alternative titles to name a unit as we move through the text, but Heil's wording remains the best guide to the chiastic parallels.[2]

1. *Colossians: Encouragement to Walk in All Wisdom as Holy Ones in Christ*, Early Christianity 4 (Atlanta: Society of Biblical Literature, 2010).
2. The following outline appears in ibid., 37. I omit his account of the minichiasms that structure each of the ten units. The full outline and the criteria for recognizing the chiastic structures are best understood in the context of Heil's detailed study.

## Outline of the Chiastic Structure of Colossians

A  Grace from Paul an apostle by the will of God (1:1–2)

  B  Thanking God when praying for you to walk in wisdom (1:3–14)

    C  The gospel preached to every creature under heaven (1:15–23)

      D  We are admonishing and teaching every human in all wisdom (1:24–2:5)

        E  Walk and live in Christ, with whom you have died and been raised (2:6–23)

        E′  You died and were raised with Christ from living as you once walked (3:1–7)

      D′  In all wisdom teaching and admonishing one another (3:8–16)

    C′  You have a master in heaven (3:17–4:1)

  B′  Pray for us in thanksgiving and walk in wisdom (4:2–6)

A′  Full assurance in the will of God and grace from Paul (4:7–18)

# Greeting, Thanks to the Father, and Prayer

## Colossians 1:1–14

As we have seen in Philemon and Philippians, Paul shapes the elements of a typical introduction to a Greco-Roman letter in ways that deftly prepare his audience for the message to follow. In the greeting (vv. 1–2) and in a prayer that looks backward in thanksgiving (vv. 3–8) and forward in petition (vv. 9–14), Paul subtly plants the seeds of themes he will elaborate throughout the rest of the letter: realize what you have received through the gospel; grow into and walk in the wisdom you already have in Christ! These fourteen verses move seamlessly into the famous "hymn" of 1:15–20, which turns out not to be a free-standing artifact but a development of the prayer that then flows into the application in verses 21–23. The editorial headings in the NABRE translation (Greeting, Thanksgiving, Prayer), appropriate though they may be, can give the impression of discrete units and obscure to the reader the seamless continuity of Paul's thought.

### Greeting (1:1–2)

¹Paul, an apostle of Christ Jesus by the will of God, and Timothy our brother, ²to the holy ones and faithful brothers in Christ in Colossae: grace to you and peace from God our Father.

NT: Philem 1; Phil 1:1
Catechism: apostles as sent by Jesus, 858–60

As in our other two Prison Letters, Paul names **Timothy** as cosender.[1] Given      1:1
that Paul's greeting at the close of the letter implies the use of an †amanuensis, or
secretary ("The greeting is in my own hand, Paul's"), it is possible that Timothy
is functioning as Paul's scribe. Unlike Philemon and the Philippians, where
he implies no further reference to Timothy after the greeting, here Paul does
include Timothy by using "we" in verses 3–12, as he moves into the thanksgiving and †prayer report. I use the phrase "prayer report" since verses 3–12 are
not, strictly speaking, a prayer but rather a *description* of Paul's and Timothy's
habitual prayer for the Colossians.

Paul's self-identification as **an apostle of Christ Jesus**[2] does not simply mean
that he is one who preaches Jesus as Messiah; the word *apostolos* means one
who is sent by and represents the sender—Jesus the Messiah and risen Lord.
Dead men don't send. Jesus is alive! **By the will of God** may seem superfluous
(would the Son not do the will of the Father?), but the phrase serves as a reminder that Christ Jesus does indeed serve the Father's will, an expression that
lends weight to Paul's authority (see also 1 Cor 1:1; 2 Cor 1:1; Eph 1:1; 2 Tim
1:1). Paul spells out what this way of identifying himself means in the opening words of Galatians: "Paul, an apostle not from human beings nor through
a human being but through Jesus Christ and God the Father who raised him
from the dead" (Gal 1:1).

Paul addresses the Colossian community as the **holy ones** (or "saints," RSV),      1:2
that venerable Old Testament name for the covenant people of God (who are
holy in the sense of "dedicated to God") that we met in Philem 5–7 and Phil
1:1; 4:21–22. He adds the epithet **faithful brothers in Christ.** "Brothers," of
course, includes both men and women and emphasizes that the members of the
church have become one family (see Matt 23:8). The Greek word for "faithful"
is *pistos*, which like its cognate *pistis* ("faith" or "faithfulness") can be active or
passive. In the active sense, *pistos* can mean "trusting" (that is, having trust in
another); in the passive sense it can mean "faithful" or "trustworthy" (that is,
worthy of another's trust). Here Paul probably has both senses in mind. In this
letter *pistos* is a favorite term of approval: Epaphras is a "trustworthy minister"
(1:7), and both Tychicus (4:7) and Onesimus (4:9—yes, the slave we met in the
Letter to Philemon) are beloved and trustworthy, faithful brothers.

There follows Paul's usual benediction: **grace to you and peace from God
our Father.** Absent, however, is Paul's usual "and the Lord Jesus Christ."[3] As

---

1. See also 2 Cor 1:1; 1 Thess 1:1; 2 Thess 1:1.
2. See Rom 1:1; 11:13; 1 Cor 1:1; 2 Cor 1:1; Gal 1:1; Eph 1:1; 1 Tim 1:1; 2 Tim 1:1; Titus 1:1.
3. See 1 Cor 1:3; 2 Cor 1:2; Gal 1:3; Eph 1:2; Phil 1:2; 1 Thess 1:1; 2 Thess 1:2.

will immediately become clear, this highlighting of God the Father is deliberate (see 1:3, 12; 3:17).

## Prayer Report, Part 1: Thanksgiving (1:3–8)

³We always give thanks to God, the Father of our Lord Jesus Christ, when we pray for you, ⁴for we have heard of your faith in Christ Jesus and the love that you have for all the holy ones ⁵because of the hope reserved for you in heaven. Of this you have already heard through the word of truth, the gospel, ⁶that has come to you. Just as in the whole world it is bearing fruit and growing, so also among you, from the day you heard it and came to know the grace of God in truth, ⁷as you learned it from Epaphras our beloved fellow slave, who is a trustworthy minister of Christ on your behalf ⁸and who also told us of your love in the Spirit.

OT: Gen 1:28; Jer 3:16, 18; 23:8; Ezek 36:11
NT: 2 Cor 5:17; Gal 6:15
Catechism: theological virtues, 1812–29; living the truth, 2465–70; Trinity, 232–56; intercession, 2634–36

1:3–5a       The missing element of Paul's usual greeting—**our Lord Jesus Christ**—turns up here in this thanksgiving. The plural form, **we always give thanks**, is consistent with Timothy's coauthorship. The present verses do not themselves *constitute* a prayer of thanksgiving, since a prayer is addressed to God whereas these words are addressed to the Colossian community. Rather, they are an *account* of Paul and Timothy's regular prayer, which is filled with gratitude for the grace of God at work among the Colossians. The three classic theological virtues—faith, hope, and love—are evident in their lives: **for we have heard of your faith in Christ Jesus and the love that you have for all the holy ones because of the hope reserved for you in heaven.** The hope here obviously refers not to the virtue itself but to *what is hoped for*, namely, that which awaits the Christian in heaven. The Colossians have faith in the Messiah and Lord Jesus, and they have learned to love their fellow Christians, a virtue supported by their shared confidence in a heavenly future. Even in a letter that will emphasize the *present* grace of the Christian life, Paul reminds the Colossians of the future fulfillment of this grace still awaiting them.

1:5b–6       Paul already begins here to address the temptation the "philosophy" may present (see 2:8). If the practitioners of the philosophy would seduce them with promises of gaining ultimate *truth* and full contact with *reality* (both expressed in the Greek word *alētheia*) in their special practices, Paul reminds them that

## Loosed from the Chains of the Ancient Captivity

**LIVING TRADITION**

Pope St. Leo the Great reminds Christians to remain faithful to the gift we have received in baptism.

> Snatched from the powers of darkness at such a great price, and by so great a mystery, and loosed from the chains of the ancient captivity, make sure, dearly beloved, that the devil does not destroy the integrity of your souls with any stratagem. Whatever is forced on you contrary to the Christian faith, whatever is presented to you contrary to the commandments of God, it comes from the deceptions of the one who tries with many wiles to divert you from eternal life, and, by seizing certain occasions of human weakness, leads careless and negligent souls again into the snares of death. Let all those reborn through water and the Holy Spirit consider the one whom they have renounced.[a]

a. *Sermon* 57.5.1–2, quoted in ACCS 9:9.

they **have already heard** what they need through **the word of truth** (*alētheia*), **the gospel** that **has come** to them. The gospel is not mere theological speculation or comforting ideas, but the truth about God and the world. Further, the Colossians are part of a growing movement much greater than their local church life: **Just as in the whole world** (*kosmos*) the gospel **is bearing fruit and growing, so also among you, from the day you heard it and came to know the grace of God in truth.** Their faith community is a participation in a larger work of God—indeed, the *cosmic* work of the Creator of the universe. The fact that this same faith is flourishing elsewhere is a reminder that no local enhancement or variation, such as the new Colossian "philosophy," is necessary.

To anyone familiar with the creation account in Genesis, Paul's phrase "it is bearing fruit and growing" recalls God's mandate to Adam and Eve at Gen 1:28, most familiar to English speakers in the translation, "Be fruitful and multiply" (NRSV, NJB). As in other short letters such as Philemon and Philippians, Paul does not explicitly *quote* Scripture here, but he does engage his biblical heritage by way of allusion or echo. There are a number of possibilities for Paul's intention in echoing Gen 1:28. On the one hand, it could be a mere rhetorical flourish to underscore his words. On the other hand, further occurrences of that phrase in the Old Testament itself suggest a fuller connection. Throughout Genesis, the patriarchs are repeatedly referred to as "increasing and multiplying." Then in the prophets the phrase describes the fertility that will accompany the end of exile and the restoration of Israel (see Jer 3:16, 18; 23:3; Ezek 36:11). Thus Paul likely chose the phrase because it evokes that whole tradition of God-given fertility in the beginning and in the end times, for much of this letter will emphasize the newness that Christians have entered by being baptized into Christ. Indeed, they have become "a new creation" (2 Cor 5:17; Gal 6:15), a new creation that manifests itself in the fruits of the Holy Spirit (Gal 5:22–23).[4]

**1:7–8**  If the Colossians feel that the purveyors of the "philosophy" offer the fullness of knowledge, Paul reminds them that the knowledge of the truth is something they learned **from Epaphras** at the foundation of their community. Since Epaphras is the living link between Paul and this community that he has not yet met face-to-face, Paul affirms the worth of this emissary by describing him as **our beloved fellow slave, who is a trustworthy minister of Christ on your behalf.** "Fellow slave" translates a single word—*syndoulos*—which Paul will use later to describe his coworker Tychicus (4:7). The full phrase applied to Tychicus is "fellow slave *in the Lord*," which helps us understand Paul's meaning here: Epaphras is a slave of the Lord Jesus Messiah. This is the sense in which Paul identifies himself as "slave" elsewhere (Rom 1:1; Gal 1:10; Phil 1:1). This self-designation may seem to conflict with his claim to the high-sounding title of "apostle" in 1:1; but it should be remembered that "apostle" essentially means "one who is sent," and being dispatched to deliver a message was often the function of a slave in the first-century world of the Roman Empire. The point is that Paul, Epaphras, Tychicus, and others are all servants of the one Lord and Master, Jesus.

This affirmation of Epaphras's trustworthiness is intended to revive the Colossians' confidence in the "word of truth, the gospel," which they received through this servant of Christ. Paul's reference to their **love in the Spirit** also serves as a reminder of the vitality of their community life—the faith, hope, and love for one another mentioned in verses 4–5—that began with their first reception of the good news.

Along with the triad of theological virtues, the thanksgiving also names the three divine Persons who in later Church teaching will be formally articulated as the Trinity—the "Father" and "Lord Jesus Christ" in verse 3, and "the Spirit" in verse 8.

### Prayer Report, Part 2: Petition (1:9–14)

[9]**Therefore, from the day we heard this, we do not cease praying for you and asking that you may be filled with the knowledge of his will through**

---

4. Christopher A. Beetham, *Echoes of Scripture in the Letter of Paul to the Colossians* (Boston: Brill, 2008) has produced an illuminating study of this dimension. The material in the present paragraph draws on his treatment in 41–59.

all spiritual wisdom and understanding ¹⁰to live in a manner worthy of
the Lord, so as to be fully pleasing, in every good work bearing fruit and
growing in the knowledge of God, ¹¹strengthened with every power, in
accord with his glorious might, for all endurance and patience, with joy
¹²giving thanks to the Father, who has made you fit to share in the inheritance of the holy ones in light. ¹³He delivered us from the power of darkness and transferred us to the kingdom of his beloved Son, ¹⁴in whom we
have redemption, the forgiveness of sins.

OT: 2 Sam 7:11–14; Isa 11:1–9
NT: Acts 26:17–18
Catechism: Christian prayer, 2697–745; Son of God, 238–48; baptism and forgiveness of sins, 2839
Lectionary: 1:12–20 Christ the King (Year C)

Having spent six verses telling of his and Timothy's gratitude to the Father      1:9
for the grace he has given the Colossian Christians, Paul now spends six
verses telling of his and Timothy's intercession for continuation and growth
of those very same gifts, especially knowledge and power. They are praying
for knowledge not simply in the speculative sense, but specifically practical
knowledge for Christian living. Given that the erroneous teaching appears to
offer *fulfillment*—something that will become evident in Paul's use of "fullness" (*plērōma*) and "fill" (*pleroō*) at key moments in the letter—Paul prays
that the Colossians may be **filled with the knowledge of his will through all
spiritual wisdom and understanding.** We might hear this as a reference to
theological information. But the focus is on the knowledge of God's *will* and
on *spiritual* wisdom and understanding—that is, knowing how to apply the
truth of God to daily life. These are the fruits of the Spirit that characterize
the "shoot from the stump of Jesse" in Isa 11:1–3, which Jewish tradition
understood as a prophecy of the messiah. Paul declares that this Spirit has
been given to Christian believers so that they too can increasingly take on the
character of the Messiah.

Paul's desire is that the Colossians learn **to live in a manner worthy of the**      1:10
**Lord.** The Greek word for "live" here literally means to "walk"—the common
biblical expression for carrying out the will of God in one's daily life, as in
our contemporary saying, "She doesn't just talk the talk; she walks the walk."
Both Isa 11 and Paul are asserting that such faithful walking is empowered
by the Holy Spirit.[5] The result is a life **fully pleasing** to God, **in every good
work bearing fruit.** Living according to the gospel causes people to flourish,
which in turn delights and honors God. Jesus speaks in a similar way in the

5. See Beetham, *Echoes of Scripture*, 61–79.

Gospel of John: "By this is my Father glorified, that you bear much fruit" (John 15:8).[6]

The impression of wordiness and repetition that one gets reading verses 3-14 derives from Paul's effort to make his intercessory prayer in verses 9-14 a kind of mirror image of his thanksgiving in verses 3-8. Both speak of "the holy ones" and of "giving thanks" to the Father. The echo of Genesis in verse 6, about responding to what is heard and "bearing fruit and growing" in knowledge, is paralleled in verse 10. But Paul does not simply repeat himself. Whereas verse 6 speaks of the growth of the word on the universal scale ("in the whole world"), verses 9-14 focus on the growth in the local community. A further sense of design and completeness derives from the inclusion of Father (vv. 3, 12), Lord Jesus Christ (vv. 3, 4, 7, 10), and Spirit (v. 7).[7]

**1:11**     Paul and Timothy pray not only that the Colossians will *know* God's will but also that they be **strengthened with every power** to carry out that will—as is Paul himself (v. 29). God's **glorious might** is the power of the risen Christ, which will enable them to do God's will with **all endurance and patience,** even in adverse circumstances. And the special grace of the Christian life is to endure such difficulties not with grim resignation but **with joy.**

**1:12**     Paul envisions the new Christians of Colossae and Laodicea as **giving thanks to the Father, who has made you fit to share in the inheritance of the holy ones in light.** To say that the Father has made them fit (or "qualified," RSV) is a reassurance they need in view of the situation Paul will address in chapter 2—namely, that some members of the church are insisting that those who do not follow *their* beliefs and practices are not fully qualified Christians (2:18). Here, Paul is reminding the Colossians that they have already definitively passed from darkness to light, as he will elaborate in verses 13-23.

Verses 12-14 contain a complex of images that echo the biblical story of the exodus. In the Old Testament "the holy ones" are the covenant people of Israel, and their "inheritance" is life in the land God promised them. In the New Testament the inheritance of the holy ones is life in the kingdom of God, already begun through baptism into the body of Christ, the Church.

**1:13-14**  Paul moves from the you-plural form to the inclusive "we" as he summarizes this good news, the "grace of God" that both the senders and the receivers of the letter have already known: **He (the Father) delivered us from the power of darkness and transferred us to the kingdom of his beloved Son, in whom we**

---

6. See also Rom 7:4; Gal 5:22-23; Phil 1:11; Heb 12:11.

7. Indeed, it is the kind of "mirror" balancing we find in 1:3-14 that provides the basis for the chiastic pattern Heil finds here and throughout the whole of the letter. On this passage see Heil, *Colossians,* 47-61.

**have redemption, the forgiveness of sins.** "Deliver" is the term used in the Old Testament for God's rescue of Israel from enslavement to Pharaoh's oppressive power—into freedom and communion with God (Exod 6:6). While people tend to think and live as though most of life is spiritually neutral, Paul through this statement implies that there are only two kingdoms—that of darkness and that of Christ. To become a Christian is to be transferred from one to the other. Very similar wording appears in Paul's speech before Agrippa II in Acts, where Paul says the risen Lord sent him to Jews and Gentiles "to open their eyes that they may turn from darkness to light and from the power of Satan to God, so that they may obtain the forgiveness of sins and inheritance among those who have been consecrated by faith in me" (Acts 26:18).

As Gentiles, most Colossians before their Christian conversion probably lived with a worldview populated by various spiritual powers that threatened their existence and required appeasements or special defenses (amulets, sacrifices, and other practices) to ensure their safety. Their conversion to Christ, however, enabled them to live free of fear of such powers and supplied them with a supporting community that leaned together on Jesus as Master of all. They shared a common hope of future life with Jesus and found themselves surprisingly enabled to love and forgive one another. Although the full sharing in "the inheritance of the holy ones in light"—the hope reserved for them in heaven (v. 5)—remains in the future, their *rescue from the power of darkness* is a reality already inaugurated by the Father through the life, death, and resurrection of his beloved Son.

"Son" can refer to Christ in three modes of his existence:

1. as the divine Person through whom all things were made, whom the prologue of John calls "the Word" (*ho logos*),
2. as the same eternal Son incarnate as Jesus in his earthly life, and
3. as the incarnate Son raised from the dead, the Church's risen Lord.

The poem of verses 15–20 will evoke all three aspects of Christ's existence. Here in verses 13–14 the focus is on the Son as risen Lord. Further, the phrase "kingdom of his beloved Son" alludes to Nathan's prophecy to David: "I will raise up your offspring after you, sprung from your loins, and I will establish his kingdom. He it is who shall build a house for my name, and I will establish his royal throne forever" (2 Sam 7:12–13). Originally this prophecy applied to David's temple-building son, Solomon, but ultimately it points to the end-time messiah who would establish God's kingdom over a restored Israel.[8] The risen Jesus fulfills this prophecy.

8. Beetham, *Echoes of Scripture*, 97–112.

## The Editing of Modern-Language Editions of the Bible

The original Greek text of the New Testament not only lacked headings but also had neither punctuation nor chapter and verse divisions. Translators and editors of modern editions of the Bible are faced with the challenging task of rendering an ancient text into contemporary English that is accurate and readable, whether read silently by an individual at home or aloud in the liturgy. That sometimes requires breaking long Greek sentences into short English ones to make the thought process easier to follow. To help readers find their way around a given biblical book, editors have supplied headings and subheadings as helpful markers of changes of topic or transitions in an argument. All of this is in the service of understanding the text in a way that will serve the life and mission of the Church. When I make reference to differences between the English version (in our case, the NABRE) and the Greek original, the point is to listen to what the format and phrasing of the Greek original can contribute to our understanding of the Word of God. This, too, is in the service of the life and mission of the Church.

The full stop here in the NABRE translation, together with the section heading and special title for the poem to follow—"The Preeminence of Christ—His Person and Work"—can give the impression that a new unit begins at this point. However, verse 14 does not end the sentence in the Greek text, but is part of a sentence that began at verse 9 and continues into verse 15: ". . . who is an image of God the unseen, the firstborn of all creation." Paul moves seamlessly from a report of his prayer for the Colossians into a hymn celebrating the supremacy of Christ.

### Reflection and Application (1:3–14)

Paul and Timothy's carefully articulated account of their intercessory prayer carries powerful reminders of three perennial realities of Christian life: the place of giving thanks to God, the power of evangelization, and the "already/ not yet" paradox of the Christian life.

*The place of thanksgiving.* Paul and Timothy begin and end this †prayer report with expressions of thanksgiving. This emphasis underscores the reality that the young community at Colossae already has much to be thankful for. It also serves as a reminder that prayer, and indeed faith itself, is rooted in gratitude to God. When we sometimes feel at a loss as to how to begin private or public prayer, the easiest and most natural way is to look around us and recognize the gifts of God for which we are thankful—everything from the last meal to the gift of existence itself. Gratitude is the easiest starting point of prayer, the prevailing atmosphere of a prayerful life.

*The power of evangelization.* Those of us fortunate enough to have grown up with the support of a believing family and a robust faith community can be tempted to merely maintain that way of life with practices that have become second nature to us. Paul's focus on what the young Colossian community has been enjoying since Epaphras first evangelized them can alert us to the reality that the Christian life really is *good news* to those who have lived in darkness and even despair. Evangelization is not a matter of persuading others to think as we do. It is sharing the good news of a remedy for what most ails the world—coldness, guilt, fear, hopelessness, unruly attachments, alienation, and violence. These (mainly) Gentiles of Colossae found a new beginning, a born-again experience, in the gospel of Christ that Epaphras brought to them. If we are alert to the joys and the hopes, the grief and the anguish of those around us, the sharing of our faith will come naturally, and we can replicate what Epaphras initiated in the Lycus Valley. Of course, evangelization also includes the *ongoing* evangelization that we Christians continually need in order to grow in the life of the Spirit—the challenge and nurturing that comes from regular, well-prepared homilies, good conversation and reading, spiritual direction, and occasional retreats.

*The "already/not yet" paradox of Christian life.* When scholars summarize the New Testament's presentation of the coming of the kingdom of God, they often use the phrase "already/not yet." That is, the kingdom of God that Jesus announced is *already* inaugurated in his life, death, and resurrection; but it has *not yet* reached the fulfillment that will occur only with his final coming at the end of history. We met this understanding in the prayer at the beginning of Colossians: "the love you [already] have" and "the hope reserved for you in heaven" (1:4–5). This view of how God's plan and the Church's present historical moment mesh is equally applicable to our own day. We have *already* been rescued by God from enslavement to sin through incorporation into the body of the risen Lord; and we also live in the hope of inheriting the full blessing *yet to come* in the †parousia of Christ and the risen life of the faithful. We encapsulate that understanding when, at the Eucharist, we recite: "We proclaim your Death, O Lord, and profess your Resurrection until you come again."

# Beloved Son of the Father, Head and Redeemer of All

## Colossians 1:15–23

We come now to the jewel of the Letter to the Colossians, sometimes referred to as the cosmic Christ hymn (1:15–20). These verses make powerfully good sense when considered as a free-standing hymn. Yet they flow from verses 13–14 and really find completion in verses 21–23. The previous section celebrated the redemption that "we"—the Colossian Christians and Paul and Timothy as well—have received in being delivered from the power of darkness into the kingdom of the Son. This section will put that personal experience of salvation into the larger, cosmic story of the eternal Son, first as "firstborn" of all creation (vv. 15–17) and then as "firstborn" of the *new* creation (vv. 18–20)—a story that extends even to the present life of the Colossians themselves and the ministry of Paul (vv. 21–23).

### The Preeminence of Jesus Christ (1:15–23)

[15]He is the image of the invisible God, the firstborn of all creation. [16]For in him were created all things in heaven and on earth, the visible and the invisible, whether thrones or dominions or principalities or powers; all things were created through him and for him. [17]He is before all things, and in him all things hold together. [18]He is the head of the body, the church. He is the beginning, the firstborn from the dead, that in all things he himself might be preeminent. [19]For in him all the fullness was pleased to

dwell, [20]and through him to reconcile all things for him, making peace by the blood of his cross [through him], whether those on earth or those in heaven.

[21]And you who once were alienated and hostile in mind because of evil deeds [22]he has now reconciled in his fleshly body through his death, to present you holy, without blemish, and irreproachable before him, [23]provided that you persevere in the faith, firmly grounded, stable, and not shifting from the hope of the gospel that you heard, which has been preached to every creature under heaven, of which I, Paul, am a minister.

---

**OT:** Exod 12:12; Ps 68:17
**NT:** Matt 5:9; John 1:1–18; Rom 5:10–11; 2 Cor 5:18–21; Eph 1:20–23; 2:14–16; 4:4, 16; 5:23–30
**Catechism:** Christ, head of the Church, 669, 792; creation, work of the Trinity, 290–92; prayer of praise, 2639–43
**Lectionary:** 1:12–20: Christ the King (Year C)

Paul begins his marvelous hymn by describing the preeminence of God's **1:15** beloved Son as image of God and as firstborn of all creation. Describing Christ as **the image** (Greek *eikōn*, from which our word "icon" is derived) **of the invisible God**, he turns the focus to the incarnate Son, Jesus, since only the *enfleshed* Son is visible. This means that to look upon Jesus of Nazareth is to see the face of the eternal, invisible God. The word "image" echoes Gen 1:26–27 ("Let us make man in our image") and prepares the way for understanding Christ as the new Adam (see Col 3:10). When he calls the Son **the firstborn of all creation**, he uses the rich biblical notion of a firstborn son as preeminent in a family in two ways: (1) the firstborn is chronologically first to be born to his parents; (2) he has greater privilege and honor (e.g., in measure of inheritance) than other siblings.[1] Paul proceeds to apply this concept to the eternal Son in two different ways, each of which uses both senses of "firstborn." First, the Son is firstborn in the sense that he is, with the Father, the source and sustainer of all created things (vv. 16–17). As firstborn, he is heir to the entire universe. Second, he is chronologically the first to rise from the dead; and as risen Lord he is the foundation and capstone of the *new* creation, the Church (vv. 18–20). In both the original creation and the new creation, Christ is prior in time and supreme in honor.

In verse 16 Paul speaks of the eternal Son before his incarnation. A vast world **1:16** of things was created over the course of the enormous era we call BC (some 13.7 billion years, astronomers tell us). The Son was not himself created. He is

---

1. For scriptural precedents for this sense of "firstborn," see Exod 4:22, where God declares that "Israel is my son, my firstborn," and Ps 89:28, where God declares about the Davidic king that "I myself make him the firstborn, Most High over the kings of the earth."

## The Image of the Invisible God

LIVING TRADITION

St. Gregory of Nazianzus, a fourth-century father of the Church, explains how Christ is the image of the invisible God.

> He is called "image" because he is of one substance with the Father; he stems from the Father and not the Father from him, it being the nature of an image to copy the original and to be named after it. But there is more to it than this. An ordinary image is a motionless copy of a moving being. Here we have a living image of a living being, indistinguishable from its original to a higher degree than Seth from Adam [Gen 1:26] and any earthly offspring from its parents. Beings with no complexity to their nature have no points of likeness or unlikeness. They are exact replicas, identical rather than like.[a]

a. *Orations* 30.20, quoted in ACCS 9:11.

"firstborn" of all creation because of his status as *agent* of all creation from the beginning—as we say in the Nicene Creed, "begotten, not made."

The sense of "firstborn" that we discerned in the previous verse is confirmed here: **For in him were created all things.** The firstborn's preeminence consists in being the one through whom the Father created *everything* from the beginning. The whole world, with all its beauty, complexity, and mystery, is his workmanship. And Paul finds several ways to express that "all things" really includes everything that is or ever was: (1) **in heaven** (literally, "in the heavens") **and on earth** embraces the totality of what exists spatially: "heaven" is everything "up there," like the sun, moon, and stars; "earth" stands for everything "here below." (2) **The visible and the invisible** is not simply another way of saying "in heaven and on earth" but another way of looking at all creation, this time distinguishing *sensible* objects ("the visible": the physical universe, including the sun, moon, and stars; the perceptible persons, places, and things that reside on earth; and the elements—earth, air, fire, water) from *spiritual* entities ("the invisible"). Both these expressions are examples of merism, a figure of speech in which a totality is referred to in terms of contrasting components (as in "high and low," "young and old").

The phrase **whether thrones or dominions or principalities or powers** is best understood as an elaboration of "the invisible." Principalities and powers *can* refer to earthly rulers. (The same phrase is translated "rulers and authorities" in Luke 12:11 and "magistrates and authorities" in Titus 3:1.) But this language is also used of angelic powers, whether benign or hostile. (See Eph 1:21, where

## The Principalities and Powers

Sprinkled through 1 Corinthians, Ephesians, and Colossians are a number of terms referring to spiritual beings that exercise power in the world: principalities, rulers, authorities, powers, dominions, thrones, and world rulers. Although all of these terms can be used for human political authorities, the contexts in which they occur indicate that Paul intends spiritual beings, and uses these terms somewhat flexibly without explaining the differences among them.

Jewish tradition held that God allowed angelic beings to exercise power over territories and nations, an understanding based on Deut 32:8: "When the Most High allotted each nation its heritage, / when he separated out human beings, / He set up the boundaries of the peoples / after the number of the divine beings" (see also Dan 10:13, 20–21; 12:1). Events on earth are influenced by, though not controlled by, what is happening in the heavenly realm among these beings. God's people are under the protection of the archangel Michael, while the affairs of other nations are affected by principalities opposed to God and his people. These spiritual beings were linked with the pagan gods that the Gentiles worshiped (Exod 12:12; Deut 32:17; 1 Cor 10:20).

The Pauline Letters presume this worldview but insist on several points: all heavenly powers were created in, through, and for Christ (Col 1:16). Christ triumphed over them in the cross (Col 2:15) and has been raised to a place "far above them" (Eph 1:21). Evil powers and authorities under the control of the devil presently wage warfare against Christians (Eph 6:11–12), but Christians can stand against them (Eph 6:10–11), and Christ will destroy them at his second coming (1 Cor 15:24–26). Johannine literature (the Gospel and Letters of John and the book of Revelation) offers similar perspectives on the devil and other evil spiritual beings. The canonical Scriptures do not explain the relationship among the various heavenly beings or how some of them came to oppose God.

---

Paul describes the risen Christ as seated far above every principality, authority, power, and dominion.)[2] The similarity of contexts between Col 1:16 and Eph 1:21 implies that both refer to the *invisible* created ruling forces in the universe. The fact that the sequence differs slightly, and Colossians has "thrones" where Ephesians has "powers," suggests that the list of four is a sampling, not an exhaustive list or a hierarchical ranking. For those Colossians who were tempted to worship angels (see 2:18), Paul's affirmation that Christ ranks supreme over

2. See the sidebar on the *stoicheia* on 196.

all these spiritual beings was a call to return to the truth of the gospel about the lordship of Jesus Christ.

The assertion that **all things were created through him** reiterates the beginning of verse 16, but the next phrase, **and for him,** introduces a new thought, that the eternal Son is also the *goal* of all creation. Apart from this it might be possible to think of the Son's role as merely instrumental, the means. But "for him" suggests that all creation exists as the Father's gift to his beloved Son. Some interpreters find these cosmic references to Christ the Son as somehow novel, and thus alien to Paul's worldview. But one has only to revisit 1 Cor 8:5–6 to see how comfortable Paul is with this kind of cosmic thinking about Christ:

> Indeed, even though there are so-called gods in heaven and on earth (there are, to be sure, many "gods" and many "lords"), yet for us there is one God, the Father, *from whom* all things are and *for whom* we exist, and one Lord, Jesus Christ, *through whom* all things are, and *through whom* we exist. (italics added)

This passage, like the hymn of Col 1:15–20, speaks of the Lord Jesus Christ as the mediator through whom God the Father created and sustains *all* things (Greek *ta panta,* as in Col 1:16, 17, 20), including ourselves. What Paul says of the Son's role in creation is parallel to what the prologue of John says of the eternal Word: "All things came to be through him. . . . He was in the world and the world came to be through him, but the world did not know him" (John 1:3, 10).

1:17    In verse 17 Paul summarizes what he has said in verses 15 and 16: **He is before all things.** Paul uses the preposition "before" (Greek *pro*) in the same two senses that we heard in the word "firstborn" (*prototokos*)—temporal priority, and priority of status and privilege. The Son is "before all" as the mediator through whom all things were created, and he is also "before all" in the sense that he possesses God-given preeminence of honor. And the Son continues to give order to the universe and uphold all things in existence: **in him all things hold together.** Creation was not just an initial event that set the world in motion but also a divine work that continues throughout all time.

1:18    In verse 18 Paul moves from the cosmic to the ecclesial: **He is the head of the body, the church.** Although Paul usually employs the word "church" (*ekklēsia*) to refer to a local Christian community, like the church in Corinth or the church in Rome, the cosmic framework of this passage suggests that here *ekklēsia* refers to the universal Church—the network of all the Christian communities considered as one body. "Church" occurs three more times in the letter, once referring to all the communities considered as a body (1:24) and twice referring to local churches—the one that met in Nympha's house (4:15) and the one in Laodicea (4:16).

In 1 Corinthians and Romans the church is called the body of Christ with special stress on the relationship of members to one another ("we, though many, are one body in Christ and individually parts of one another," Rom 12:5). But in Colossians the Church is called the body of Christ with special emphasis on the relationship of members to *Christ as head*.[3] What Paul means by "head" will become evident later, when he will refer to the risen Christ as "the head, from whom the whole body, supported and held together by its ligaments and bonds, achieves the growth that comes from God" (Col 2:19). There is a unity of shared life between members and head. That perspective will enable the Colossians to understand that chaste behavior (3:5), true and loving speech (3:8), and patience and forgiveness (3:12–13)—all within the community, the one body of Christ—derive not simply from their efforts but come as a gift ("grace," 1:6) of the Father through the headship of the risen Lord.

That the Son **is the beginning** may sound at first like Paul is reiterating what he has already stated in the previous three verses. But the Greek word for "beginning" (*archē*) means not just the first in a series but also the origin and active cause of the rest. Paul probably intends to echo Gen 1:1: "In the beginning God created the heavens and the earth." The beginning in whom he created them is Jesus Christ! **The firstborn from the dead** refers to a particular moment in history, the *new* beginning of the resurrection of the incarnate Son, Jesus, on the third day after his crucifixion. Thus "firstborn" has here a strong temporal meaning. The incarnate Son is first in a quite literal sense: he is the first to rise from the dead. This is not a return from the dead in the sense of resuscitation (a return to biological life, as in the cases of Lazarus and the son of the widow of Nain) but in the sense of *transformation* into a new mode of existence.[4] Jesus' resurrection marks the beginning of a new creation. He is the first to pass through human existence and the defeat of death into a new and glorious life, having won a victory that infinitely surpasses the prestige of the highest angels.

The purpose and result of the resurrection is **that in all things he himself might be preeminent**. As man, Christ has emerged triumphant over all cosmic powers and even over death itself. The perspective has again moved from the Son's agency in the *origin* of all things to his role as the *goal* of all.

**In him all the fullness was pleased to dwell.** "All the fullness" is a way of         1:19
referring to God the Father, as becomes clear at 2:9: "For in him dwells the

---

3. See also Eph 1:22–23; 2:16; 4:4, 12, 16; 5:23, 28–30.
4. Paul spells out this notion of resurrection as transformation in 1 Cor 15:35–44.

## Through Him All Things Were Made

Christ's role in the creation of the world is not something contemporary Christians focus on, even though at least once a week on Sunday we assert, "Through him all things were made." Some may even think that the Son's participation in creation is a later, postbiblical development in Christian faith. We do well, then, to review the broad witness to that truth already present in the New Testament.

In 1 Cor 8:6 Paul presumes that Christ's centrality in creation is a conviction shared by the Church as a whole: "There is one God, the Father, / from whom all things are and for whom we exist, / and one Lord, Jesus Christ, / through whom all things are and through whom we exist."

In a more familiar passage, the Gospel of John uses the term *logos* ("Word") to say the same thing:

> In the beginning was the Word,
> and the Word was with God,
> and the Word was God. . . .
>
> All things came to be through him,
> and without him nothing came to be. . . .
>
> And the Word became flesh
> and made his dwelling among us,
> and we saw his glory,
> the glory as of the Father's only Son,
> full of grace and truth.
>
> John 1:1, 3, 14

*continued on next page*

whole fullness of the deity bodily." All God's creative and redeeming power is present and at work in the risen body of Jesus. The notion of God's indwelling evokes the Jerusalem temple, where God dwelled in the midst of his people. The very wording "*in him* all the fullness *was pleased to dwell*" echoes verbatim the Greek version of Ps 68:17, which describes the temple mount as "the mountain that God *was pleased to dwell in*." The prologue of the Gospel of John expresses the same thought: "The Word became flesh and made his dwelling"—literally, pitched his tent—"among us" (1:14).[5] Both passages refer to the incarnate Son as the new and living temple in which God dwells.

---

5. See Christopher A. Beetham, *Echoes of Scripture in the Letter of Paul to the Colossians* (Boston: Brill, 2008), 143–55.

The letter to the Hebrews celebrates the supremacy of the eternal Son in its opening words:

> In times past, God spoke in partial and various ways to our ancestors through the prophets; in these last days, he spoke to us through a son, whom he made heir of all things, *and through whom he created the universe*, who is the refulgence of his glory and very imprint of his being, and who *sustains all things by his mighty word* . . . as far superior to the angels as the name he has inherited is more excellent than theirs.
>
> Heb 1:1–4, italics added

It is noteworthy that Hebrews, besides paralleling the Colossians hymn in speaking of the Son as creating and sustaining all things, also like Colossians emphasizes the Son's superiority to the angels. In verse 10, Hebrews applies these words of Ps 102:26 to *the Son*:

> At the beginning, O Lord, you established the earth,
> and the heavens are the works of your hands.

Finally, it is striking that in the book of Revelation, the letter addressed to the angel of the church in Laodicea identifies Christ as "the Amen, the faithful and true witness, the source of God's creation" (Rev 3:14). It is fascinating that only for this church does Christ identify himself as the "source of God's creation." The Laodiceans, as recipients of the circular letter delivered to the Colossians (Col 4:16), with its cosmic celebration of Christ as sovereign agent of the Father's creation, would be especially ready to understand that language.

**And through him to reconcile all things for him** (literally, "to him"). God, **1:20** called "the fullness" in verse 19, works through his incarnate Son to reconcile not just persons but *all things*, **whether those on earth or those in heaven.** It is significant that Paul does not say that *God* needs to be reconciled, but that his creatures need to be reconciled to him. As the whole created world shares in the estrangement and disorder caused by human sin, so it will share in Christ's redemption and be restored to its full beauty, harmony, and magnificence (see Rom 8:20–21). The verb for **making peace** occurs only here in the New Testament, although its noun counterpart ("peacemakers") appears in the seventh Beatitude (Matt 5:9).[6] In a biblical context, "peace" means not only the absence

---

6. "Peace" appears twice in this letter, in the blessing of the greeting ("Grace to you and peace from God our Father," 1:2) and at the center of the exhortation on Christian living in 3:1–4:6 ("And let the peace of Christ control your hearts, the peace into which you were also called in one body," 3:15). Peace comes both as a gift of God and as the fruit of Christian love. In Ephesians Paul elaborates this peacemaking through Jesus' crucifixion: Christ has broken down the wall of enmity between Jew and Gentile (Eph 2:14–15) and reconciled both to God in one body (Eph 2:16–17).

## The Son of God, Creator and Servant

The Office of Readings for the fifth week of Lent offers a reflection by Saint Augustine from his commentary on Psalm 85. In his reflection, Augustine ponders the paradox of Christ as both the One to whom we pray and the One who prays with us.

God could give no greater gift to men than to make his Word, through whom he created all things, their head and to join them to him as his members, so that the Word might be both Son of God and son of man, one God with the Father, and one man with all men. The result is that when we speak with God in prayer we do not separate the Son from him, and when the body of the Son prays it does not separate its head from itself. It is the one Savior of his body, our Lord Jesus Christ, the Son of God, who prays for us and in us and is himself the object of our prayers.

He prays for us as our priest, he prays in us as our head, he is the object of our prayer as our God.

Let us then recognize both our voice in his, and his voice in ours. When something is said, especially in prophecy, about the Lord Jesus Christ that seems to belong to a condition of lowliness unworthy of God, we must not hesitate to ascribe this condition to one who did not hesitate to unite himself to us. Every creature is his servant, for it was through him that every creature came to be. . . .

We pray to him as God, he prays for us as a servant. In the first case he is the Creator, in the second a creature. Himself unchanged, he took to himself our created nature in order to change it, and made us one man with himself, head and body. We pray then to him, through him, in him, and we speak along with him and he along with us.

of conflict but also the fullness of well-being and harmony in relationships. Whereas disciples are called to be peacemakers in Matthew, here in Colossians God himself is celebrated as the source of all peacemaking. He has done so **by the blood of** Jesus' **cross**, healing the relationship that was fractured by sin. "The cross," of course, is short for Jesus' passion and death by crucifixion.

1:21–22          With the words **and you** (plural), Paul moves from the big picture of God's creation and reconciliation of all things in Christ to his immediate audience, the Colossian Christian community. And to drive home again the transformation Christ brought about in their lives, he employs the strongest possible language: **you who once were alienated and hostile in mind because of evil deeds**.[7] The stark language about once being hostile "because of evil deeds" reminds us that the Colossians were mainly, if not entirely, Gentiles, whose

7. For "alienated" Paul uses a seven-syllable word (*apēllotriōmenous*), found in the New Testament only here and at Eph 2:12 and 4:18, where the meaning is the same. And to say "he has reconciled," he

culture tolerated behavior that was absolutely taboo for Jews—for example, the use of prostitutes (see 1 Cor 6:15–20 and the list of vices in Col 3:5). For many Colossians, becoming Christian would have entailed changes in behavior that Jews typically would not have needed to make, since the Hebrew Scriptures already had high standards for sexual conduct, although the conversion of Jews to recognizing Jesus as Messiah also entailed a profound reorientation to and reconciliation with God, as shown by Paul's including himself in such language in Rom 5:10; 8:7–8; Eph 2:3.

**He has now reconciled** you **in his fleshly body through his death, to present you holy, without blemish, and irreproachable before him.** Exactly who is meant by "he" and "him" is hard to determine. Is it God, "the fullness," who in verse 19 is said to reconcile all things to the Son? Or is it the Son, the main subject of the hymn, whose death reconciles us to the Father and who as risen Lord will one day present the perfected Christians to the Father (v. 28)? Either interpretation fits Paul's theology. Just as the Father and the Son are co-creators, so they are also co-redeemers.[8] In saying that the Colossians are now reconciled in Christ's fleshly body through his death, Paul has moved from the picture of God's cosmic reconciliation of "all things" to the dramatic changes in their own individual lifestyles right there in Colossae. The new creation parallels the original cosmic creation. They have been made holy by their baptism, and God's purpose is to bring that holiness to perfection.

The goal of being presented to God fully perfected requires a Christian response to God's initiatives of creation and redemption, celebrated in verses 15–20 and applied to the Colossians in verses 21–22. Hence the proviso of verse 23: **provided that you persevere in the faith, firmly grounded, stable, and not shifting from the hope of the gospel that you heard.** The possibility of being doctrinally unstable and "shifting" from the gospel no doubt alludes to the "philosophy" that Paul will address in the next chapter. So again, as in verses 7–8, Paul harks back to the Colossians' initial reception of the good news from the evangelist Epaphras, their community's founder. They have been the beneficiaries of a gospel addressed **to every creature under heaven,** which Paul, by means of this very letter, preaches with the same authority Epaphras exercised with them in the beginning—**Paul** being, like Epaphras, a **minister** (*diakonos*) of that same gospel. "Preached to every creature" is rhetorical hyperbole, but

1:23

---

uses another impressively polysyllabic word (*apokatallassō*), used only in the chiastically parallel v. 20, just above, and at Eph 2:16, where it makes the same point.

8. Apart from two passing references (1:8, Epaphras "also told us of your love in the Spirit"; and 2:5, "I am with you in spirit"), in this letter Paul does not choose to elaborate on the Holy Spirit's role. (Compare Ephesians, where there are fourteen references to the Spirit.)

it points to the fact that the gospel is destined for the whole world, that is, to all human beings, as in Mark 16:15: "Go into the whole world and proclaim the gospel to every creature."

### Reflection and Application (1:15–23)

Although this commentary has emphasized the continuity of the "hymn" of Col 1:15–20 with the preceding and following material of the letter, there is

LIVING TRADITION

## God's Creative Action: Immensely Cosmic, Intimately Personal

The English poet and Jesuit priest Gerard Manley Hopkins (1844–89) possessed a profound appreciation of God as Creator on both the cosmic and the personal level. Both dimensions come through powerfully in his poem celebrating St. Alphonsus Rodriguez, who grew into sanctity in the humblest of circumstances, as doorkeeper of a Jesuit residence on the Island of Majorca. Cannot the God who shapes mountains and continents, the poem asks, forge holiness in the soul of a man who performs no heroic military exploits but simply carries out his humble duties faithfully, year after year? In the tenth line, "all" catches wonderfully what the Colossians hymn means by "everything." The poem's movement from the cosmic dimension of God's creation of *all* to the intimate service of a brother's hospitality in Majorca mirrors the movement of Col 1:15–23, from the vastness of the cosmos to the intimacy of the Christian community.

> Honour is flashed off exploit, so we say;
> And those strokes once that gashed flesh or galled shield
> Should tongue that time now, trumpet now that field,
> And, on the fighter, forge his glorious day.
> On Christ they do and on the martyr may;
> But be the war within, the brand we wield
> Unseen, the heroic breast not outward-steeled,
> Earth hears no hurtle then from fiercest fray.
>
> Yet God (that hews mountain and continent,
> Earth, all, out; who, with trickling increment,
> Veins violets and tall trees makes more and more)
> Could crowd career with conquest while there went
> Those years and years by of world without event
> That in Majorca Alfonso watched the door.[a]

a. W. H. Gardner and N. H. MacKenzie, eds., *The Poems of Gerard Manley Hopkins*, 4th ed. (New York: Oxford University Press, 1967), 106.

no denying the power that these six verses carry as a subunit. Along with the prologue of the Gospel of John, the beginning of the Letter to the Hebrews, and the self-emptying hymn of Philippians 2, these verses of Colossians constitute a key source of Christian theology. Christ the eternal Son of the Father, mediator of all creation and redemption, source of reconciliation—these major themes are celebrated and illuminated in this passage. At the same time, it is important to recognize that Paul writes of these mysteries of the faith not simply to nurture wonder and speculation in his audience. His purpose is pastoral. He writes to help his addressees appreciate where *they* fit into this cosmic scheme of things. They—the Christians who meet at Philemon's house in Colossae, at Nympha's, and in Laodicea—are the object of the eternal Father's reconciling love. The cosmic context makes the reality of their call in Christ all the more impressive. In showing how their Christian life is part of this cosmic scenario, Paul means to encourage them to persevere in this grace into which they have entered through their response to Epaphras's preaching and their own baptism into the body of Christ.

We, of course, are meant to hear this passage in the same way as the Lycus Valley Christians. In fact, with the help of our growing sense of the age, vastness, complexity, and beauty of the cosmos, what this passage says about the Father, the Son, and *all things*, is all the more dramatic for us. That the Creator of this expanding, fourteen-billion-year-old cosmos, with its billions of galaxies and multiple planetary systems, makes us the object of his love in Christ should be all the more encouraging. We simply need to take time to pay attention and contemplate the realities intimated by this passage within the universe as we are coming to know it in our day. Our science can enhance our prayer.

# Paul Rejoices in His Ministry to the Gentiles

## Colossians 1:24–2:5

Having brought the lofty vision of the supremacy of Christ down to its practical consequences in the Colossians' own conversion though the preaching of Epaphras, Paul now ponders his own participation in that ministry. He rejoices in the fact that, in God's vast plan, he was especially sent to Gentiles like them to unveil the †mystery of God's work of salvation through the Messiah of Israel (1:24–28). He also tells of his strenuous apostolic labors, which are animated by Christ's power (1:29–2:1). Finally, he prays that their good order and faith in Christ may unite their hearts in love so that they may be fortified against the deception of "specious arguments" (2:2–5).

### Paul Rejoices in His Apostolic Labors (1:24–29)

²⁴Now I rejoice in my sufferings for your sake, and in my flesh I am filling up what is lacking in the afflictions of Christ on behalf of his body, which is the church, ²⁵of which I am a minister in accordance with God's stewardship given to me to bring to completion for you the word of God, ²⁶the mystery hidden from ages and from generations past. But now it has been manifested to his holy ones, ²⁷to whom God chose to make known the riches of the glory of this mystery among the Gentiles; it is Christ in you, the hope for glory. ²⁸It is he whom we proclaim, admonishing everyone and teaching everyone with all wisdom, that we may present everyone perfect in Christ. ²⁹For this I labor and struggle, in accord with the exercise of his power working within me.

NT: Matt 5:10; Luke 6:23; Phil 1:12–18; 1 Thess 3:4–5
**Catechism:** collaboration with God through prayer, work, and suffering, 307; participation in Christ's sacrifice, 618, 1508

As we saw in the Letter to the Philippians, Paul boldly speaks of himself in **1:24** terms of the same self-emptying that he applied to Christ's own †incarnation and death (Phil 2:17). Here Paul describes his joyful suffering in his imprisonment for the gospel with language that mirrors Jesus' vicarious suffering for the Church. Paul's paradoxical claim, **Now I rejoice in my sufferings for your sake,** is a fulfillment of Jesus' eighth Beatitude: "Blessed are they who are persecuted for the sake of righteousness" (Matt 5:10) or, in Luke's version, "Rejoice and leap for joy on that day!" (Luke 6:23). Paul probably refers to the sufferings of his incarceration, and his rejoicing parallels the rejoicing he expresses in Philippians regarding his imprisonment (Phil 1:12–18).

The statement that follows has, understandably, puzzled many: **and in my flesh I am filling up what is lacking in the afflictions of Christ on behalf of his body.** Paul seems to imply that the atoning sacrifice of Christ was somehow incomplete. That understanding would, of course, fly in the face of the basic message of the letter, which is the absolute sufficiency of God's creative and redemptive work in Christ (see 1:13–22). Careful attention to the diction and immediate context of the passage shows a way of reading verses 24–27 that coheres with the thrust of the letter.

The Greek word for "filling up" (*antanaplēroō*), which occurs only here in the New Testament, has a nuanced meaning in extrabiblical Greek: "to take one's turn in filling up."[1] **What is lacking** can be rendered "what remains to be completed," that is, what remains for the full establishment of Christ's kingdom throughout the world. And **the afflictions of Christ** can mean the afflictions that inevitably accompany the mission of any follower of Christ.[2] As Paul learned on the road to Damascus, Jesus is intimately united with his disciples such that their sufferings are his (Acts 9:4–5). Paul writes to the Thessalonians about the tribulations that attend Christian discipleship in a hostile world: "Even when we were among you, we used to warn you in advance that we would undergo affliction (*thlipsis*), just as has happened" (1 Thess 3:4; see Rom 8:17). This joyful Christian demeanor in the midst of adversity is nicely captured in 1 Thess 1:6: "And you became imitators of us and of the Lord, receiving the word in great

1. BDAG 87. Paul "takes his turn" here in the sense of exercising his ministry in the context of vv. 13–23, the story of the creating and redeeming work of the Father and Son, reconciling all things through the ministry of evangelists like Epaphras, and now, taking *his* turn in the lineup, Paul.
2. The New Testament most often uses *thlipsis* to refer to tribulations that come with the Christian mission, such as persecutions, rejections, even stoning (John 16:33; Acts 14:22; Rom 5:3; Phil 1:17; 4:14).

---

## Augustine on Filling Up "What Is Lacking in the Afflictions of Christ"

LIVING TRADITION

Here is St. Augustine's comment on Col 1:24.

The Apostle says: "that I may fill up what was lacking in the afflictions of Christ in my flesh" (Col 1:24). Note what Paul says: "that I may fill up what was lacking," not in *my* "afflictions," but in "Christ's"; and not in *Christ's* "flesh," but in "*mine*." Christ is still suffering, he says, not in his own flesh that he ascended into heaven with, but in *my* flesh, which still labors hard on earth. Christ, as Paul says, is still suffering in my flesh: "I live, no longer I, but Christ lives in me" (Gal 2:20). If Christ were not suffering real affliction in his members, that is, his faithful, Saul on earth would not have been able to persecute Christ seated in heaven. In fact, Paul openly explains in a certain place, "Just as a body is one and has many members, and still all the members of the body, though many, are one body, so also Christ" (1 Cor 2:12). He does not say: "So also Christ *and His body*," but "one body, many members, so also Christ." All, therefore, is Christ; and because the whole Christ is one, for that reason, the Head from heaven spoke: "Saul, Saul, why are you persecuting me?" (Acts 9:4).[a]

a. *Expositions of the Psalms*, Ps 142:3, in *Augustine in His Own Words*, trans. and ed. William Harmless, SJ (Washington, DC: Catholic University of America Press, 2010), 194–95.

---

affliction, with joy from the holy Spirit, so that you became a model for all the believers in Macedonia and in Achaia."[3]

**1:25**      That Paul has in mind the afflictions of his unfinished mission to the †Gentiles becomes clear as the sentence continues: on behalf of his body, the church, **of which I am a minister in accordance with God's stewardship given to me to bring to completion for you the word of God**. This mainly Gentile Christian community of Colossae had first heard the "word of God"—the gospel—from Epaphras; now Paul, exercising the same ministry with this letter, is bringing that ministry a further step toward completion. Paul's work helps to complete God's grand design to extend the blessings of the Jewish Messiah to the Gentiles.

**1:26–27**      **The mystery hidden from ages and from generations past** is the surprising revelation that Israel's Messiah is also for the *Gentiles*. In a biblical context, "†mystery" refers to something in God's plan that was previously hidden but is now revealed (see sidebar). Paul elaborates: **But now it has been manifested to**

---

3. Jerry L. Sumney, in "'I Fill Up What Is Lacking in the Afflictions of Christ': Paul's Vicarious Suffering in Colossians," *CBQ* 61, no. 4 (October 2006): 664–80, makes the case that Col 1:24 presents Paul's suffering of imprisonment as benefiting his fellow Christians by way of example, to encourage their commitment to the truth of the gospel.

**his holy ones, to whom God chose to make known the riches of the glory of this mystery among the Gentiles.** For Paul, as for all the early Christians, that Gentiles were now fully included in God's covenant people and could receive all his rich blessings was a never-ending source of wonder. That universal scope of God's saving plan was already foreseen in the Old Testament as far back as God's promises to Abraham (Gen 12:3), but has been fully revealed only to "his holy ones," that is, Christians. Paul considers himself specially privileged as a bearer of this mystery (see Eph 3:1–10).

The mystery is, in short, **Christ in you, the hope for glory.** Since "you" here is plural, the phrase "in you" can be rendered either *collectively* as "Christ among you"—that is, in the community—or *distributively* as "Christ in *each* of you."

---

## What Does "Mystery" Mean in the Bible?

**BIBLICAL BACKGROUND**

The biblical meaning of "mystery" contrasts with both (a) the meaning of the word among the pagan religions contemporary with early Christianity, where it referred to a secret, esoteric teaching or practice not to be disclosed to outsiders, and (b) the usual meaning in modern English, where mystery usually denotes some kind of puzzle, as in a detective mystery. In Scripture, mystery means something about God revealed by means of prophecy and the Holy Spirit. It is almost the opposite of meanings (a) and (b). Contrary to the ancient pagan meaning, God's mystery is secret only in the sense that it was hidden until God revealed it; and it is revealed precisely to be communicated to others, not to be kept secret. And in contrast to our usual modern meaning, a biblical mystery is precisely *not* a puzzle but a clarification, a revelation, though it always remains more than we can comprehend.

In the Greek Old Testament (the Septuagint), the word appears exclusively in the book of Daniel, mainly in chapter 2, where it refers to the meaning of Nebuchadnezzar's dream that God reveals to the boy Daniel. Daniel explains to the king that his dream of the four-metal statue shattered and replaced by the great stone not hewn by hand is really about the kingdom of the one God soon to replace the evil empires of the world, including that of Babylon.

In that biblical sense, "mystery" is the perfect word for Paul to use for the good news about Jesus Christ—a revelation by God about his plan for the salvation of all. And indeed, this mystery is meant not to be kept secret but to be shared with everyone.[a] The word occurs in a saying of Jesus about "the mystery," or "mysteries," of the kingdom, which appears in all three Synoptic Gospels (Matt 13:11; Mark 4:11; Luke 8:10).

a. Paul uses "mystery" in this sense in three letters: 1 Cor 2:1, 7; 4:1; 13:2; 14:2; 15:51; Eph 1:9; 3:3, 4, 9; 5:32; 6:19; Col 1:26–27; 2:2; 4:3.

Both renderings ring true in this context; indeed, it is possible that Paul meant to have it both ways. The former has the value of emphasizing the fact that the Messiah of Israel has been sent *among you Gentiles*. And that surely fits the context of Paul's reflection on his special mission to Gentiles like the Colossians. At the same time, "Christ *in* you" catches Paul's interest in helping the Colossians fully realize what they already possess and experience interiorly—Christ dwelling in them and empowering them to love one another, overcome social barriers, forgive injuries, and place others first. Paul will refer to his own inner experience of Christ's "power working within me" in verse 29.[4]

**1:28**     As Paul describes his mission, he emphasizes Christ as the totality of wisdom for *everyone*: **It is he whom we proclaim, admonishing everyone and teaching everyone with all wisdom.** Paul aims to foster the Colossians' continuous growth in understanding and living out the mystery that has been revealed to them. The universality of the thrice-mentioned "everyone" is even more emphatic in Greek, where we hear a threefold repetition of "every human being." Paul insists that there is no Christian teaching reserved for an elite. God's life-transforming word is for every member of his people.

The purpose of Paul's continuous teaching and exhortation is **that we may present everyone perfect** (or "mature," RSV) **in Christ**. Christ is the *means* of this process of maturation, since it occurs by his grace. But he is also the *goal*, as maturity is ultimately union with him. Paul's pastoral goal is leading people not simply to faith, baptism, and church membership (something already accomplished in this case by Epaphras) but also to the perfection of holiness. As each individual believer is brought into deeper conformity with Christ, the whole body "achieves the growth that comes from God" (2:19). Paul describes his pastoral method as an extended *process* that entails constant preaching and instruction. The goal is ultimately to present them mature "in Christ" to the Father—a work that will be completed only at Christ's second coming (see 1 Thess 3:13; 5:23).

**1:29**     Paul brings the description of his ministry to its climax by confiding to his readers how strenuously he toils, expending all his energy to bring the Christian converts to full maturity. **For this I labor and struggle, in accord with the exercise of his power** (*energeia*) **working** (*energeō*) **within me.** The word for "struggle" is *agonizō*, the root of our English word "agonize." Paul labors and

---

4. A good example of Paul using the phrase *en hymin* ("in you [plural]") distributively ("in each of you") is Rom 8:9, 11: "But you are not in the flesh; on the contrary, you are in the spirit, if only the Spirit of God dwells *in you*.... If the Spirit of the one who raised Jesus from the dead dwells *in you*, the one who raised Christ from the dead will give life to your mortal bodies also, through his Spirit that dwells *in you*."

struggles not by his own strength but by Christ's power at work in him, the same collaboration of God's power and human effort he describes in Phil 2:13: "God is the one who, for his good purpose, works in you both to desire and to work." The Church would later turn to these texts in clarifying the delicate interplay between the grace of God and human free will. Our reliance on grace does not mean that we do a certain percentage and God does the rest, but rather that *all* the strength by which we do God's will is *entirely* dependent on him.[5] The union of Paul's own efforts with Christ's empowerment is captured in four clauses at the center of the minichiasm of 1:24–2:5. (See the full outline of Colossians above.)

> C   For this I also labor, *struggling*
> > D   according to his *working*
> > D′  that is *working* in me in power.
> C′  For I wish you to know how great a *struggle* I am
> > having (1:29–2:1).[6]

It is noteworthy that, in a letter that treats of various powers in the cosmos (thrones, dominions, principalities, and powers), Paul reserves important Greek power words—*dynamis* and *energeia* (sources of our English words "dynamic" and "energy")—exclusively for *God's* activity at work in human beings (see Col 1:29; 2:12).

## Reflection and Application (1:24–29)

Paul's expression of joy during his imprisonment is striking. We saw it in the joy-filled letter to the Philippians, and we encounter it here in Colossians. We might at first be inclined to take this as a special character trait of Saint Paul. But he expects his readers to rejoice with him. And we need only revisit the final beatitude as it appears in both Matthew's Sermon on the Mount and Luke's Sermon on the Plain (Matt 5:11–12; Luke 6:22–23) to realize that Jesus, and the evangelists after him, understood joy in apostolic affliction as simply part and parcel of Christian discipleship. "Blessed are you when they insult you and persecute you and utter every kind of evil against you [falsely] because of me. Rejoice and be glad, for your reward will be great in heaven" (Matt 5:11–12; see

---

5. See Catechism, 308, 1742.

6. Translation and outline from John Paul Heil, *Colossians: Encouragement to Walk in All Wisdom as Holy Ones in Christ*, Early Christianity 4 (Atlanta: Society of Biblical Literature, 2010), 83. The traditional chapter break at 2:1 disturbs a passage that is structured as a unity.

Luke 6:22–23). To understand this joy in suffering, it may be helpful to recall how Paul speaks of his nurturing the faith of his converts as that of a father for his children. Recall his fathering of Onesimus mentioned in the Letter to Philemon. Although it was not he but Epaphras who fathered the Colossians into the new life of faith, he can speak of the joy entailed in his "agonizing" for them now as he labors in intercessory prayer and in the work of this communication by letter. He is like a parent taking joy in the labors entailed in fostering the life of a growing child. The joy comes from being part of a process larger than himself, knowing that his work is the work of God, that he labors by God-given energy. The suffering involved in all this is transformed into joy by love, and by the awareness that the new Christians are beginning to share in a wisdom whose fruits he has already experienced.

### The Best Defense against Specious Arguments (2:1–5)

<sup></sup>

¹For I want you to know how great a struggle I am having for you and for those in Laodicea and all who have not seen me face to face, ²that their hearts may be encouraged as they are brought together in love, to have all the richness of fully assured understanding, for the knowledge of the mystery of God, Christ, ³in whom are hidden all the treasures of wisdom and knowledge. ⁴I say this so that no one may deceive you by specious arguments. ⁵For even if I am absent in the flesh, yet I am with you in spirit, rejoicing as I observe your good order and the firmness of your faith in Christ.

**NT:** Phil 1:30
**Catechism:** perseverance in faith, 162

2:1    Paul elaborates on the toil of his ministry-at-a-distance for these new Christians of the Lycus Valley: **For I want you to know how great a struggle I am having for you and for those in Laodicea and all who have not seen me face to face.** The Greek word for "struggle" (*agōn*, source of the English word "agony") is literally "wrestling match." Paul uses this same sports image in Philippians: "Yours is the same struggle as you saw in me and now hear about me" (Phil 1:30). What exactly is this struggle? The context suggests that Paul's struggle is threefold: First, his imprisonment, which he gladly undergoes because he can offer his suffering as a form of prayer for the flourishing of these budding communities of faith; second, the exertion of intense intercessory prayer (see Col 4:12; Rom 8:26; Eph 6:18); and, third, perhaps, the labor of composing this letter, his struggle to communicate a truth he sees as crucial to their maturation in Christ. Under the tutelage of Epaphras, these communities have made a great beginning. Now Paul wants them to stand fast and remain faithful to the mystery of Christ, which holds *everything* they need to remain secure and to flourish spiritually.

The intent of his prayer and of the composition of this very letter is **that** **2:2–3** **their hearts may be encouraged as they are brought together** (literally, *knit* together) **in love.** The word for encourage (*parakaleō*) means to comfort, buoy up, or exhort those who are dispirited so that they can meet challenges with courage and confidence. Paul knows the young community will be encouraged as they experience Christ's presence among them, knitting their hearts together in affection and love. This presence of the risen Lord in their midst is precisely what will lead them to **all the richness of fully assured understanding** and **the knowledge of the mystery of God, Christ, in whom are hidden all the treasures of wisdom and knowledge.** Against the temptation to seek spiritual fulfillment in novel, esoteric teachings, Paul emphasizes the completeness they already have in Christ. It is important to catch the biblical connotations of several key words here. For "mystery," the biblical sense of which differs considerably from ordinary usage, see the sidebar on page 187. The biblical senses of "wisdom" and "knowledge" also differ from common parlance today. Biblical knowledge is no mere information; it is relational and personal. And "wisdom" in Scripture is not speculative insight so much as practical know-how. Paul is speaking of personal knowledge of Jesus, who is the mystery of God revealed, and the wisdom of knowing how to live in accordance with his ways, in the sense in which Jesus is called "the way" in John 14:6. This is the hidden "treasure" that is worth giving everything to possess (see Matt 13:44). As the members of the church grow in love for one another, they grow in knowledge of Christ, experiencing the power of his love at work among them.

At this point Paul reiterates the note of admonition, to prepare for the warn- **2:4–5** ing that will occupy the remainder of chapter 2: **I say this so that no one may deceive you by specious arguments.** The tone of this statement, suggesting that the deception is not yet a prevalent evil within the communities but rather a threat from which they are to be protected, is confirmed by the next verse: **For even if I am absent in the flesh, yet I am with you in spirit, rejoicing as I observe your good order and the firmness of your faith in Christ.** Paul's observation of their well-ordered community life and stable faith in Christ, as well as their being knit together in love (mentioned above) comes, no doubt, through the report of Epaphras, who has recounted to Paul his experience of evangelizing these Lycus Valley communities.

Although the majority are holding firmly to what they have learned from Epaphras, the following portion of the letter suggests that some have already yielded to the seduction.

### Reflection and Application (2:1–5)

Paul makes much of the fact that he is commissioned specifically to the Gentiles and even of the fact that such is the plan of God. Part of that enthusiasm likely derives from his own surprise as a Pharisee whose life prior to the Damascus road experience had focused on helping his fellow Israelites live as good Jews. In Romans 9 he laments the fact that the good news of the Messiah Jesus is gaining a far better reception from non-Jews than from the original people of the covenant. This was pain and scandal for him. Indeed, it was a significant part of his suffering (had God abandoned the people of the covenant?). Yet he grew to understand this development as part of God's plan, for Israel's rejection of Jesus as Messiah had deflected the Christian mission toward the Gentiles (see Rom 11:11). In fact, he learned to see this as part of the biblical vision. Being a "light to the nations" was, after all, the vocation of Servant Israel (Isa 49:6).

Paul's quandary about the place of Israel in God's plan offers some important challenges for twenty-first-century Gentiles. First, it is important to take seriously the Jewishness of Jesus, and, for that matter, the Jewishness of Paul. Who they were, and are, is only understandable against the background of the story of Israel's life with God as spelled out in the Old Testament, which is one reason we continue to read these texts in Christian worship. Understanding that connection only becomes possible when we invest some time reading, studying, and praying from the whole Bible.

Second, the anti-Jewish teaching and behavior that has characterized much of Christian history must be acknowledged and overcome, and its effects healed by the way we worship and the way we talk about and relate to the contemporary descendants of ancient Israel, whom we are gradually learning to recognize as our elder brothers and sisters.[7] We are fortunate to be living at a time when the Church is beginning to acknowledge these realities. This new understanding of our Jewish roots has been spelled out in such documents as *Nostra Aetate* (*Declaration on the Church's Relation to Non-Christian Religions*), promulgated in 1965 by Vatican Council II, and *The Jewish People and Their Sacred Scriptures in the Christian Bible*, a study issued in 2001 by the Pontifical Biblical Commis-

---

7. A phrase coined by John Paul II in his famous speech at the synagogue in Rome, April 13, 1986.

sion, both available on the Vatican website. The recent Vatican instruction on avoiding the use of the Hebrew name of God, Yahweh, in the liturgy, a source of puzzlement to some, was based on a thoughtful response to the long-standing Jewish practice of refraining from pronouncing the sacred name of God. It is a reasonable act of respect for Judaism and reverence for God that Christians do the same.

# The Wisdom of Christ versus the "Philosophy"

## Colossians 2:6–23

Now that Paul has reminded the Colossians of their fullness of life through faith in Christ (1:15–2:5), he is ready to challenge them to stand firm in Christ and reject the false "philosophy" that is threatening their new identity. This section is the fifth of the ten units that make up the overall chiastic structure of the letter. Together with the next section (3:1–7), its parallel twin, it sits at the heart of Paul's communication with his audience.[1]

In this chapter Paul uses four vivid images to portray what happens when a person is baptized into Christ:

1. a spiritual circumcision (of the heart),
2. a burial and rising with Christ,
3. the cancelation of a debt, an IOU that is erased and even nailed to the cross, and
4. a victory over spiritual enemies.

Further, with the word "stripping" in verses 11 and 15, Paul alludes to the Christian baptismal rite of taking off an old garment and donning a new, white one, a symbol that will be further elaborated in 3:8–10.

---

1. This unit is itself a †chiasm, whose framing members are signaled by verbal parallels: "love of wisdom" (*philosophia*, 2:8) and false "wisdom" (*sophia*, 2:23); "elemental powers of the world" (vv. 8 and 20) and "principality(s) and power(s)" (vv. 10 and 15); and "circumcision not made with *hands*" (v. 11) and "the *hand*-written charge" (v. 14). See John Paul Heil, *Colossians: Encouragement to Walk in All Wisdom as Holy Ones in Christ*, Early Christianity 4 (Atlanta: Society of Biblical Literature, 2010), 101–33, for details.

## You Share in the Fullness of God (2:6–10)

⁶So, as you received Christ Jesus the Lord, walk in him, ⁷rooted in him and built upon him and established in the faith as you were taught, abounding in thanksgiving. ⁸See to it that no one captivate you with an empty, seductive philosophy according to human tradition, according to the elemental powers of the world and not according to Christ. ⁹For in him dwells the whole fullness of the deity bodily, ¹⁰and you share in this fullness in him, who is the head of every principality and power.

OT: Isa 29:13
NT: Gal 4:3, 9
Catechism: Mary and the bodily indwelling of God, 484; Jesus as mediator of divine presence, 515; the Church and divine indwelling, 772; incarnation and sacred art, 2502

"Walk in him" is the core of Paul's imperative. Believers must move forward    **2:6–7**
in Christ and in the way of life they have begun, for failure to move forward is
to go backward. Paul again uses "walk" in the metaphorical sense that we met
in Phil 3:17–18—to mean acting, behaving, or, more broadly, living. In 1:10,
in Paul's prayer that the Colossians *live* "in a manner worthy of the Lord," it is
properly translated "to live." Paul also uses the same verb to describe how they
"conducted themselves" before they heard the gospel (3:7) and how they are to
"conduct themselves" toward outsiders (4:5). **So, as you received Christ Jesus
the Lord, walk in him, rooted in him and built upon him and established
in the faith as you were taught.** If the use of both "walk" and "rooted" seems
to mix metaphors, it helps to consider the implications of the horticultural
image: When baptized into Christ, the Colossians were like a plant nurtured
in rich soil (see Matt 13:8; 1 Cor 3:7); breaking loose from that connection
would be like uprooting a sapling. To remain rooted even as one walks the way
of Christ is to continually draw life and strength from him, overflowing with
**thanksgiving** to God.

What is it that threatens their walking in the faith they learned from Epa-    **2:8**
phras? It is a competing way of thinking and behaving, which Paul characterizes in three vivid ways. (1) There are those in the neighborhood of the Lycus
Valley who would **captivate** the new Christians. This is a colorful verb. It means
"to gain control by carrying off as booty."[2] What the advocates of this teaching
intend to do with the new Christians is tantamount to enslaving them, tearing
them away from their rootedness in the Messiah. (2) The adversaries' means for

2. BDAG 955.

## The "Elemental Powers of the World"

**BIBLICAL**
**BACKGROUND**

Book-length studies have been devoted to the "elemental powers of the world" (*stoicheia tou kosmou*), what they meant in Paul's social environment, and how best to translate the phrase into English. Here is my understanding of the issues.

First, what are the basic meanings of the Greek word *stoicheia*? The most common meaning is "basic components of something, elements." This meaning appears in 2 Pet 3:10–12, where the *stoicheia* are the elements that compose the material universe—not of course in our current sense of the periodic table but in the ancient sense of the basic four elements: earth, air, fire, and water. It can also include heavenly bodies and constellations, like the twelve signs of the zodiac.

*Stoicheia* can also mean "fundamental principles," as in the first things one learns in school, such as the alphabet, our phrase "*elementary* school," or Sherlock Holmes's frequent comment, "Elementary, my dear Watson." This meaning shows up in Heb 5:12: "Although you should be teachers by this time, you need to have someone teach you again the basic elements of the utterances of God."

The other major meaning of *stoicheia* is "elemental spirits" or "transcendent powers that are in control over events in this world." Scholarly research has found plenty of evidence that *stoicheia* was used in ancient times to describe cosmic entities like the sun, moon, stars, planets, and the four elements *as managed by spirits, angels, and demons.* A ready example appears in the book of Wisdom, where Solomon is portrayed as boasting about his special God-given knowledge of the elements of creation.

> For he gave me sound knowledge of what exists, that I might know the structure of the universe and the force of its elements [*stoicheia*], The beginning and the end and the midpoint of times, the changes in the sun's course and the variations of the seasons.
>
> Wis 7:17–18; see 19:18

*continued on next page*

captivating them is **an empty, seductive philosophy**. A common word in our vocabulary today, *philosophia* appears only here in the New Testament. Paul's use of the word in this context suggests not so much speculative knowledge, as in the philosophies of Aristotle and Plato, but *a way of life* entailing both an ideology and certain practices, something like the way "wisdom" is used in other biblical writing. (3) Moreover, this philosophy is not rooted in biblical revelation but in **human tradition**, the kind of idolatrous human precepts that were confronted long ago by the prophet Isaiah (Isa 29:13; see commentary on Col 2:23) and more recently by Jesus himself (Mark 7:6–7).

Then in Wis 13:2 pagans are described as foolish for *worshiping* these things as gods.

> Either fire, or wind, or the swift air, or the circuit of the stars, or the mighty water, or the luminaries of heaven, the governors of the world, they considered gods.

Translated literally, Paul's phrase *stoicheia tou kosmou* is "elements of the cosmos." Given that Paul writes of these elements as something to which the baptized Colossians "have died" (2:20), it is clear that he has in mind something more than the material components of the universe. The Christian does not die to earth, air, fire, and water, or sun, moon, and stars. The *stoicheia* here, then, are personal forces that human beings can be enslaved to or freed from. Indeed, in writing to the Galatians, Paul can speak of pre-Christians as "enslaved to the *stoicheia tou kosmou*" (Gal 4:3). This relational language has prompted contemporary translators to add a word to clarify "elements" in Col 2:8–10—for instance, "elemental *powers* of the world" (NABRE), "the ruling *spirits* of this world" (Good News), "the elemental *spirits* of the universe" (NRSV). One scholar summarizes his research on teaching about "the elements" and Paul's response to it this way.

> For Paul the *stoicheia* were an integral part of the present evil age. They function as masters and overlords of unredeemed humanity working through various means—including the Jewish law and pagan religions—to hold their subjects in bondage. The rules and regulations imposed by these "powers," ostensibly through sacred and venerable religious tradition, are therefore entirely unnecessary and actually represent a reversion to a form of slavery to the "powers" themselves. A reaffirmation of the community's freedom from this demonic tyranny is expressed by the author, who stresses the complete identification of believers with Christ. The identification includes death to the former lords, the *stoicheia tou kosmou*, who would still seek to impose their control.[a]

This seems to reflect Paul's intended meaning of the *stoicheia tou kosmou* in Colossians.

a. Arnold, *Colossian Syncretism*, 194.

---

These human traditions have to do not with Christ but with spiritual forces called **the elemental powers of the world** (*stoicheia tou kosmou*).[3] Given the evidence for the variety of spiritual powers, both hostile and benevolent, in the folk religions of the Lycus Valley, these "elemental powers" are probably synonymous with the "thrones or dominions or principalities or powers" mentioned in 1:16. All these powers, Paul declares, are wholly subordinate to Christ the Lord.

3. This phrase turns up only three times as is in the New Testament—twice in this letter (2:8, 20) and once in Galatians (Gal 4:3); and once in shorthand form, *stoicheia* (without *tou kosmou*) in Gal 4:9.

2:9–10    In contrast to these competing spiritual powers, the risen Christ is the embodiment of God himself: **For in him dwells the whole fullness of the deity bodily.** Here Paul builds on his affirmation in the Christ hymn: "in him all the fullness was pleased to dwell" (1:19). The One whose presence and spirit fills all creation (Ps 104:27–30; Isa 6:3; Jer 23:24) has chosen to make that presence fully accessible in his incarnate Son. To put it another way, the fullness of God dwells in the transformed risen humanity of Jesus, such that all divine life, grace, and power are found in him.

Paul means to convince his addressees that they have all they need in Christ. There is no reason to call on other spiritual powers or to fear their influence; in fact, to do so is to return to enslavement. **And you** (plural) **share in this fullness in him.** Because Christians are part of the body of Christ, his divine life is imparted to them (see John 1:16). Moreover, Christ **is the head of every principality and power.** He is the uncreated *Master* of these mere creatures, whatever function they may have in the structure of the universe. "Head," in this context, has a different meaning from its other two instances in Colossians, where Christ Jesus is declared head of the *Church* in the organic sense of providing life, unity, vigor, and growth (1:18; 2:19). Christ is "head of every principality and power" in the sense of being *sovereign over* every spiritual force in the universe.

### Raised Up and Alive in Christ (2:11–14)

[11]In him you were also circumcised with a circumcision not administered by hand, by stripping off the carnal body, with the circumcision of Christ. [12]You were buried with him in baptism, in which you were also raised with him through faith in the power of God, who raised him from the dead. [13]And even when you were dead [in] transgressions and the uncircumcision of your flesh, he brought you to life along with him, having forgiven us all our transgressions; [14]obliterating the bond against us, with its legal claims, which was opposed to us, he also removed it from our midst, nailing it to the cross. . . .

OT: Deut 10:16; Jer 4:4; 9:25–26, 31–33; Ezek 36:26–27; 44:7, 9; Dan 2:34

NT: Mark 14:58; Rom 6:3–11; 2 Cor 5:1; Gal 3:27; Phil 3:3

Catechism: Jesus' circumcision and Christian baptism, 527; baptism as burial with Christ, 628, 1214; Christians as "already risen with Christ," 1002; the ritual of baptism, 1229–45

2:11    As we learned when we explored Paul's statement in Philippians, "We are the circumcision" (Phil 3:3), the use of circumcision in a spiritual sense (as in "circumcision of the heart") was already alive in the Old Testament. If literal circumcision of the flesh was a sign of covenant dedication and membership in the people of God, "circumcision of the *heart*" meant an interior disposition that truly matched the meaning of the external sign.[4] Paul, then, could in Phil 3:3 Christianize that Hebrew understanding to refer to the renewed covenant through baptism into the body of Christ.

Here in Colossians, Paul develops that metaphor more fully. When he writes, **In him** (Christ) **you were also circumcised with a circumcision not administered by hand**, Paul emphasizes an action of *God* rather than human beings.[5] Christians have received a fully efficacious "circumcision" by God himself. They have no need for the Jewish rite of circumcision, despite what the false teachers are apparently claiming.

The biblical background for this is Deut 30:6, the only Old Testament passage that speaks of *God* circumcising anybody. There Moses foretells Israel's future return from exile, a restoration to their land, when God himself will "circumcise your hearts and the hearts of your descendants so that you will love the Lord, your God, with your whole heart and your whole being, in order that you may live." God himself will transform his people interiorly so that they can respond to him with true covenant love and fidelity. The same idea is later expressed in different terms by Jeremiah and Ezekiel: "I will place my law within them, and write it upon their hearts" (Jer 31:33); "I will give you a new heart, and a new spirit I will put within you. I will remove the heart of stone from your flesh and give you a heart of flesh. I will put my spirit within you so that you walk in my statutes, observe my ordinances" (Ezek 36:26–27). As Paul will make clear in verse 12, circumcision is a figure for Christian baptism. Just as circumcision was the initiation ritual, for males, into the people of Israel in covenant with God, baptism is the initiation ritual, the "new circumcision," into the New Covenant in Christ—one that truly accomplishes a circumcision of heart. That it is "not administered by hand" means that it is an end-time act of God—the sense this phrase has in Dan 2:34.[6]

Instead of the removal of a small piece of flesh, baptism truly entails **stripping off the carnal body**. The meaning of "the carnal body" becomes clear at 3:9, where Paul makes the same point by saying "you have taken off"—literally, "you have stripped off"—"the old self with its practices." The clinical vividness

---

4. See Deut 10:16; 30:6; Jer 4:4; 9:24–25; Ezek 44:7, 9.

5. The phrase "not administered by hand" translates a single word that occurs only two other times in the New Testament (Mark 14:58; 2 Cor 5:1). See the similar phrase in Dan 2:34.

6. For an in-depth treatment of circumcision in Colossians, see Christopher A. Beetham, *Echoes of Scripture in the Letter of Paul to the Colossians* (Boston: Brill, 2008), 157–79.

of the image of cutting off the foreskin in circumcision, challenging though it may be to some modern sensibilities, is well chosen to stress the cutting away from one's life of all that is opposed to the will of God. There is a double meaning here in that "stripping" also recalls the divestment of an old garment and the putting on of a new white garment in the baptismal rite.

The **circumcision of Christ** does not refer to Jesus' own circumcision as a baby, nor is it a metaphor for his death; rather it is a reference to baptism, the means by which Christ becomes the Lord of the person baptized in his name.[7] Baptism marks the moment when the new Christian begins to experience their rescue from the dominion of darkness and their transfer to the kingdom of the Son (1:13).

**2:12**   If there was any doubt that the previous verse was about baptism, verse 12 makes it perfectly clear. **You were buried with him in baptism, in which you were also raised with him through faith in the power of God, who raised him from the dead.** Here Paul moves from the analogy of circumcision to the even stronger analogy of death, burial, and resurrection from the dead. Christian baptism is truly a death to *self*, a surrender of the core of the human personality with all its drives toward self-preservation and self-promotion (see Gal 2:20; 5:24). It is dying to a worldview, a set of behaviors and relationships, and commencing a completely new way of life and new relationships. Paul says the same thing in Rom 6:3–11, especially in 6:4: "We were indeed buried with him through baptism into death, so that, just as Christ was raised from the dead by the glory of the Father, we too might live"—literally, "walk"—"in newness of life." In the early Church, when baptism was practiced by full immersion, the symbolism of dying and rising was all the more vivid.[8]

**2:13**   Both analogies for baptism—circumcision and death-and-resurrection—are joined in verse 13. It helps to remember that Paul is mainly addressing former pagans, people not formed within the moral constraints of the Torah. This accounts for his presumption that they were **dead [in] transgressions.** This deadness precedes the dying with Christ that happens in baptism. It refers to the moral and spiritual lifelessness of their former state of separation from God. At the same time, Paul includes himself, and presumably other Jewish Christians, when he adds **having forgiven us all our transgressions.** For, making the point that *everyone* needs redemption in Jesus Christ, he could write to the Christians of Rome, "We have already brought the charge against Jews and Greeks alike that *they are all under the domination of sin*" (Rom 3:9) and

7. Petr Pokorný, *Colossians: A Commentary* (Peabody, MA: Hendrickson, 1991), 125.
8. See Catechism, 628, 1239, 1262.

"there is no distinction; *all have sinned and are deprived of the glory of God*" (Rom 3:22–23, italics added).

**The uncircumcision of your flesh** might seem, at first, to refer to their literal uncircumcision as Gentiles; but of course Paul's whole point is that they were not then, nor are they now, in need of literal circumcision. Paul does some wordplay here with a biblical phrase that occurs several times in the Torah: "the flesh of the foreskin," meaning literally the foreskin that is cut off in circumcision (Gen 17:11, 14, 23, 24, 25). Paul reverses this phrase by writing, "the foreskin [or 'uncircumcision'] of your †flesh." By flesh here, Paul clearly does not mean flesh in the ordinary, neutral sense but with the meaning he gave that word in verse 11, namely, the sinful tendencies of fallen human nature. This is the meaning we also meet elsewhere in this letter (2:18, 23; see also Gal 5:13–24).[9] So "uncircumcision of your flesh" is another name for what has been stripped off in baptism. While this flesh has been stripped off in the sense that its domination of the human person is over (as in Rom 6:6; Gal 5:24), the flesh remains something to be reckoned with in Christian life. One must choose over and over again to walk according to the Spirit rather than according to the flesh.

Paul's words, that God **brought you to life with him, having forgiven us all our transgressions,** clarify what he put succinctly in 1:14, describing what the Father has done for us in the Son, "in whom we have redemption, the forgiveness of sins."

To the things that they have already "died to" and "stripped off" through baptism into the Messiah, Paul adds **the bond** against us. The word for "bond" (*cheirographon*) literally means "a hand-written document." The qualifying phrase **against us, with its legal claims, which was opposed to us** gives it the specific meaning of a certificate of indebtedness.[10] God has "obliterated," or "erased, wiped out," this record of our debts, leaving a clean parchment. That he **removed it from our midst, nailing it to the cross** powerfully images the assertion in verse 13: he forgave us our transgressions. Debt was the prevailing image for sin during the period of Second Temple Judaism (from the return from exile and rebuilding of the temple in 515 BC up to the Roman destruction of the temple in AD 70). Paul's picture of the Father not only erasing the text of the IOU but even nailing the blank parchment to the cross of Christ is perhaps the most vivid expression of the definitive nature of God's forgiveness of our sins through baptism.[11]

2:14

---

9. My discussion of the circumcision references draws on Beetham, *Echoes of Scripture*, 157–92.
10. BDAG 1083.
11. This understanding of sin as debt shows up in the Lord's Prayer: "forgive us our debts, as we forgive our debtors" (Matt 6:12); "forgive us our sins for we ourselves forgive everyone in debt to us" (Luke 11:4).

## Our Decree of Indebtedness Torn to Pieces   LIVING TRADITION

St. John Chrysostom, the eloquent fourth-century patriarch of Constantinople, exhorted a group of baptismal candidates,

> See to it that we do not again become debtors to the old contract. Christ came once; he found the certificate of our ancestral indebtedness which Adam wrote and signed. Adam contracted the debt; by our subsequent sins we increased the amount owed. In this contract are written a curse, and sin, and death, and the condemnation of the Law. Christ took all these away and pardoned them. Saint Paul cries out and says: "The decree of our sins which was against us, he has taken it completely away, nailing it to the cross." He did not say "erasing the decree," nor did he say "blotting it out," but "nailing it to the cross," so that no trace of it might remain. This is why he did not erase it but tore it to pieces.[a]

a. *Baptismal Catecheses* 3.21, quoted in ACCS 9:33.

Reading this passage in Greek, one cannot help but notice a playful resonance between *acheiropoiētos* ("not administered by hand," that is, administered by God) and *cheirographon* ("hand-written document," in this case an IOU written by a debtor). The word for "hand" (*cheir*) refers to human hands. Paul wants his Greek audience to hear the sharp contrast between the merely human IOU, written by the hand of the debtor (i.e., the sinner), and therefore a transient thing, and the act of God in baptism. The cancellation of sin by God easily supersedes the human "manuscript" of our guilt.[12] As Paul says in Romans, "Hence, now there is no condemnation for those who are in Christ Jesus" (Rom 8:1).

### Reflection and Application (2:11–14)

The way this passage speaks of Christian baptism as a kind of circumcision serves as a helpful reminder that just as circumcision is for Jews an initiation into the covenant community (the current Jewish term for circumcision is *bris*, from the Yiddish version of the Hebrew *berith*, "covenant"), so the sacrament of baptism is also an initiation into the covenant community of the Church, the body of Christ. Further, the language of stripping off and putting on (Col 2:11; 3:9–10; Gal 3:27; Eph 4:22–24) alludes to that part of the baptismal rite

12. For an excellent exposition of the cultural background of the IOU image entailed in v. 13, see Gary A. Anderson, *Sin: A History* (New Haven: Yale University Press, 2009), 113–21. This study also explores the full story of sin imaged first as a weight and then as a debt to be paid up, or canceled.

where the newly baptized person is dressed with a white garment as a sign of "putting on" Christ. While that symbolism pertains to the dignity and fresh innocence of the individual and the person's intimate relationship to Christ, it also signifies putting off the old life and taking on a whole new way of life shared with all the baptized, as Paul will further elaborate in 3:1–16.

## Don't Be Duped by False Spiritual Advice (2:15–19)

[15]. . . despoiling principalities and the powers, he made a public spectacle of them, leading them away in triumph by it. [16]Let no one, then, pass judgment on you in matters of food and drink or with regard to a festival or new moon or sabbath. [17]These are shadows of things to come; the reality belongs to Christ. [18]Let no one disqualify you, delighting in self-abasement and worship of angels, taking his stand on visions, inflated without reason by his fleshly mind, [19]and not holding closely to the head, from whom the whole body, supported and held together by its ligaments and bonds, achieves the growth that comes from God.

NT: 1 Cor 8:1; Eph 2:12–22; 4:15–16

Paul alludes to a scene that was well known in the ancient world: a triumphal    **2:15** march, in which a conquering Roman general paraded his vanquished enemies through the streets to humiliate them and to celebrate the victory in the most public manner possible. The verb for **despoiling** the enemy—that is, taking away their weapons and martial regalia—has the same root as "stripping off" in verse 11. The †**principalities and the powers** are disarmed by a divine act—the same act of baptism that strips away the old self. How is this victory a **public spectacle**? Paul probably has in mind the resurrection of Jesus the Messiah and its visible effects in the prodigious expansion and vitality of the Church. The "principalities and powers" are best understood as the spiritual powers first mentioned in 1:16 and later referred to as "elemental powers" (*stoicheia*, 2:8, 20).

The phrase **in . . . it**, meaning "in the cross" just mentioned in verse 14, can also be rendered "in him," that is, in Christ. "In Christ" is the more likely meaning, for since 2:9 Paul has been speaking of what God has done in and with Christ (vv. 9, 11–13). Christ is the general leading the victory parade—a startling declaration, considering that in the eyes of the Roman Empire, the crucified Jesus was the defeated and humiliated foe! In reality, Paul says, in the death and resurrection of Jesus Christ God has definitively triumphed over the powers of evil, publicly humiliating them and stripping off their armor. It is a powerful

Fig. 10. An illustration of Roman soldiers carrying the spoils of war on Domitian's arch celebrating Titus' siege of Jerusalem.

way of convincing the Colossians that they do not need the ideas and practices of the "philosophy" to defend themselves against the principalities and powers. While there may still be some skirmishes, the war has been won.

**2:16**    The warning not to let others **pass judgment on you in matters of food and drink or with regard to a festival or new moon or sabbath** surely pertains to matters of Jewish law. What is in question, however, is not simply following the law of Moses but human additions to those biblical mandates (see Mark 7:6–9). The false teaching seems to be a mix that includes some Jewish practices; the false teachers are judging the Gentile Christians as somehow unfit because they fail to practice the false teachers' own, more Jewish, brand of Christianity.

**2:17**    Paul speaks of the ceremonial practices of the Old Covenant—laws about food, drink, feasts, and sabbaths—as **shadows** pointing to the infinitely greater **reality** of the New Covenant in Christ (see Heb 8:5; 10:1). This is another way of phrasing the common New Testament affirmation that the former things are †types or figures pointing to the **things to come** (Rom 5:14; Heb 8:5; 1 Pet 3:21)—that is, the deliverance from sin and full communion with God that have already come to be in the new age inaugurated by the life, death, and resurrection of Jesus Christ.

The word for "reality" (*sōma*) is literally "body."[13] Given that the Church as the body of Christ is a key concept in this letter (1:18, 24; 2:19) it is quite likely

13. In combination with *skia* ("shadow"), *sōma* takes on the meaning "substance" or "reality," as in the writings of Philo and Josephus. See BDAG 929.

that Paul is using wordplay here. The "reality" to which the "shadows" point is indeed the body of Christ, which is the Church. For what is said in the Old Testament regarding the people of God rescued from slavery, Israel restored from exile, and Servant Israel who becomes a light to the nations (e.g., Isa 49:6) is fulfilled in the Church.[14]

Paul proceeds to describe the false teachers with language drawn from the worlds of sports and litigation. Some of the terms are so rare, appearing only here in the New Testament, that this verse has long challenged translators. Recent research has uncovered texts that illuminate the imagery Paul uses here. When he writes **let no one disqualify you** (*katabrabeuō*), he is using a sports term. A *brabeus* is an umpire, and *katabrabeuō* means "to decide against," as an Olympic official might, and so rob of a prize.[15] So the false teachers were ruling out or disqualifying the faithful of Colossae as authentic Christians because they did not participate in **self-abasement and worship of angels**. "Self-abasement" (*tapeinophrosynē*) is elsewhere simply "humility," a virtue to be desired (Acts 20:19; Eph 4:2; Phil 2:3) or indeed "put on" (Col 3:12; 1 Pet 5:5). But in this context it refers to false humility, a humiliating self-abasement (as in v. 23).

2:18

The "worship of angels" is an ambiguous phrase in Greek as in English; it can be read as referring either to worship that angels *do*, or to angels as the *object* of human worship. But the context seems to call for the latter. The false teachers have insisted on the need to pay homage to angels, detracting from the all-sufficiency of Jesus Messiah. This becomes especially clear if the "principalities and powers" and "elemental powers of the world" of this letter refer to angelic spirits.

Paul further describes the typical exponent of the "philosophy" as **taking his stand on visions**. The verb, *embateuō*, is another rare word that appears only here in the New Testament. Recent research in the legal language of Hellenistic law courts has revealed a meaning that fits the context especially well. Certain papyri (texts written on papyrus, a common writing material in the ancient Mediterranean world) use *embateuō* to refer to coming into possession of property, as in claiming an inheritance.[16] The visions, then, are the basis on which the false teachers claim a heavenly inheritance, a claim that they deny to Christians who have not had such mystical experiences.

---

14. Eduard Lohse (*Colossians and Philemon*, Hermeneia [Philadelphia: Fortress, 1971], 117) also acknowledges a reference to Church as the body of Christ, an understanding also implied in the NJB: "These are only a shadow of what is coming; the reality is the body of Christ."
15. BDAG 515.
16. Beetham provides the details in *Echoes of Scripture*, 206–7.

In this light we can see the pertinence of Paul's assurance at the beginning of the letter that the Father has made the Colossians "*fit* to share in the inheritance with the holy ones" (1:12, italics added). This picks up on the legal meaning of *embateuō*. What human judge can *dis*qualify persons whom God the Father himself has qualified as his heirs?

The typical follower of the "philosophy" is also **inflated without reason by his fleshly mind** (literally, "his mind of flesh"). †Flesh here carries the meaning established in verse 11: the fallen way of thinking and living that was stripped off in the spiritual circumcision of their baptism into Christ. The image of an "inflated" windbag parallels a statement Paul makes in 1 Cor 8:1: "Knowledge puffs up, but love builds up" (NRSV). Even though the practitioners of the "philosophy" are presumably baptized Christians, they have not appropriated into their living what they received objectively. Their minds, inflated with pride at their supposed special knowledge, in fact remain unrenewed. By practicing a *syncretistic Christianity, they have lost their grip on their "head," the risen Christ.

What is especially wrong with these false teachers, preoccupied with self-abasement, worship of angels, and visions, is their failure to hold **closely to the head**, Christ, the source of their life. From him **the whole body, supported and held together by its ligaments and bonds, achieves the growth that comes from God.** Paul's vision of the Church is intensely communal: it is an organic unity of those who are joined to Christ through baptism, growing together into maturity in him. It is through their union with Christ that the members function in harmony with one another, each fulfilling his or her unique and indispensable role in supporting the body. The Letter to the Ephesians has a parallel description of the ecclesial body in union with Christ as head:

> Living the truth in love, we should grow in every way into him who is the head, Christ, from whom the whole body, joined and held together by every supporting ligament, with the proper functioning of each part, brings about the body's growth and builds itself up in love.[17]
>
> Eph 4:15–16

That the practitioners of the "philosophy" do not "hold fast to the head" suggests that they are indeed members, or past members, of the church, for it would make little sense to speak this way of people who had no allegiance to Christ. It would seem that they have compromised Christ's headship in their

17. See, too, the combination of body and temple images in Eph 2. Whereas Col 2 stresses the union of members to head, Eph 2 underscores the union of Jews and Gentiles in one body/temple.

lives by considering him simply one of many heavenly powers to whom it is necessary to pay homage.

## Reflection and Application (2:15–19)

The problem of the false teachers in Colossae, who "pass judgment on" and "disqualify" the faithful majority that Paul and Timothy address (vv. 16–18), evokes phenomena that one can sometimes encounter in the Church today. Members of church movements or new religious communities, for instance, are sometimes tempted to look down on Catholics as not belonging to their particular expression of Christianity. Adherents of traditional devotions or liturgy can slip into viewing their practice as necessary and quasi-identical with the faith. Catholics on the left or right ends of the political or theological spectrums can too hastily disqualify one another. When one slips into dismissive language about fellow Christians, the Colossian elitists stand as a cautionary example. It is helpful to consider the famous "Presupposition" St. Ignatius of Loyola places at the head of his *Spiritual Exercises*:

> That both the giver and the maker of the Spiritual Exercises may be of greater help and benefit to each other, it should be presupposed that every good Christian ought to be more eager to put a good interpretation on a neighbor's statement than to condemn it. Further, if one cannot interpret it favorably, one should ask how the other means it. If that meaning is wrong, one should correct the person with love; and if this is not enough, one should search out every appropriate means through which, by understanding the statement in a good way, it may be saved.[18]

## Don't Submit to False Spiritual Practices (2:20–23)

**[20]If you died with Christ to the elemental powers of the world, why do you submit to regulations as if you were still living in the world? [21]"Do not handle! Do not taste! Do not touch!" [22]These are all things destined to perish with use; they accord with human precepts and teachings. [23]While they have a semblance of wisdom in rigor of devotion and self-abasement [and] severity to the body, they are of no value against gratification of the flesh.**

OT: Isa 29:13
NT: Matt 15:7–9 // Mark 7:6–7; 1 Cor 5:9–13

18. *The Spiritual Exercises of Saint Ignatius: A Translation and Commentary*, trans. George Ganss (St. Louis: Institute of Jesuit Sources, 1992), par. 22.

2:20     This unit is the final and climactic portion of the minichiasm of 2:6–23 (see the outline of Colossians above), in which Paul exhorts the Colossians not to be seduced by false teachings that would deny their dignity and the fullness of life they have in Christ. Both this unit and its parallel at 2:6–8 reference the elemental powers of the world, human precepts, and wisdom (*sophia*, echoing *philosophia* in 2:8). The key words mentioned at the beginning of the section are here repeated in reverse order, framing the unit as a whole:

philosophia—human tradition—elements of the world (v. 8)

elements of the world—human precepts—sophia (vv. 20–23)

Paul's rhetorical question, **why do you submit to regulations as if you were still living in the world**, may sound as if he sees Christian discipleship as a radical withdrawal from "the world," in the sense of society in general. But such an understanding would fly in the face of what he says elsewhere (see 1 Cor 5:9–13; Col 4:5–6). As we saw early in this very letter, Paul reported his and Timothy's gratitude for the way the gospel has borne fruit and grown "in the whole world" (1:6). Paul speaks of the "world" (*kosmos*) much as John the Evangelist does—sometimes neutrally, where "world" means everyone and all creation (as in John 3:16, "For God so loved the world"), and sometimes negatively, where "world" means the realm of unbelief (as in John 17:14, "I gave them your word, and the world hated them, because they do not belong to the world any more than I belong to the world"). Paul would agree with John's way of describing Jesus' followers as being *in* the world but not *of* the world (John 17:15–16). For Paul, Christians no longer live in the world in the sense that they no longer look to the emperor as head but to the Lord Jesus, and they now live in the spirit of service rather than in competition with one another.

Submitting to regulations refers not to the ceremonial laws of Moses but to the adversaries' practices that integrate Torah laws into their own special discipline, as verse 22 makes clear.

2:21     The generalized string of prohibitions—**Do not handle! Do not taste! Do not touch!**—sounds like a parody of some Levitical legislation (see Lev 11:1–47; 13:45–52; Num 19:11–22). For Paul, to return to these ceremonial precepts that have been set aside by Christ (see Eph 2:15) is to return to slavery (Rom 7:6; Gal 2:19; 5:1).

2:22     The NABRE translation **These are all things destined to perish with use** takes "these" as referring not to the laws themselves but to the subjects of the laws (dead bodies, blood, food, drink), which are insignificant because of their inevitable decomposition. This catches the spirit of Jesus' remark at Mark 7:18–19: "Do you not realize that everything that goes into a person from outside cannot defile, since it enters not the heart but the stomach and passes out into the latrine?" When Paul says, **they accord with human precepts** (*entalmata*) **and teachings**, he is alluding to Isa 29:13, the same passage Jesus quotes in a controversy with the Pharisees: "Well did Isaiah prophesy about you hypocrites, as it is written: 'This people honors me with their lips, but their hearts are from me; in vain do they worship me, teaching as doctrines human precepts [*entalmata*]'" (Mark 7:6–7 // Matt 15:7–9).[19] Paul's meaning is much the same. Jesus denounces the way human traditions such as extra purification practices (Mark 7:1–5) and abuses such as supporting the temple to the neglect of one's parents (Mark 7:8–13) have become a pretext for neglecting the more important laws of Scripture, such as honoring one's father and mother. The Gospel understanding of Isa 29:13 matches well Paul's point in our passage. Paul had characterized the Colossian "philosophy" as functioning "according to human tradition" (2:8; see Mark 7:8).[20]

**Wisdom** (*sophia*) in the biblical sense means knowing how to live in the fear of the Lord, that is, in right relationship with God. For Paul wisdom is, furthermore, knowing how to apply in daily life the truth of God's revelation in Christ. Paul and Timothy constantly prayed that the Colossians be filled with spiritual wisdom (1:9), and Paul's aim in his ministry to Gentiles was to teach "everyone with all wisdom" (1:28). Christ is the one "in whom are hidden all the treasures of wisdom and knowledge" (2:3). The Colossians themselves are to teach one another with wisdom (3:16) and conduct themselves wisely toward outsiders (4:5). But the practices of the false teachers—which Paul here characterizes as **rigor of devotion**,[21] **self-abasement**, and **severity to the body**—only *look* like the fruit of religious wisdom. In fact, **they are of no value against gratification of the flesh**. The NRSV paraphrase of this last clause catches the meaning nicely: "but they are of no value in checking self-indulgence." The Greek word *sarx* (literally, "flesh") can be rendered "self-indulgence" because here it carries the negative sense it has in verses 11, 13, and 18. It stands for the self-indulgent drives of the old life that the spiritual circumcision of baptism has stripped off—not just sensual forms of sin, as we tend to use the term today, but also pride, anger, jealousy, and other sins of the mind (1 Cor 3:1–3; Gal 5:19–21).[22] Paul is saying that, apart from Christ, ascetic rigors have no value

2:23

---

19. Like Jesus in Mark 7:7–8, Paul parallels "human precepts" (Col 2:22) and "human traditions" (2:8).

20. Beetham, *Echoes*, 210–18.

21. Danker translates the Greek term *ethelothrēskia* as "self-made religion," BDAG 276.

22. Like *kosmos* ("world"), *sarx* in Christian writings sometimes has a negative meaning and sometimes a neutral one. It can mean simply the concrete humanity of an individual, as in Col 1:22 (of Christ), 24; 2:1, 5 (of Paul). Here *sarx* has the negative meaning.

*in themselves* for checking the human inclination to sin, since they can leave pride intact or even increase it.

The practitioners of the false philosophy are acting as if they can get right with God through their own activities, turning religious practice into a kind of idolatry. This accords well with the context of the Isaiah passage alluded to in verse 22. Purporting to promote a *philosophia* (love of wisdom—2:8), the adversaries are actually promoting a counterfeit *sophia*. They have lost touch with the head, Christ, who teaches the true wisdom.

## Reflection and Application (2:20–23)

*Christ the Head.* While we may never be satisfied that we have completely figured out the doctrines and practices of the "philosophy" that threatens the integrity of the Colossians' faith, I think we get the gist of it. They have taken up ways of thinking and behaving that detract from the sovereignty of God's eternal Son, the risen Lord Jesus Christ. As exotic as this heresy may sound to our ears, with its severe physical discipline and talk of visions and "worship of angels," it represents a perennial temptation for Christians—the readiness to let a human mind-set or practice become so important that it threatens to compromise the place of Jesus in our faith. Even good practices can become a kind of idol.

*Human traditions.* Many good and helpful traditions—devotions and practices—have grown up among Christians over the millennia. I submit that there are none that will not profit from being measured against the Christ-centered vision of the Letter to the Colossians. As the Catechism cautions, "superstition . . . can even affect the worship we offer the true God, e.g., when one attributes an importance in some way magical to certain practices otherwise lawful or necessary. To attribute the efficacy of prayers or of sacramental signs to their mere external performance, apart from the interior dispositions that they demand, is to fall into superstition" (2111). However, Paul's strong critique of what he calls "human tradition" (v. 8) and "human precepts and teachings" (v. 22) has led some Christians to dismiss Catholic practices that have developed since the writing of the New Testament (for instance, canonization of saints, feast days, religious celibacy) as exactly the sort of things Paul condemns in this passage. But that is to espouse a Puritanism that denies authentic development and the enculturation that has always been part of the practice of the faith. Paul's concern is to avoid whatever detracts from the centrality of Jesus Christ, a concern that entails ongoing discernment regarding any development of the living tradition of the Church.

# You Have Died and Been Raised with Christ

## Colossians 3:1–7

Having just spent eighteen carefully crafted verses on the folly of yielding to the empty seduction of the false "philosophy" (2:6–23), Paul now, in a much briefer parallel unit (3:1–7), addresses the other strong temptation for many of these Colossian converts—the pull of their previous pagan lifestyle. He reminds them that they are united with Christ and therefore what is true of him is true of them: they have died to this world and are no longer dominated by its values, influences, and agendas. They have been raised with Christ and have already begun to share in his divine life and glory, though in a hidden way. Their life now is a preparation for the day when that glory will be fully revealed.

### Preparing for Glory (3:1–7)

¹If then you were raised with Christ, seek what is above, where Christ is seated at the right hand of God. ²Think of what is above, not of what is on earth. ³For you have died, and your life is hidden with Christ in God. ⁴When Christ your life appears, then you too will appear with him in glory. ⁵Put to death, then, the parts of you that are earthly: immorality, impurity, passion, evil desire, and the greed that is idolatry. ⁶Because of these the wrath of God is coming [upon the disobedient]. ⁷By these you too once conducted yourselves, when you lived in that way.

OT: Ps 110:1
NT: Phil 2:2, 5; 3:14

---

## Seeking What Is Above, Living More Intensely Below

**LIVING TRADITION**

Addressing the issue of the relationship of the Church to the modern world, the bishops at Vatican Council II recalled the exhortation of Col 3:1, "seek what is above," even as they were urging more active participation in the human family on earth:

> In their pilgrimage to the heavenly city Christians are to seek and value the things that are above; this involves not less, but greater commitment to working with everyone for the establishment of a more human world. Indeed, the mystery of their faith provides Christians with greater incentive and encouragement to fulfill their role more willingly and to assess the significance of activities capable of assigning to human culture its honored role in the complete vocation of humanity.
>
> By the work of our hands or with the help of technology, we till the earth to produce fruit and to make it a dwelling place fit for all of humanity; we also play our part in the life of social groups. In so doing we are realizing God's plan, revealed at the beginning of time, to subdue the earth and perfect the work of creation; at the same time we are perfecting ourselves and observing the command of Christ to devote ourselves to the service of our sisters and brothers.[a]

a. *Gaudium et Spes* (*Pastoral Constitution on the Church in the Modern World*), 57.

---

**Catechism:** Christians as already participating in Christ's risen life, 655, 1002–4, 2796
**Lectionary:** 3:1–4: Easter Sunday (Years A, B, C)

**3:1–2**    As in Philippians, where Paul speaks of "God's upward calling" and "our citizenship . . . in heaven" (3:14, 20), his exhortation here to **seek what is above**, where "your life is hidden with Christ in God," is not so much about *location* as *orientation*. Since Christians have truly died and been **raised with Christ** in baptism, the concerns of this world can no longer dominate their attention. This does not mean being so otherworldly that you're no earthly good, but just the opposite: relating to others with the purity and selflessness that come from knowing Christ's victory and sovereignty over all things. Just as Paul spoke of Christians' having left the world without denying their flesh-and-blood existence on earth (2:20), so here he reminds them to orient their daily lives toward union with their exalted and risen head, Christ. This is similar to his words in Eph 2:6, about our being seated with Christ in the heavenly places. For the only time in this letter, he uses that habits-of-the-heart word he used ten times in Philippians: **Think of** (*phroneō*). Keeping in mind that **Christ is seated at the right**

---

## Your Life Is Hidden with Christ in God

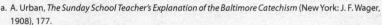

**LIVING TRADITION**

The story is told that when St. Catherine of Siena was granted a vision of a baptized soul,

> it was so beautiful that she could not look on it; the brightness of that soul dazzled her. Blessed Raymond, her confessor, asked her to describe to him as far as she was able the beauty of the soul she had seen. St. Catherine thought of the sweet light of that morning, and of the beautiful colors of the rainbow, but that soul was far more beautiful. She remembered the dazzling beams of the noonday sun, but the light that beamed from that soul was far brighter. She thought of the pure whiteness of the lily and of the fresh snow, but that is only an earthly white-ness. The soul she had seen was bright with the whiteness of heaven, such as is not to be found on earth. "Father," she answered, "I cannot find anything in this world that can give you the smallest idea of what I have seen. Oh, if you could but see the beauty of a soul in the state of grace, you would sacrifice your life a thousand times for its salvation. I asked the angel who was with me what had made that soul so beautiful, and he answered me, "It is the image and likeness of God in that soul, and the divine grace that made it so beautiful."[a]

a. A. Urban, *The Sunday School Teacher's Explanation of the Baltimore Catechism* (New York: J. F. Wager, 1908), 177.

---

**hand of God**, the place of highest sovereignty, is the best possible perspective for handling affairs on earth.[1]

Further, Paul says, **your life is hidden with Christ in God**—that is, the divine glory already present and at work within you is for the time being invisible. This heavenly orientation of our earthly lives will eventually be heavenly in the literal sense at Christ's †parousia, or second coming, when **you too will appear with him in glory**. The contrasting orientations Paul speaks of here, heavenly versus earthly, are the same as those he expresses in Galatians as walking in the Spirit versus doing the works of the flesh (Gal 5:13–26). 

3:3–4

When Paul urges his audience to **put to death, then, the parts of you that are earthly**, this may sound as if he is using the image of self-mutilation to advocate severe discipline of the body. But given his recent warning that the false teachers have "a semblance of wisdom in rigor of devotion and self-abasement [and] severity to the body" (2:23), that meaning can scarcely be his intent. Rather, he seems to be extending the image of stripping off the carnal body to 

3:5

1. The imagery for the Messiah seated at the right hand of God derives from Ps 110:1, a verse that appears frequently in the New Testament (e.g., Matt 22:44; Acts 2:34–35; 1 Cor 15:25; Heb 1:13).

213

behavior that specifically involved the body, namely, the sexual misbehavior common in the pagan lifestyle that they had left behind. That sort of behavior is "earthly" in that it is not oriented to holy living in the body of Christ. The strong language of this verse is something like the scolding tone of the idiom, "Now cut that out!" While the five vices that illustrate "earthly" behavior—**immorality, impurity, passion, evil desire**, and **greed**—can each carry a generic meaning that is not necessarily sexual, each of them occurs in Paul's Letters mainly in contexts dealing with disordered sexual conduct. "Greed," further characterized as **idolatry** (*eidōlatria*), might seem to be the exception, but possessive and addictive sexual indulgence can so dominate one's life that it is a God-substitute, an idol. Indeed, the parallel passage in Ephesians (5:5) uses idolatry in exactly that way: "Be sure of this, that no immoral or impure or greedy person, that is an idolater, has any inheritance in the kingdom of Christ and of God." Some contemporary readers may fault Paul for being preoccupied with sexual morality, but it is important to recognize that his audience in this letter is mainly Gentile in background, and the pull of the previous lifestyle for many of them was still strong. (See 1 Cor 6:12–20 for a similar problem in another community.) Paul alludes to this past life in verse 7: **By these you too once conducted yourselves**, that is, "walked." Old habits die hard.

3:6–7      The **wrath of God** is a traditional biblical image that uses human language to portray divine judgment and punishment of sin. Although the language refers to the human emotion of anger, God's "wrath" is not arbitrary or impulsive, but an expression of his justice. A helpful analogy: the light of the sun is necessary for exercising the sense of vision; however, if we relate to the sun inappropriately—for example, by looking directly at it—the injury that follows does not come from some evil intent of the sun but from our faulty way of relating to what is in itself a great good. God's holiness hurts if we reject it.

## Reflection and Application (3:1–7)

How countercultural is Christianity? Even in asking the question in those words, we must recognize that the relationship between Christian faith and culture is far too complex to be addressed so simplistically. Paul's Letters show that how Christians relate to the culture in which they are embedded is a matter requiring constant discernment. In the days of Jesus and Paul, some Jews—the Essenes—formed a countercultural movement that espoused living apart from their fellow religionists because the current temple leadership was not faithful to the Torah. Apparently some Essenes, the authors of the Dead Sea Scrolls, judged it necessary to form a commune in the wilderness area at Qumran, on the northwest shore of the Dead Sea. Paul never advocates that way of life for any of his churches. As a diaspora Jew who grew up in the Greek city of Tarsus, he had the experience of belonging to a community that was countercultural in some ways, especially in matters of religious belief and sexual fidelity, without the need to withdraw entirely from the surrounding culture. Paul addresses this issue as a Christian in 1 Cor 5:9–13. But just as many pagans who converted to Judaism had to change their behavior regarding, for example, the use of prostitutes, pagan converts to the *Christian* faith also had to begin living according to a standard of holiness not shared by the surrounding culture (1 Cor 6:12–20).

The challenge of discerning in what way Christians should affirm the values of the culture in which they find themselves, and in what way they should resist or counter that culture, has continued throughout the millennia. Given the prevailing attitudes toward promiscuity, adultery, pornography, and abortion in much of Western culture in our day, the sexual fidelity that Jesus mandates in the Sermon on the Mount (Matt 5:27–32) requires the support of a strong community of faith. In these things we are called to be countercultural.

# Let the Peace of Christ Rule in Your Hearts

## Colossians 3:8–16

In this unit Paul elaborates on the positive behavioral consequences of having "died with Christ" and having been "circumcised" in him through baptism. Our first parents were created in the image of God, a resemblance marred by the fall. We are now being renewed in that image through our baptismal union with Jesus, becoming a new creation. Yet these converted Gentiles of Colossae remain a work in progress as they grow further into the new self that they have put on.

### You Have Stripped Off the Old Self (3:8–11)

[8]But now you must put them all away: anger, fury, malice, slander, and obscene language out of your mouths. [9]Stop lying to one another, since you have taken off the old self with its practices [10]and have put on the new self, which is being renewed, for knowledge, in the image of its creator. [11]Here there is not Greek and Jew, circumcision and uncircumcision, barbarian, Scythian, slave, free; but Christ is all and in all.

OT: Gen 1:26–27
NT: 1 Cor 13:1–13; Gal 3:28
Lectionary: 3:9–17: Ritual Mass for Christian Initiation apart from Easter Vigil; Mass for Unity of Christians

3:8     When Paul writes, **But now you must put them all away**, the postbaptism "now" contrasts with the prebaptism lifestyle he has been describing. The mandate to "put away"—literally "put off" or "strip," as in discarding soiled garments—evokes the long-standing baptismal practice of removing one garment and putting on another (typically, white) to signify the transformation occurring in baptism, an image Paul will sustain in this passage. Paul summarizes what is put off in a further list of five vices (as in v. 5): **anger, fury, malice, slander, and obscene language**. While the first three can manifest themselves in a variety of human misbehaviors, the inclusion of slander and obscene language, plus the redundantly emphatic **out of your mouths**, suggests that the full quintet is meant to focus on sins of speech. The *emotion* of "anger" and its hotter cousin, "fury," usually a spontaneous response to a personal offense, is in itself morally neutral. Paul had just spoken of the wrath of God (v. 6), where "wrath" translates the same word as "anger" in verse 8. Anger becomes sinful when it is expressed in hostile action, most commonly in hurtful speech, here called "slander." "Malice" names a disposition of general ill-will, often the product of unresolved anger. Obscene language comes not so much from anger as from the emptiness of sexual promiscuity and a general disregard of sexuality as a gift of God.

The very structure of this vice list reflects the link between one's interior life and exterior speech, which Jesus emphasizes in some of his sayings; for example, in his reprimand of the Pharisees:

> You brood of vipers, how can you say good things when you are evil? For from the fullness of the heart the mouth speaks. A good person brings forth good out of a store of goodness, but an evil person brings forth evil out of a store of evil. I tell you, on the day of judgment people will render an account for every careless word they speak. By your words you will be acquitted, and by your words you will be condemned.
>
> Matt 12:34–37; see Luke 6:43–45

The next verse confirms this: **Stop lying to one another**. Paul pointedly im- plies that, new Christians though they may be, some Colossians continue the **practices** of **the old self** (literally, "the old human being," or "the old humanity") that they had cast aside at the time of baptism. Even with the donning of the **new self**, they are still God's work in progress. God is still fashioning them into **the image of** their **creator**, restoring the divine image in humanity (Gen 1:27) that had been disfigured by the fall. The reference to the Creator looks back to the Christ hymn (1:15–20) in its celebration of the Church as the *new creation*, of which Jesus, the "firstborn from the dead," is the head. In that capacity, the risen Jesus is the creator of Christians in his image.[1]

3:9–10

---

1. See Rom 8:29, where it is *God* who conforms the new creature (the baptized Christian) to the image of his Son, whereas here, in the context of the new creation as spelled out in the hymn, Christ is the one creating.

3:11        This verse is the centerpiece of the minichiasm of verses 8–16: **Here there is not Greek and Jew, circumcision and uncircumcision, barbarian, Scythian, slave, free; but Christ is all and in all.** Scholars have pondered what brings this particular list together. The eight elements are four contrasting pairs. "Jew and Greek" is a Jewish way of looking at the main religious and ethnic division of humanity, where "Greek" is everybody other than "Jew." "Circumcision and uncircumcision" was a more common way of naming the same division, but in reverse order. "Barbarian" is a Greek-speaker's way of naming those who do not share Hellenistic culture, and "Scythian" is someone from north of the Black Sea, considered to be particularly uncouth, even by other barbarians; so "barbarian and Scythian" names a local sociocultural category of the uncivilized. "Slave, free" is another obvious social distinction. Given that Scythians in the Colossians' world were commonly slaves, it has been suggested that there is reverse balance in the last two contrasting pairs, just as with the first two pairs.[2]

In saying that "here" these divisions "are not," Paul is not denying that cultural identities and social distinctions exist; rather, he is asserting that *here*, in the body of Christ, these distinctions are transcended and the persons they label are united in **Christ, who is all and in all.** There is no difference in spiritual status among Christians. Writing to the Galatians in a different context, that of the unity of the baptized as "Abraham's descendants," Paul speaks in similar language: "For all of you who were baptized into Christ have clothed yourselves with Christ. There is neither Jew nor Greek, there is neither slave nor free person, there is not male and female; for you are all one in Christ Jesus" (Gal 3:27–28). This unity among members of the Church, a remarkable phenomenon in the ancient world, is a consequence of putting on "the new self" described in verse 10. It also provides the basis for the relationships characterized by unity and love spelled out in verses 12–15.

## Reflection and Application (3:8–11)

The language of this letter regarding the unity of the Christian community and the diversity of its members presents an apparent paradox and invites reflection. On the one hand, Paul can say that "here there is not Greek and Jew, circumcision and uncircumcision . . . slave, free" (3:11); and yet, a few verses later, he will address Christian slaves and masters individually (3:22–4:1) and will distinguish between Christians who are "of the circumcision" (4:11) and

---

2. John Paul Heil refers to this pattern in *Colossians: Encouragement to Walk in All Wisdom as Holy Ones in Christ*, Early Christianity 4 (Atlanta: Society of Biblical Literature, 2010), 151.

those who are not. Thus the "new self" Christians put on is nothing less than Christ, and this is a communal, not merely an individual, matter—a union of individuals of diverse backgrounds and social roles, which people nevertheless retain as they grow into the body of Christ and are "conformed" to his image. Rather, as we also learn from other letters of Paul (especially 1 Corinthians), this unity is expressed in our transformed way of relating to one another, precisely through heartfelt compassion, kindness, humility, gentleness, and patience, loving one another and recognizing our basic equality as sisters and brothers in Christ (3:12–14).

## Put On Love, Let the Peace of Christ Reign (3:12–16)

[12]Put on then, as God's chosen ones, holy and beloved, heartfelt compassion, kindness, humility, gentleness, and patience, [13]bearing with one another and forgiving one another, if one has a grievance against another; as the Lord has forgiven you, so must you also do. [14]And over all these put on love, that is, the bond of perfection. [15]And let the peace of Christ control your hearts, the peace into which you were also called in one body. And be thankful. [16]Let the word of Christ dwell in you richly, as in all wisdom you teach and admonish one another, singing psalms, hymns, and spiritual songs with gratitude in your hearts to God.

OT: Lev 19:18
NT: Matt 6:14; Eph 5:19; Phil 2:1–4
Catechism: love as bond, 1827; singing and music, 1156–58;
Lectionary: 3:12–21 (or 3:12–17): Feast of the Holy Family; Ritual Mass for Marriage; Consecration of Virgins and Religious Profession; Mass for Peace and Justice; Mass in Thanksgiving

Having reviewed what Christians are to continue to "take off," Paul picks up     **3:12–13**
the other side of the baptismal clothing imagery. Reminding them that they
are **God's chosen ones, holy and beloved**—epithets that describe the people
of God in the Old Testament (Deut 7:6–8)—he invites them to **put on then**,
another set of five, this time a quintet of virtues: **heartfelt compassion, kindness, humility, gentleness, and patience**. These are virtues that Paul would
commend to any community. See, for example, his exhortation in Phil 2:1–4,
which leads into the Christ hymn, and his similar urging in Eph 4:1–3. But in
the context of this letter, "humility" (*tapeinophrosynē*) carries special nuance.
In the chapter just above, the Colossians heard him use that word negatively, in
the sense of "self-abasement" (2:18) and a kind of humiliation associated with
severity toward the body (2:23). Against that background, *tapeinophrosynē* in

its more usual sense of "humility" in this list comes across as saying: "*Genuine* humility, humility that pleases God, is what comes from deferring to one another in community life, as opposed to the false humility affected by the exponents of the 'philosophy.'"

To that list of five virtues Paul adds a practice essential to community life: **bearing with one another and forgiving one another, if one has a grievance against another.** Putting up with the troublesome (not forgetting that we ourselves are often troublesome) is a necessary lubricant in Christian life together. The rationale for forgiveness is the familiar one found in the Lord's Prayer (Matt 6:14): **As the Lord has forgiven you, so must you also do.** This is dramatized powerfully in the parable of the unforgiving servant (Matt 18:23–35).

3:14    Like a further garment over that layer of virtues, Paul urges the Colossians to **put on love.** Love is **the bond of perfection** in the sense that it completes and unifies the virtues, and more importantly it perfects, or matures, the community itself. This is parallel to Paul's well-known praise of love in 1 Cor 13, where he presents love as the "more excellent way," the virtue that animates and guides the exercise of the spiritual gifts, sometimes called "charisms," that he discusses in the adjoining chapters of that letter. Early in Colossians, Paul and Timothy referred to what they had heard from Epaphras regarding "the love you have for all the holy ones" (1:4) and "your love in the Spirit" (1:8). Again in 2:2, Paul refers to the Christian communities of the Lycus Valley as "brought together in love."

3:15    **And let the peace of Christ control your hearts, the peace into which you were also called in one body.** Apart from Paul's benediction in the prescript of the letter (1:2), this is the only other occurrence of the noun "peace" (*eirēnē*, as in the name Irene). But Paul surely chooses the word with awareness of his reference to Christ's "making peace [*eirēnopoiēsas*] by the blood of his cross" in the climactic line of the Christ hymn (1:20). Obviously, "the peace of Christ" is not merely the absence of war or violence but also the serenity and good order in relationships that proceeds from self-giving and self-denying love practiced in the Christian community, which participates in the self-emptying love of the Son.

And how exactly does one let the peace of Christ "control" one's heart? The verb for "control" is another rare word, used only here in the New Testament. It carries the connotation of decisiveness. The imperative is addressed to the community as a whole, so it could be paraphrased, "Beloved brothers and sisters, let the reign of Christ's peace be the determining factor in all your personal and community relationships."

The image of **the word of Christ** dwelling **in you richly** draws on the cosmic
poem in chapter 1. As the fullness of divinity dwells in Christ (1:19), the word
of Christ dwells in the gathered worshiping community. Although one might
easily hear "dwell in you" as applied to the individual, the pronoun is plural
and the phrase can also be translated "among you," and probably should be in
this context. How does this indwelling of the word of Christ come about? By
way of teaching and admonition, and by **singing psalms, hymns, and spiritual
songs with gratitude in your hearts to God.** Thus Paul gives us a fascinating
interpretation of what actually goes on in liturgical song. Even as we are praising God musically, we are supporting and teaching one another by way of this
shared prayer of praise (see the parallel sentiment in Eph 5:18–20).

The whole vision of chapter 1 stands in the background of these verses.
Moreover, verse 16 echoes 1:28:

> A  It is he whom we proclaim, *admonishing* everyone
>  B  and *teaching* everyone
>   C  with *all wisdom,*
>    D  that we may present everyone perfect in *Christ* (1:28).
>    D′ Let the word of *Christ* dwell in you richly,
>   C′ as in *all wisdom*
>  B′ you *teach*
> A′ and *admonish* one another (3:16).

Notice that this echo entails not simply a repetition of four words but also a
precise chiastic reversal of the order.[3] Such patterns are more a matter for the
ear than for the eye; for the alert audience of the oral reading of the letter, they
reinforce the unity and development of Paul's thought. Everything that stands
between 1:28 and 3:16 illustrates the wisdom of Christ that is fostered in the
community's teaching and admonishing. Christians help one another grow into
maturity as the body of Christ both individually and communally.

## Reflection and Application (3:8–16)

*Let the word of Christ dwell in you richly.* We have good reason to presume
that the typical setting for the communication of Paul's Letters was the gathering
of a house church on Sunday for worship. Colossians 3:16 gives us a sense of
Paul's understanding of this liturgical gathering and also provides a wonderful

---

3. See Heil, *Colossians*, 146.

stimulus for meditation on what we do in our day when we participate in the liturgy of the Eucharist. The "word of Christ" is the gospel, the mystery of Christ that Paul and his coworkers, such as Epaphras, proclaim. It is also, no doubt, the word of the Scriptures as fulfilled in Jesus. Paul may even have in mind the sharing of a Christian writing such as a letter from the likes of himself, James, or John. In our contemporary eucharistic liturgy, the service of the word is designed to enable this rich indwelling of the word of Christ within the assembled community. If we take some time to prepare individually through reading, study, meditation, and contemplation—focusing on the Scripture readings of the day—we contribute to the rich indwelling of the word in one another.

*As in wisdom you teach and admonish one another.* Our study of this letter has helped us appreciate that, for Paul, "wisdom" is the understanding and behavior that flows from recognizing everything as coming from the Father through his eternal Son, who is Lord of all creation. In his humanity, Christ redeems all who respond to what his Father has revealed through him. It is the goal of readers and homilists to mediate some of that wisdom of the word in their teaching and admonition.

*Singing psalms, hymns, and spiritual songs with gratitude in your hearts to God.* Does the "singing" here modify "teach and admonish one another"? It is not impossible that Paul recognizes that the *content* of the hymns teaches and challenges us as we proclaim the gospel to one another with voices raised in song. But even apart from that possible meaning, the language he chooses to describe worshipful singing helps us realize that we do not raise our voices together in song simply to feel good. This singing is from the heart and directed to God. Investing the extra energy that singing requires helps us recognize that we do indeed find a deep kind of unity precisely when we acknowledge and address our Father together. Singing at the liturgy—indeed, singing the liturgy itself—is no mere ornament. As St. Augustine put it, "Whoever sings prays twice." In a culture where many of us are a bit shy about raising our sometimes uncertain and often untrained voices in song, the act of liturgical singing calls for a commitment of healthy self-forgetfulness. This can only be a good thing.

# Work for the Lord and Not for Human Beings

## Colossians 3:17–4:1

This unit constitutes what scholars call a "household code," a standard feature in ancient moral exhortation, in which an author addresses the topic of inter-personal relationships in the typical Mediterranean household—those between husband and wife, father and children, and master and slaves. Paul Christianizes his approach to these relationships by showing how they are transformed in light of the lordship of Christ.

As the eighth unit in the overall ten-part chiastic structure of the letter, this part relates to its parallel member (1:15–23) by illustrating again how the heavenly lordship of Jesus plays out in, and transforms, the earthly relation-ships of daily life.[1]

### Living as the Household of the Lord of All (3:17–4:1)

[17]And whatever you do, in word or in deed, do everything in the name of the Lord Jesus, giving thanks to God the Father through him. [18]Wives, be subordinate to your husbands, as is proper in the Lord. [19]Husbands, love your wives, and avoid any bitterness toward them. [20]Children, obey your parents in everything, for this is pleasing to the Lord. [21]Fathers, do not provoke your children, so they may not become discouraged. [22]Slaves, obey your human masters in everything, not only when being watched,

1. The unit itself also forms a simple minichiasm: A (v. 17), B (18–21), B′ (22), A′ (3:23–4:1).

223

as currying favor, but in simplicity of heart, fearing the Lord. [23]Whatever you do, do from the heart, as for the Lord and not for others, [24]knowing that you will receive from the Lord the due payment of the inheritance; be slaves of the Lord Christ. [25]For the wrongdoer will receive recompense for the wrong he committed, and there is no partiality. [4:1]Masters, treat your slaves justly and fairly, realizing that you too have a Master in heaven.

---

**NT:** Eph 5:21–4:9; 1 Pet 2:13–3:12
**Catechism:** the Christian family, 2201–31
**Lectionary:** 3:14–15, 17, 23–24: Joseph the Worker

**3:17**   Verse 17 is better understood as the beginning of this unit rather than the end of the previous passage, because **whatever you do** (repeated in v. 23) and **do everything in the name of the Lord** is a perfect introduction to a passage about living fully under the lordship of Christ.[2] The follow-through, **giving thanks to God the Father through him,** puts the reader back in touch with the big picture established at 1:3—God the Father is the ultimate source of the creation and salvation of the universe, through the Lord Jesus Christ.

**3:18**   When we read **wives, be subordinate to your husbands,** we may hear a manifestation of patriarchy. In fact, two things mark this imperative as countercultural: (1) Whereas Greco-Roman household codes addressed the husband as head of the family, Paul first addresses the woman, and (2) he addresses her as a free agent, which is also exceptional for the time.[3] Moreover, when he adds **as is proper in the Lord** (*en kyriō*), he casts this mandate in an entirely new light: the context of Christian community lived as the body of Christ, precisely as spelled out in verses 11–16. This subordination to one another is "proper in the Lord" in the same way that humbly regarding others "as more important than yourselves" (Phil 2:3) is proper "in Christ" in Phil 2:1–4.

**3:19**   Moving to the other side of the spousal relationship, he refers not to domination but rather to love: **Husbands, love your wives, and avoid any bitterness toward them.** Note that, in this letter, as in Paul generally, *love* is always more than spontaneous attraction; it is a deliberate Christian choice to care for the other (see 1:4; 2:2; 3:14), and such love is animated by the Holy Spirit (see 1:8). Although Paul's instruction to wives occurs in the setting of traditional culture and can seem offensive to modern sensibilities, it helps to realize that Paul's teaching to spouses did not merely mirror the patriarchal culture of his day, but reenvisioned and modified the relationships between husbands and wives in light of Christ.

---

2. Also v. 16, with its echoing of 1:26, is more obviously a climax.
3. In the household code of the Letter to the Ephesians, the subordination is mutual: "Be subordinate to one another out of reverence for Christ" (Eph 5:21).

The charge to **children** is to **obey your parents in everything, for this is**     3:20–21
**pleasing to the Lord**. That last phrase might be better rendered, as it was in
the mandate to wives, "in the Lord," meaning in the Church as the body of
Christ. When it comes to the child-parent relationship, Paul says "parents,"
acknowledging a parental authority that *both* parents share with respect to
their children. But when he addresses parental attitudes toward the children,
he focuses solely on the father: **Fathers, do not provoke your children, so they**
**may not become discouraged**. Is it because mothers are more spontaneously
gentle with their children? Or is it because in the ancient Roman world the
*paterfamilias* had an absolute authority that could easily shade into harshness?
We can only guess. In any case Paul chooses to warn against what may have
been a common proclivity in a traditional society.

Having spent one verse apiece on four relationships, Paul now proceeds to     3:22
devote five verses to the relationship of slaves to masters. He repeats the phrase
used for children relating to parents: **obey your human masters in everything**.[4]
Pointedly, Paul calls them "*human* masters"—literally, "lords [*kyrioi*] according
to the flesh"—clearly distinguishing them from *the* Lord (*kyrios*), the risen Jesus.
The obedience is further specified: **not only when being watched, as currying**
**favor, but in simplicity of heart, fearing the Lord**. The first two clauses can be
paraphrased, "not only in *eye-service, as people-pleasers*." And, of course, "fearing the Lord"—the real Master, Christ—is not a matter of craven fear but the
fundamental posture of authentic religion in both Old and New Testaments.
Thus Paul's more elaborate counsel for the attitude of slaves is really a description of a habit of the heart that should inform all Christian relationships. The
inclusive nature of this mandate becomes evident in the three verses that follow.

**Whatever you do, do from the heart, as for the Lord and not for others**.     3:23–25
This is a mandate that even free persons can take to heart, for anyone can be
tempted to be motivated by people-pleasing—choosing to behave in a way that
will put me on the good side of those who can benefit me, rather than making choices consistent with my deepest commitments. The best curb against
that motivation is to be a "*Lord*-pleaser," **knowing that you will receive from**
**the Lord the due payment of the inheritance**. To drive home this point, Paul
returns to his favorite way of referring to discipleship: **be slaves of the Lord**
**Christ**. Paul has used the phrase "slaves of Jesus Messiah" of Christians generally
(e.g., Rom 6:20–23) and of himself in particular (1:7), as he will again in this
letter (4:7, 12). What prevents this from being a servile vision of Christianity

---

4. *Kyrios* can mean either "Lord," as a divine title for Jesus Christ, or "master" of a slave, a distinction
obvious in Greek but obscured in English translation.

## Did Paul Change His Mind about Slavery?

BIBLICAL BACKGROUND

When some contemporary readers read Paul's advice to slaves and masters with the Letter to Philemon fresh in their minds, they are amazed that he appears to simply take the institution of slavery for granted. If he could write the Colossian slaveholder expressing such love and compassion for the slave Onesimus, and even hint that he expects the master to release the slave, how can he discuss the relationship of slaves and masters without challenging the social structure that supports those roles? Indeed, this household code is sometimes cited to support the theory that Colossians is not an authentic letter of Paul, since it seems to compromise the attitude of his letter to Philemon, thus understood.

There is, however, no necessary contradiction between Paul's attitude toward slavery in Philemon and his advice to slaves and masters in Colossians. Indeed, Onesimus himself, who accompanied Tychicus as he carried both letters to Colossae (Col 4:9), would not have found the two letters contradictory. The Letter to Philemon, after all, does not challenge slavery as an institution. Within the conventions of the Roman Empire, Paul urges Philemon to honor the new relationship that has emerged with his slave's conversion to the Christian faith; Onesimus has become his brother and deserves the special love owed a member of the body of Christ. But that is not Paul's reason for requesting the slave's release. Paul has another purpose: he wants Philemon to release this Christian slave early so he can help Paul spread the gospel. Paul requests Philemon's manumission of Onesimus not as a moral obligation but as a free-will sacrifice. None of this confronts the Roman institution of slaveholding. What Paul mandates in Colossians is, however, a new perspective: in the Christian community *both* masters and slaves ought to live out this legal structure as "slaves" of the Master Christ, to whom both slave and master are answerable.[a]

a. This understanding of being both Christian and slave is in line with Paul's words in 1 Cor 7:20–24. See the comment on those verses in George Montague, *First Corinthians*, CCSS (Grand Rapids: Baker Academic, 2011), 126.

is that the framework is not that of captivity but of a loving household. "The inheritance" recalls the fact that the Christian is an adopted child of God, not literally a slave, and thus a coheir with the Son of the kingdom (1:12–13; see Rom 8:15–17). To be a people-pleaser is to miss out on the inheritance. If your earthly master is unresponsive to your good service and even harsh, don't worry. **For the wrongdoer will receive recompense for the wrong he committed, and there is no partiality** in God's ultimate judgment.

Finally, Paul completes the household code with a charge to slave masters     4:1
that flows inevitably from what he has been teaching. **Masters** (*kyrioi*), **treat
your slaves justly and fairly, realizing that you too have a Master** (*kyrios*) **in
heaven.** Thus the challenge addressed to slaves relative to masters holds true
for masters relative to the Master of us all.

### Reflection and Application (3:17–4:1)

*Applying Scripture today.* Our study of this household code gives rise to
several questions about applying Scripture. It highlights the importance of attending to cultural contexts—that of the original author and our own—when
we interpret any ancient text, especially a biblical one. It also reminds us of the
need for discernment in applying a biblical text to our own lives. Regarding
one's approach to social structures, the difference that Christian faith makes,
now as then, pertains primarily to the orientation of one's heart, and secondarily
to the transformation of the structure itself. The gospel has led to a slow but
world-transforming recognition of how certain social structures are incom-
patible with human dignity. This gradual process, of course, does not excuse
individual Christians from making a countercultural choice when so led by their
consciences. Blessed Franz Jägerstätter's refusal to fight for Hitler is a modern
example of such courageous witness.

*The need for discernment in interpretation.* The contemporary feminist critique
of patriarchy and our consequent growing sensitivity to the role of women, especially in North America, has made many understandably resistant to language
like "Wives, be subordinate to your husbands." In this case, our own cultural
setting can distract us from the fact that this imperative is qualified by "as is
proper in the Lord" and is followed immediately by "Husbands, love your wives
and avoid any bitterness toward them," advice that would not spring naturally
out of the Greco-Roman context. Similarly, we might hear the charge to Christian slaves that they obey their masters in all things as if it applied to slaves in
our own national history (as indeed it *was* so applied, for the wrong reasons).
But that social situation was not at all parallel to that of the first-century Roman
Empire, as explained in our study of Philemon. These insights remind us always
to attend, as well as we are able, to the differences between the cultural context
of the biblical passage and our own.

*The need for discernment in contemporary application.* Paul's failure to condemn slavery is no more surprising than Jesus' silence on that topic in his encounter with the centurion (Luke 7:1–10), who as an official of the occupying

Roman militia was clearly a slave owner ("I say . . . to my slave, 'Do this,' and he does it"). Yet Jesus praises his faith (7:9) without taking up the topic of slaveholding itself. There are two false applications regarding Jesus' and Paul's silence. One is to use that silence as an implied divine approval of the institution, as indeed some American slaveholders did to justify their practice of owning other human beings—now recognized as a violation of human dignity and rights. The other false move is to criticize Jesus and Paul for not acting as Abraham Lincoln did in his emancipation proclamation. Although social structural change was not feasible in the culture in which Jesus and Paul lived, the change they did bring about was in the way human relationships were lived out. Jesus affirms the centurion for acting in faith and compassion as he sought the healing of his dying slave. And Paul calls all Christians, male and female, slave and free, to live within the social structures of the Roman Empire as people who are themselves transformed by their ultimate allegiance to the Lord Jesus Christ rather than to the Lord Caesar. The first Christian difference is in the human heart; later, when the opportunity arises, the structure itself can be transformed. It takes time for the full implications of the gospel regarding human dignity to be fully recognized and then reflected in social structures. And of course such development is still ongoing.

*The Christian difference today.* Nowadays, when we are very much aware of both cultural diversity on planet Earth and the possibility of change in social structures through legislation in democratic systems, the Christian difference more often calls for efforts to change those structures when they are discovered to be unjust. The Serenity Prayer, of uncertain origin but made popular by Alcoholics Anonymous, provides a helpful perspective here. "God, grant me serenity to accept the things I cannot change, courage to change the things I can, and wisdom to know the difference." For citizens in the United States, where structural change remains desirable and possible (for instance, in the situation of immigrants, the urban poor, the unborn), it may be time to say that prayer with special emphasis on *courage* and *wisdom*.

# A Request for Prayer

## Colossians 4:2–6

In this unit Paul moves from the I-mode to the we-mode, implicitly including Timothy once again as coauthor, and returns to the themes of prayer, thanksgiving, grace, the word, and walking in wisdom, which were first established in 1:3–14. There he and Timothy told of their prayers for the new Christians of Colossae; here they reveal how they in turn count on the Colossians' prayers for the fruitfulness of their apostolic mission—prayers that God would give them both opportunities for and clarity in preaching the word.

### Pray for Our Mission and Walk in Wisdom (4:2–6)

²Persevere in prayer, being watchful in it with thanksgiving; ³at the same time, pray for us, too, that God may open a door to us for the word, to speak of the mystery of Christ, for which I am in prison, ⁴that I may make it clear, as I must speak. ⁵Conduct yourselves wisely toward outsiders, making the most of the opportunity. ⁶Let your speech always be gracious, seasoned with salt, so that you know how you should respond to each one.

**NT:** Matt 5:13; Acts 14:27; Eph 5:15–16; 1 Pet 3:15
**Catechism:** prayer of intercession and thanksgiving, 2634–38; vigilance, 2849

With the mandate **persevere in prayer**, Paul returns to a theme first sounded  **4:2–3**
in his and Timothy's prayer for the Colossians at the beginning of the letter. That
they are to be **watchful in it with thanksgiving** supports his ongoing theme that

---

## The Battle and Labor of Prayer

**LIVING TRADITION**

St. John Chrysostom reminds us why it is necessary to "persevere" and "be watchful" in prayer.

> Paul realizes that continuing in prayer can frequently produce restlessness. Therefore he writes, "watching," that is, be sober, avoid wandering. For the devil knows, yes he knows, how great a good prayer is. Hence, he presses heavily on us as we pray. And Paul also knows how careless many are when they pray. Thus he says "continue" in prayer, as something that takes hard work, "watching therein with thanksgiving." . . . This is how the saints normally pray, giving thanks for the benefits shared by all.[a]

a. *Homilies on Colossians* 10, quoted in ACCS 9:54.

---

Christians should not forget the grace and freedom they have already come to experience in Christ. Paul's move into the first person plural brings to the listeners' awareness that Timothy is still there in the background as coauthor of this communiqué: **pray for us, too, that God may open a door to us**. The **word** of course is "the word of truth, the gospel" (1:5), "the word of Christ" (3:16) that they first received from Epaphras. The prayer that God open "a door . . . for the word" recalls Acts 14:27, where Luke writes that Paul and Barnabas "reported what God had done with them and how he had opened the door of faith to the Gentiles." The word Paul proclaims is further described as **the mystery of Christ**, God's secret, now divulged, that the Jewish Messiah is for Gentiles too (1:26–27). Although Paul has alluded to the larger growth of the Church beyond the Lycus Valley communities ("just as in the whole world it is bearing fruit and growing," 1:6), here for the first time he rouses the Colossians to their own part in this missionary outreach, in this instance by their intercessory prayer.

4:4        The side note, "for which I am in prison" (literally, "for which I am bound"), can and probably does carry a double meaning, especially as Paul follows it with **that I may make it clear, as I must speak** (literally, "as I am bound to speak"). Paul is "bound" in two senses: commissioned by God, he is bound to speak in the sense of being divinely compelled; and because his mission runs up against both Jewish and Roman opposition, he is bound in prison.[1]

4:5        Now Paul picks up the ongoing theme of "walking in wisdom" (1:9–10; 2:6), that is, putting faith into action: **conduct yourselves wisely toward outsiders**,

---

1. On this see John Paul Heil, *Colossians: Encouragement to Walk in All Wisdom as Holy Ones in Christ*, Early Christianity 4 (Atlanta: Society of Biblical Literature, 2010), 180.

**making the most of the opportunity.** Paul uses another rich word from his fertile vocabulary, "make the most of" (*exagorazō*), which has "marketplace" (*agora*) in the middle of it, suggesting the readiness and opportunism of an entrepreneur with great street sense. Evangelization is a matter of being alert to the opportunities to share one's faith in the flow of daily life.

Their conversation is to be **gracious** and **seasoned with salt.** Just as a good     4:6
cook uses salt in a way that renders foods more tasty and attractive, Christians are to present the good news gracefully and attractively. The personal testimonies of those touched by Christ and the Holy Spirit are powerful when communicated with the spontaneity and plain talk that people use in discussing sports, politics, their favorite music, or their grandchildren. This is much like the advice of Peter: "Always be ready to give an explanation to anyone who asks you for a reason for your hope" (1 Pet 3:15). And Jesus calls his disciples to be a community of salt and light (Matt 5:13). This, too, is a matter of prayer and watching (v. 2), **so that you know how you should respond,** for Christians are "bound" to do so, just as Paul is.


## Reflection and Application (4:2–6)

This short passage provides fertile material for reflection on our Christian vocation as evangelists, that is, people who spread the good news of Jesus Christ.

*God opens the door.* Luke in Acts, and Paul in his letters, are clear that sharing the gospel is a participation in something *God* is doing. Shortly after the text quoted above (Acts 14:27), Luke writes that Paul and Barnabas reported to the church in Jerusalem "what God had done with them" (Acts 15:4). No doubt this experience underlies Paul's reference to himself and others as God's coworkers (4:11). He spoke of the same experience of the power of God working through him earlier in this letter: "For this I labor and struggle, in accord with the exercise of his power working within me" (1:29).

*God calls us to be "opportunists" in this enterprise.* This idea is captured beautifully in Col 4:5–6: "Conduct yourselves wisely toward outsiders, making the most of the opportunity." The opportunity is given; this is what is meant by God "opening the door." But it calls for response, alertness, and creativity on the part of the Christian. We can easily be tempted to delegate the spread of the gospel to those ordained to preaching and teaching roles in the Church, or to people especially trained in apologetics and ready to take on the enemies of Christianity. But Paul addresses his mandate to share the gospel to his entire audience, and so to all of us. His way of putting it can help us see that we evangelize best when we are simply alert to the opportunities that arise when we encounter people who hunger, perhaps unknowingly, for the good news we enjoy. If we readily share our enthusiasm about relatively trivial news (a great recipe, a terrific movie, the victory of our favorite football team), is it too much of a stretch to be ready to share our experience of Christ just as spontaneously?

# Commendations, Greetings, and Blessing

## Colossians 4:7–18

After providing a note of recommendation for Tychicus and Onesimus, the bearers of the letter, Paul relays greetings from his Jewish Christian companions and his Gentile coworkers, including Epaphras, whom the Colossians know well. Then Paul sends greetings to the Christians of Laodicea and to a house church near Colossae, and an exhortation to a church leader, before adding a greeting in his own hand. Even these seemingly mundane pleasantries reward a close reading.

### Commendation of Two Coworkers for the Gospel (4:7–9)

⁷Tychicus, my beloved brother, trustworthy minister, and fellow slave in the Lord, will tell you all the news of me. ⁸I am sending him to you for this very purpose, so that you may know about us and that he may encourage your hearts, ⁹together with Onesimus, a trustworthy and beloved brother, who is one of you. They will tell you about everything here.

NT: Eph 6:21–22; Philem 10

We meet Tychicus in Acts 20:4, a companion of Paul on his mission to Jeru-  **4:7–8**
salem with the collection from among the Gentile churches of Macedonia and Achaia. He is mentioned in 2 Tim 4:12 as being sent to Ephesus (perhaps on the

same journey in which he carries this letter to the Colossians).[1] And the Letter to the Ephesians repeats most of the words describing him here: **beloved brother** and **trustworthy minister . . . in the Lord** (Eph 6:21). The inclusion of **fellow slave** here has a special resonance, coming as it does just after the instructions to literal masters and slaves, and also because Tychicus accompanies the slave Onesimus. Paul is quite explicit that Tychicus **will tell you all the news of me** and that he is sending him **for this very purpose, so that you may know about us and that he may encourage your hearts**. Thus, what this man will say about Paul and his companions is not idle chatter but real news that this trustworthy coworker has been authorized to share.

The fact that Col 4:7–8 is repeated verbatim in Eph 6:21–22 (except for the phrase "and fellow slave") contributes in a helpful way to discussions about the relationship between these two letters and about their authenticity. Scholars who argue that Colossians and Ephesians are †pseudonymous—that is, written by followers of Paul in his name, probably after his death—hold that such realistic details about carriers and greetings are added by the pseudonymous author to evoke the time and circumstances of Paul, "what Paul would say if he were still with us." But that would be more like forgery, something intended to deceive—not a convention of pseudonymous writing. And if verisimilitude were the motive for repeating the reference to Tychicus in Ephesians, why did the alleged pseudonymous writer not also name some of the greeters found at the end of Colossians? It makes better sense to me to understand the Tychicus reference in terms of the scenario presented above (see p. 155), namely, that Tychicus really is the bearer of the encyclical to Ephesus and perhaps letters to other Asian towns as well. On that hypothesis, the name of Onesimus is omitted from Ephesians because he stayed with Philemon's household after his return to Colossae. And the greetings from Aristarchus, Mark, Jesus-Justus, Epaphras, Luke, and Demas are dropped because they are not pertinent to the much wider and distant audiences addressed in the encyclical letter we call Ephesians.

**4:9**       We have no reason to doubt that the **Onesimus** named here is the slave we learn about in Paul's Letter to Philemon. Paul affirms him with the same adjectives with which he affirmed Tychicus, **beloved brother** and **trustworthy**. Paul reminds the recipients that Onesimus is **one of you**, not simply as a fellow Colossian but now also as a fellow Christian and thus part of the house church. Paul also authorizes him along with Tychicus as a dependable reporter of news: **they will tell you about everything here**.

---

1. As explained in the introduction to Colossians, it is not implausible that Paul was in an Ephesian jail when he sent Tychicus with a message to the Ephesian church.

## Greetings from Three Jewish Christians (4:10–11)

<sup>10</sup>Aristarchus, my fellow prisoner, sends you greetings, as does Mark the cousin of Barnabas (concerning whom you have received instructions; if he comes to you, receive him), <sup>11</sup>and Jesus, who is called Justus, who are of the circumcision; these alone are my co-workers for the kingdom of God, and they have been a comfort to me.

**NT:** Acts 12:12, 25; 13:5, 13; 15:36–39; Philem 24; 1 Pet 5:13
**Catechism:** collaborating with the creator, 307

Now comes the usual Pauline list of people sending greetings from his lo-    **4:10–11**
cation. **Aristarchus** is called literally a "co-captive," which is an unusual word for a civilian prisoner, though Paul used it of Epaphras in Philem 23 and also of Andronicus and Junia in Rom 16:7. The Greek noun for "captive" usually applies to a prisoner of war.[2] As he often does elsewhere, Paul adds the prefix *syn* to make a new word meaning "*co*-captive." So Paul appears to be think-ing metaphorically of imprisonment for the faith as being "taken captive" in the †eschatological battle against evil. In this sense, "fellow captive" is similar to calling Archippus "fellow soldier" in Philem 2. It is also like the military imagery of Eph 6:11–17, where Paul describes the Christian struggle "with the principalities, with the powers, with the world rulers of this present darkness, with the evil spirits in the heavens"—language that has much in common with that used of hostile spiritual powers in Colossians. Aristarchus, a Thessalonian, was with Paul in Ephesus (Acts 19:29). Along with Timothy and Tychicus, he was part of the group of seven that accompanied Paul in bringing the collec-tion to Jerusalem (Acts 20:4). We last hear of him sailing with Paul to Rome in Acts 27:2.

**Mark,** the son of Mary of Jerusalem,[3] is commonly considered the same Mark listed in Philemon, and is traditionally identified as the Evangelist of that name. The reference to Mark's blood relative **Barnabas**, a frequent travel companion of Paul, identifies him as the John Mark we meet in Acts and occa-sions a parenthetical note of commendation: Paul appears suddenly to recall that Colossae is on Barnabas's itinerary and wants to make sure that Mark is well received as a valued coworker when he turns up there. Regarding **Jesus, who is called Justus,** we know nothing beyond what we learn from this verse; "Jesus" is the Greek form of the common Jewish name Joshua, and "Justus" is a

2. In the New Testament only in Luke 4:18 (LXX Isa 61:1).
3. Acts 12:12, 25; 15:37–39; 2 Tim 4:11; 1 Pet 5:13; he is called simply John at Acts 13:5, 13.

Latinized second name meaning "righteous"—a moniker he could have earned either before or after his conversion to Christ.

Why does Paul make a point that these three—Aristarchus, Mark, and Jesus Justus—**are of the circumcision** and **alone are my co-workers for the kingdom of God**? Given that this letter to (mainly) Gentiles has made a point of the irrelevance of "circumcision made by hand" for Gentiles (2:11–13), this underscoring of the Jewish Christians who share his ministry may be an aside to the minority of Jewish Christians, to encourage them that others of their background have not succumbed to the seductions of the "philosophy." Paul's unusual use of "kingdom of God" to refer to the goal of the gospel mission[4] supports the idea that it is an aside to Jewish Christians, for the term requires some familiarity with Jewish background and would have been a more natural expression in speaking with his Jewish peers. In the synoptic Gospels, "kingdom of God" is Jesus' term for the visible sovereignty of God over the whole world, which has begun with his coming, is extended in the Church, and will be fully realized at the end of time.

## Greetings from Your Founder and Two Other Gentiles (4:12–14)

[12]**Epaphras sends you greetings; he is one of you, a slave of Christ [Jesus], always striving for you in his prayers so that you may be perfect and fully assured in all the will of God.** [13]**For I can testify that he works very hard for you and for those in Laodicea and those in Hierapolis.** [14]**Luke the beloved physician sends greetings, as does Demas.**

**Catechism:** prayer of petition, 2629, 2632

4:12–13    The greeting from their founder, **Epaphras**, with Paul's special tribute to him, is the centerpiece of this passage (4:17–18). As in the case of the slave Onesimus, Paul reminds the Colossians that Epaphras is **one of you**. Whether he means that Epaphras grew up in Colossae or that he became one of them as a fellow Christian during his evangelical ministry there we can only guess. Once again Paul uses his favorite countercultural honorific title, **slave of Christ**—recalling that he referred to Epaphras as "beloved fellow slave" when he first mentioned him (1:7), as he also complimented Tychicus as "fellow slave in the Lord" just above. Paul's climactic tribute becomes the †chiastic center of the passage:

---

4. The phrase "kingdom of God" turns up seven other times in the Pauline corpus—Rom 14:17; 1 Cor 4:20; 6:9–10 (twice); 15:50; Gal 5:21; and 2 Thess 1:5.

   C  always *striving for you* in his prayers

      D  so that you may be perfect and fully assured in all the will of
      God.

   C′  For I can testify that he *works very hard for you.* . . .

Paul's description of Epaphras's **striving** (*agonizō*) in prayer for the full spiritual *perfection* of *all* the Lycus Valley Christians echoes precisely the language
he used of his and Timothy's ministry: "that we may present *everyone perfect* in
Christ. For this I labor and struggle [*agonizō*]" (1:28–29, italics added). Epaphras
"agonizes" on their behalf for the same goal for which Paul "agonizes," namely,
that they become "perfect" (*teleios*), fully mature in Christ.

    To round off the group of local greeters, he adds the names **Luke**—yes, the      **4:14**
one traditionally identified as the author of the Gospel of Luke and the Acts
of the Apostles—and **Demas**, both also mentioned as coworkers at the end
of the Letter to Philemon. These two men are also named toward the end of
2 Timothy, where Demas is said to have abandoned Paul, whereas Luke is still
with him (2 Tim 4:9–11).

## Paul Blesses Other Lycus Valley Christians and Signs Off (4:15–18)

---

[15]**Give greetings to the brothers in Laodicea and to Nympha and to the
church in her house.** [16]**And when this letter is read before you, have it read
also in the church of the Laodiceans, and you yourselves read the one
from Laodicea.** [17]**And tell Archippus, "See that you fulfill the ministry that
you received in the Lord."** [18]**The greeting is in my own hand, Paul's. Remember my chains. Grace be with you.**

---

**NT:** Rev 3:14–22

    Finally, Paul himself extends greetings to Christians in **Laodicea** and to a     **4:15–18**
house church leader named **Nympha**, presumably also in the Lycus Valley,
though no location is specified, nor does the New Testament tell us anything
else about this person. The gender is ambiguous, as the form used here can
either be the accusative of *Nymphas*, a man's name, or of *Nympha*, a woman's name. The uncertainty of the gender of the name led to variation in the
manuscripts regarding the possessive pronoun modifying house—"her" or
"his." Since the manuscript evidence favors "her," our translation (along with
the NIV and NRSV) identifies her as a female house church leader called

Nympha.[5] This reading of the text is consistent with the other New Testament testimony regarding female leadership in first-century Christian churches—see the hospitality of Mary, mother of John Mark, in the Jerusalem community (Acts 12:12) and that of Lydia in Philippi (Acts 16:14–15, 40); the ministry of Chloe and Phoebe in Corinth and nearby Cenchreae (1 Cor 1:11; Rom 16:1); that of Prisca in Rome, Corinth, and Ephesus (Acts 18:2, 26; 1 Cor 16:19); and of Euodia and Syntyche in Philippi (Phil 4:2–3).

The phrase **when this letter is read before you** provides a reminder that this letter, like most documents of the ancient world, was a script intended not for silent reading but for oral performance before an audience gathered for the occasion. The "you" is plural, as usual. We learn here that this letter is also meant to be read before the Christian community of **Laodicea.** Apparently the church in this much larger town, just a few miles down the Lycus River, was subject to the same challenge that the "philosophy" presented to the Christians in Colossae. It is fascinating that the message to the church in Laodicea in the book of Revelation (Rev 3:14–22) has several things in common with the Letter to the Colossians that was also read before them:

a. a reference to Christ as *archē*—"source," "head," beginning, or ruler—of God's creation (Rev 3:14; Col 1:18, 2:10),

b. the image of an open door representing a faith response (Rev 3:20; Col 4:3), and

c. the risen Son enthroned with the Father (Rev 3:21; Col 3:1).

It is possible that John the Seer knew the **Laodiceans** would be at home with these concepts and images that Paul and Timothy had introduced to them in the Letter to the Colossians.

The instruction that the Colossians are to **read** the letter **from Laodicea** raises questions. Is this a reference to the letter we know as Ephesians? Or to a lost letter? We can only guess. Similarly, the instruction to **tell Archippus, "See that you fulfill the ministry that you received in the Lord,"** also invites hypotheses. A common Greek name, Archippus is found in the New Testament only here and as one of the three named addressees in the Letter to Philemon. Given that this final section of Colossians also includes six other names found

---

5. The KJV and Rheims have "Nymphas . . . the church at *his* house." This textual issue is similar to the question of the partner of Andronicus, *Iounian,* in Rom 16:7, which could be the accusative of either *Iounias,* a masculine name, or *Iounia,* a feminine name. Given that the female Latin name Junia appears more than 250 times in Rome alone, whereas the male name Junias is nowhere attested, editors lean toward Junia. For a discussion of these textual variants, see Bruce M. Metzger, *A Textual Commentary on the Greek New Testament* (New York: American Bible Society, 1994), 475–76, 560.

in Philemon, it is reasonable to conclude that this Archippus is the same one addressed by Paul and Timothy as "fellow soldier" in Philem 2. This has led to speculation that Archippus is the pastor of the Colossian house church, or even that he is the real master of the slave Onesimus; but the priority of Philemon's name among those addressed in Philem 1 trumps those hypotheses. At the end of the day, the letter from Laodicea and the unspecified ministry of Archippus remain mysterious. These questions are a healthy reminder of an enduring fact: on the most important level, the New Testament letters are the Word of God and carry profound meaning for Christians of any era; yet, on another level, we should not forget that we are reading "other people's mail." As another New Testament writer said regarding the Letters of Paul, "In them there are some things hard to understand" (2 Pet 3:16).

When Paul writes, **The greeting is in my own hand, Paul's,** he is not sim-    4:18
ply stating the obvious, as in, "Here I am, Paul, signing my own letter." Most scholars agree that he is following the convention of authorizing a document that another person has penned (perhaps, in this case, Timothy). We noted this custom when we commented on Philem 19: "I, Paul, write this in my own hand: I will pay." There, of course, Paul's point is that his promise to pay for any damages incurred by Onesimus takes on the nature of a legal IOU note. But it also fits the scenario of another hand inscribing the Letter to Philemon, with Paul adding verse 19, and possibly the remainder of the letter, to a text otherwise penned by a scribe (again, possibly coauthor Timothy). Once more, we are reminded of the fact that authorship did not necessarily consist of putting pen to parchment. We are quite familiar with this practice in our own day, when executive assistants not only take dictation but often work with basic ideas given by their bosses—putting them into their own expression, subject to the final approval of the official author. This is a venerable tradition, for instance, with regard to papal encyclicals.

**Remember my chains.** This plea, together with the final clause in 4:3 ("for which I am in prison"), are the only statements that mark this document as a Prison Letter, but they are enough to provide that important context. We can be sure that Paul's plea to remember his chains is no "poor me" whimper. As we know, especially from Philippians, he is convinced that, far from hindering the mission, his confinement actually advances the gospel (Phil 1:12).

His final words, **Grace be with you,** repeat the blessing with which he and Timothy began. No perfunctory good-bye, "grace" (*charis*)—meaning the gift of God—has been the topic of the whole letter. This whole communiqué has been an "agonizing" effort (see 1:29; 2:1) to refresh these new Christians of Colossae in their appreciation for the grace of God they have received in accepting the lordship of Jesus Christ into their lives—so that they are strengthened against compromising that gift by succumbing to the false philosophy and its competing spiritual powers.

### Reflection and Application (4:7–18)

Readers of Paul's Letters today may be inclined to give scant attention to the commendations, greetings, and blessings that end these documents. These can seem at first to be little more than conventional proprieties. Closer inspection, however, usually shows that even these personal details provide something to enlighten our understanding and nurture our faith.

*Evangelization as collaborative venture.* It would be easy to think of Paul as a kind of lone ranger, moving around as he was led by the Spirit, sometimes with a particular companion like Silas or Barnabas, but mainly on his own. The endings of his letters, however, remind us that he was part of a collaborative network. Sometimes the collaboration is simultaneous, for example, Paul working in the same town with the likes of Aquila and Prisca (Acts 18). Sometimes the collaboration is sequential ("I planted, Apollos watered, but God caused the growth," 1 Cor 3:6). This final section of Colossians is another rich illustration of evangelization by networking. In the case of ministry in the Lycus Valley—Colossae, Laodicea, Hierapolis, and wherever Nympha lives—it was Epaphras who did the planting. And now, by means of this letter, Paul waters, with robust confidence that God the Father will give the growth. The witness of the Pauline network should be an encouragement to the kind of networking entailed in Christian ministry in our own day. This is especially evident in the collaborative approach to Rite of Christian Initiation of Adults (RCIA) programs carried out by most parishes. Indeed, this community process, involving a variety of teachers and participating sponsors, may well be the most explicit form of evangelization practiced in the US Catholic Church today.

*Female leadership in the church.* Like the hospitable women we meet in Acts (Lydia and Mary, the mother of John Mark), and the female evangelists and ministers we learn about in the closing sections of Romans and 1 Corinthians (e.g., Junia and Prisca), Paul's reference to Nympha and the church at her house serves as yet another reminder of women's perennial role in the spreading and sustaining of ecclesial communities.

*The Colossian "philosophy" today.* The puzzle of precisely identifying the nature of the philosophy that prompted Paul's writing of this letter could lead a contemporary reader to dismiss Colossians as irrelevant to the life and mission of the Church today. That would be unfortunate. As our study of this document reveals, Paul tells us enough about the Colossian error to show us that the espousal of a particular religious practice or ideology by a dissident group, accompanied by their dismissal of others who do not share their ideology, has been a recurring threat to the centrality of Jesus Christ as sovereign Lord. Whatever the precise occasion that led to Paul and Timothy's writing of this letter, it remains a masterful teaching and celebration of the role of the eternal Son of the Father in the creation and redemption of us all—and of everything else that exists. The letter's sketch of the false teachers provides a cautionary sidebar regarding the folly of creating factions within the Christian community.

# Suggested Resources

## Introductions to Paul's Life, Writings, and Message

Gorman, Michael J. *Apostle of the Crucified Lord: A Theological Introduction to Paul and His Letters*. Grand Rapids: Eerdmans, 2004. Professor of New Testament at St. Mary's Seminary and University in Baltimore, Gorman has written a state-of-the-art introduction to Paul and his writings. After a broad introduction, he takes the reader through each of the books ascribed to Paul.

———. *Reading Paul*. Eugene, OR: Cascade, 2008. A brief summary of Gorman's 2004 book, discussing Paul's writing by way of major themes.

Harrington, Daniel J. *Meeting St. Paul Today: Understanding the Man, His Mission, and His Message*. Chicago: Loyola Press, 2008. Harrington, a Jesuit priest, provides an excellent introduction to Paul, his work, and his writings.

Heil, John Paul. *The Letters of Paul as Rituals of Worship*. Eugene, OR: Cascade, 2011. Professor of New Testament at the Catholic University of America, Heil treats each of the Pauline Letters as a script to be performed for a community gathered for worship over which Paul presides through the letter, thereby evoking and sharing in the prayer of his audience.

Matera, Frank J. *New Testament Theology: Exploring Diversity and Unity*. Louisville: Westminster John Knox, 2007. Within the context of a comprehensive theology of the New Testament, Matera devotes thirty succinct pages to Philemon, Philippians, and Colossians.

Murphy-O'Connor, Jerome. *Paul: His Story*. New York: Oxford University Press, 2004. Murphy-O'Connor, a Dominican priest, presents a moving reconstruction of Paul's life and ministry.

Wright, N. T. *Paul: In Fresh Perspective*. Minneapolis: Fortress, 2005. Wright, formerly an Anglican bishop of the Diocese of Durham, England, and now professor of New Testament and early Christianity at the University of St. Andrews, offers a helpful introduction to key themes in Paul's writings as well as a brief systematic presentation of the structures of his theology.

## Commentaries on Individual Prison Letters of Paul

Fee, Gordon D. *Paul's Letter to the Philippians*. New International Commentary on the New Testament. Grand Rapids: Eerdmans, 1995. A thorough and detailed exegesis by an evangelical scholar who works carefully with the Greek text. A good resource for in-depth work on specific passages.

Fitzmyer, Joseph A. *The Letter to Philemon: A New Translation with Introduction and Commentary*. Anchor Bible 34c. New York: Doubleday, 2000. Fitzmyer, a Jesuit priest, provides here a solid commentary with rich notes and comprehensive bibliography.

Fowl, Stephen E. *Philippians*. Two Horizons New Testament Commentary. Grand Rapids: Eerdmans, 2005. Professor of theology at Loyola College in Maryland, Fowl approaches the Letter to the Philippians within the "two horizons" of exegesis and theological and pastoral application. A full and satisfying treatment of this letter.

McDonald, Margaret Y. *Colossians and Ephesians*. Sacra Pagina. Collegeville, MN: Liturgical Press, 2000. McDonald's detailed social-scientific interpretation of Colossians occupies the first 189 pages of this volume.

Osiek, Carolyn. *Philippians, Philemon*. Abingdon New Testament Commentaries. Nashville: Abingdon, 2000. Osiek, a religious of the Sacred Heart, devotes 21 pages to Philemon and 110 pages to Philippians.

Sumney, Jerry L. *Colossians: A Commentary*. New Testament Library. Louisville: Westminster John Knox, 2008. Professor of biblical studies at Lexington Theological Seminary, Sumney has written an up-to-date, in-depth, carefully reasoned, and pastorally sensitive commentary on this letter. A recent discovery for me, this is now my favorite commentary on Colossians for consulting the state of the question on a given passage.

Thurston, Bonnie B., and Judith M. Ryan. *Philippians and Colossians*. Sacra Pagina. Collegeville, MN: Liturgical Press, 2005. Ryan's comprehensive commentary occupies the last ninety-two pages of this book; especially thorough on slavery in the ancient world.

Witherington, Ben, III. *Friendship and Finances in Philippi: The Letter of Paul to the Philippians*. The New Testament in Context. Valley Forge, PA: Trinity Press International, 1994. A fine, brief commentary on the whole letter, highlighting the themes of friendship and finances.

## More-Specialized Studies

Arnold, Clinton E. *The Colossian Syncretism: The Interface between Christianity and Folk Religion in Colossae*. Tübingen: J. C. B. Mohr (Paul Siebeck), 1995. A fascinating effort to reconstruct the historical context of the Letter to the Colossians.

Fee, Gordon D. *Pauline Christology: An Exegetical-Theological Study*. Peabody, MA: Hendrickson, 2007. A thorough exegesis of all the passages in the thirteen letters ascribed to Paul that pertain to his presentation of the person of Christ—first by document in chronological order, then by theme. For advanced students interested in the language and grammatical issues as well as the main issues in the history of interpretation for each passage.

Gorman, Michael J. *Inhabiting the Cruciform God: Kenosis, Justification, and Theosis in Paul's Narrative Soteriology*. Grand Rapids: Eerdmans, 2009. A theological study of Paul's understanding of how Jesus saves, focusing on the Christ story of Philippians 2 as Paul's "master story." For the more advanced student.

Hellerman, Joseph H. *Reconstructing Honor in Roman Philippi*. Carmen Christi *as* Cursus Pudorum. Society for New Testament Studies Monograph series 132. New York: Cambridge University Press, 2005. A detailed effort to read Philippians against what we know about the social setting of Philippi as a Roman colony, and what it must have been like to be part of the Christian minority there. Focuses especially on the meaning of the Christ hymn of Phil 2 as understood against the honor/shame culture of the Roman Empire.

# Glossary

**amanuensis**: a scribe or secretary employed to write from an author's dictation or to compose a document under the employer's authorization.

*Carmen Christi*: Latin for "song of Christ," or "Christ hymn." A traditional name for Phil 2:5–11, especially when treated as a free-standing composition.

**Chiasm, chiastic**: a pattern of writing in which words, phrases, or clauses are arranged in parallel, such that the order of elements in the first part is mirrored in reverse in the second part. The arrangement A–B–C–D–C′–B′–A′ represents a chiastic structure. The word "chiasm" derives from the Greek letter *chi*, or X, where the letter itself reflects the mirror structure, the right half reflecting a reverse image of the left half. For a familiar example, consider Isaiah 6:10:

> You are to make the *heart* of this people sluggish,     [A]
>> to dull their *ears* [B]
>>> and close their *eyes*;   [C]
>>> Else their *eyes* will see, [C′]
>> their *ears* hear,   [B′]
> their *heart* understand     [A′]
> and they will turn and be healed.

The chiasm is a common feature of ancient writing, abundantly illustrated in the Old and New Testaments. Sometimes entire documents are structured chiastically.

**Christ**: a title of Jesus, from the Greek word *Christos*, "anointed," translating the Hebrew *mashiach*, "Messiah," in English. It expresses the faith claim that Jesus fulfills Jewish expectations for an end-time "anointed one" of God—albeit in an unexpected way. Whereas most Jews were expecting a warrior-king like David, or a temple priest, or a prophet like Moses, Jesus fulfilled all of these roles, but in a transcendent way.

**Christology:** formal speculation and teaching regarding the person of Jesus Christ and his divine and human natures; the systematic unfolding of Christian faith regarding Jesus as Messiah and Lord, especially as expressed in the early councils of the Church.

**disputed letters:** six New Testament letters that bear Paul's name but whose authorship scholars have questioned: Ephesians, Colossians, 2 Thessalonians, 1 and 2 Timothy, and Titus. See also **undisputed letters.**

**docetism** (from the Greek *dokein,* "to seem"): a heretical belief that Jesus only *appeared* to have a body and that he did not really die on the cross.

**eschatology, eschatological** (from Greek *eschata,* "last things"): all that concerns the end of human history, the glorious return of Christ, the resurrection of the dead, the last judgment, and eternal life in the kingdom. According to the New Testament, the end begins with Jesus' passion and resurrection, which is the transition from the former age to the new and final age of salvation history. Like Ephesians and the Gospel of John, Colossians is often described as having a *realized eschatology* because it focuses on the blessings of the new age that Christians already enjoy—that is, the blessings that are already realized (1:13–14; 2:11–15; 3:3). Nevertheless, the letter also points to a *future eschatology* (1:5, 22, 28; 3:4).

**flesh** (Greek *sarx*): (1) the material that covers the bones of a human or animal body (Col 2:13); (2) the physical body as a functioning entity (Col 1:22, 24; 2:1, 5; Phil 1:22, 24); (3) fallen human nature characterized by sinful inclinations and disordered desires (Gal 5:19–21; Col 2:11, 13, 18, 23); (4) the outward dimension of human life (Phil 3:3–4; Col 3:22; Philem 16).

**Gentiles** (Greek *ethnē,* also translated as "nations"): (1) people of non-Jewish descent; (2) people who are not a part of God's people, who do not know God, and who live immorally and unjustly ("pagans" and "sinners"). In the letters covered in this commentary, the addressees are primarily Gentiles, though the word appears as a topic only in Col 1:27. The Christian mission to the Gentiles becomes an important topic in Galatians, Romans, Matthew, and Luke-Acts.

**gospel:** from the Anglo-Saxon *godspel,* literally, "good news," a translation of the Greek *euangelion.* While its primary reference in contemporary English is to the four documents attributed to Matthew, Mark, Luke, and John, the main meaning is the content of Christian preaching: the good news about the life, death, and resurrection of Jesus Christ—the fullness of God's revelation to humankind. Sometimes "gospel" refers to the *content* of the good news; sometimes it refers to the *process* of evangelization, as when Paul speaks of "partnership for the gospel" (Phil 1:5) or advancing the gospel (Phil 1:12). In the context of Jesus' mission ("Repent, and believe in the gospel," Mark 1:15) it refers to his proclamation of the kingdom of God.

**incarnation** (from Latin *incarnatio*, literally, "enfleshment"): the eternal Son of God's taking on of human nature in the womb of Mary. While the term itself is not found in Scripture, it is the traditional word for referring to what is said in the prologue of John: "The Word became flesh and made his dwelling among us" (1:14).

*inclusio*: a literary device indicating the unity of a passage by marking the beginning and the end with some kind of repetition, either of vocabulary or of image. For example, Rev 19:9–10 and 22:8–9 frame a unit of seven visions.

**Judaizers, Judaizing**: opponents of Paul, especially in Galatia, who compromised the good news of salvation through faith in Christ by insisting that Gentile Christians must be circumcised and adhere to the ceremonial observances of the Mosaic law.

**law**: (1) the law of Moses written in the first five books of the Hebrew Bible, the Torah; (2) Scripture in general, as in the expression "the law and the prophets." The word can also include much of the range of meaning "law" carries in ordinary English: "custom, rule, principle, norm," and "constitutional or statutory or legal system." In the Prison Letters covered by this commentary, "law" occurs only in Phil 3:5, 6, and 9.

**Lord** (Greek *kyrios*): In the oral reading of the Hebrew Bible, when Jews come to the ineffable name of God, YHWH, they say instead *adonai* ("Lord"). Therefore, in the Greek translation of the Hebrew Bible, YHWH is rendered by *kyrios*, the translation of *adonai*. Given this background, when "the Lord" is used as a title for Jesus, it carries the connotation of divinity. Philippians 2:11 is a clear example of this. Because *kyrios* was also applied to the Roman emperor in civic worship, its application to Jesus Christ can carry the countercultural message, "*Jesus*—not Caesar—is Lord!" *Kyrios* appears in the liturgical acclamation *kyrie eleēson*, "Lord, have mercy!"

**LXX**: the Roman numeral for seventy, standing for the legendary seventy translators of the Hebrew Bible into Greek around 250 BC. The name for that translation, the Septuagint, derives from this seventy. LXX is used as a marker to indicate that the citation of a biblical text comes from the Septuagint rather than from the Hebrew original.

**Macedonia**: Roman province comprising the area that is today the northern part of Greece and the republic of Macedonia. Macedonian cities in which Paul established churches are Philippi, Thessalonica, and possibly Beroea.

**Messiah**: See **Christ**.

**mystery** (Greek *mystērion*, "secret"): God's saving plan kept hidden for ages but now revealed by the Holy Spirit to the apostles and prophets for the Church (Eph 3:9). The content of the mystery is the gospel and revelation of Christ himself (Col 1:27; 2:2; 4:3) and God's intention to save Gentiles as well as Jews (1:27).

**occasional writing**: writing intended to address a specific, transient issue—written to deal with a particular occasion.

**parenesis**: moral exhortation. In classical rhetoric, parenesis often describes a section of a speech or letter in which the writer exhorts the addressee(s) to behave in a particular way. The exhortation flows from what has been said prior to it. You might think of it as answering the unspoken question, "so what?" Typically, the final section of a Pauline Letter is parenesis—for example, Rom 12:1–15:33; Col 2:15–4:6; or Eph 4:1–6:24.

**parousia**: Greek word that means "presence" or the "arrival" of a person. In the New Testament it sometimes refers to the presence or arrival of an ordinary person such as Paul (Phil 1:26; 2:12). More often, especially in Matthew (24:3, 27, 37, 39) and in the Letters of Paul (1 Cor 15:23; 1 Thess 4:15; 2 Thess 2:8), it refers to the second coming of Christ. The word has entered the English language in that sense.

**philosophy** (Greek *philosophia*): contrary to our contemporary meaning of "philosophy" as a system of thought (as found, for example, in the writings of Aristotle and Aquinas), in ancient times *philosophia* was often used to refer to practical wisdom expressed in a specific way of life. Josephus, for example, speaks of three ways of life—those of the Pharisees, the Sadducees, and the Essenes—as "three philosophies." *Philosophia* occurs only once in the New Testament, at Col 2:8, where it is used negatively, in contrast to the wisdom of the gospel.

**prayer report**: Paul's account of his regular prayer for his addressees, as distinguished from a passage in which Paul is actually writing a prayer.

**principalities and powers**: spiritual beings created by God who exercise power and influence in the world, some of whom are hostile to God and oppose his people and the spread of the gospel. Nevertheless, God has triumphed over them by means of the cross of Christ (Col 2:15) and has exalted Christ over them all (Eph 1:20–21). Christians are called to stand firm against them by drawing strength from Christ and putting on the armor of God (Eph 6:10–19); see sidebar on p. 198.

**pseudonymous:** writings attributed to someone who is not their real author. Pseudonymous writing was an honorable convention in the ancient world. Indeed, it exists in the Old Testament. For example, Jews living under the tyranny of the Syrian ruler Antiochus IV during the 160s BC understood perfectly well what their contemporary writer was doing when he took on the persona of one Daniel writing during the Babylonian captivity in the sixth century BC and facing challenges similar to the persecution of their own day. The device of pseudonymity provided a distant mirror to interpret their current situation. When scholars conjecture that a letter ascribed to Paul is pseudonymous, it is usually with the understanding that the pseudonymous author is a disciple of Paul writing after his death, intending to represent what Paul would have said had he still been alive. Whether the disputed letters ascribed to Paul are in fact pseudonymous (a question first raised in the nineteenth century) is still a matter of debate.

**realized eschatology:** see **eschatology**.

**rhetorical structure:** an argument's structure in a piece of speech or writing; the strategic arrangement of a discourse for the purpose of persuading the listeners or readers.

**righteousness:** as a human quality, being in right relationship with God; as a divine quality, God's faithfulness to his promises.

**salvation** (Greek *sōtēria*): a flexible term in the New Testament (like the verb *sōzō*, "to save") that embraces the whole range of God's care: from physical rescue from sickness and enemies (Luke 1:71) and rescue from the evils of the world ("save yourselves from this corrupt generation," Acts 2:40), to the fullness of union with God in resurrection from the dead. For Paul, salvation begins with baptism into the healing life of the body of Christ (1 Cor 1:18; 2 Cor 6:2) and is completed in the resurrection of the body (Phil 3:21).

**Septuagint** (LXX): the Greek translation of the Hebrew Bible around 250 BC by Jews in the Diaspora (the Jewish population "scattered" outside of Palestine). The term comes from the Latin *septuaginta* ("seventy") referring to the legend that seventy translators, working independently, came up with identical translations. This is the version of the Scriptures used most frequently by Paul and other New Testament writers. See **LXX**.

**Torah:** Hebrew for "law" or "teaching." In biblical contexts it usually refers to the first five books of the Hebrew Bible—Genesis, Exodus, Leviticus, Numbers, Deuteronomy—which are also known by the Greek term "Pentateuch," literally, "five scrolls." Sometimes "Torah" refers specifically to the 613 laws of Moses contained in the Pentateuch.

**type, antitype:** "type" refers to a person, event, institution, or object in the Old Testament that the New Testament sees as a prefigurement of something fulfilled in the New Covenant. The fulfillment is the antitype. For example, the Passover lamb is a type of Christ; Christ is the antitype, the fulfillment.

**undisputed letters:** In the context of modern Pauline studies, seven letters are dubbed "undisputed" because virtually no scholars dispute that Paul is their author. The seven are Romans, 1 and 2 Corinthians, Galatians, Philippians, 1 Thessalonians, and Philemon. While Paul's authorship of Ephesians, Colossians, 1 and 2 Timothy, and Titus has been disputed by many, an increasing number of scholars have argued for the authenticity of one or more of the so-called disputed letters.

**YHWH:** a transliteration of the consonants of the Hebrew name of God, which the Jerusalem Bible translated as Yahweh. It is sometimes called the Tetragrammaton—literally, the "four-letter word." In reading biblical texts aloud, Jewish tradition has called for the pronounciation of *adonai* ("Lord") in place of God's unspeakable name. The Vatican prohibition of the use of the name Yahweh in public liturgy is intended to acknowledge and respect the Jewish reverence for the ineffable name of God.

# Index of Pastoral Topics

This index highlights topics mentioned in Philemon, Philippians, or Colossians that may be useful for evangelization, catechesis, apologetics, or other forms of pastoral ministry.

# Index of Sidebars

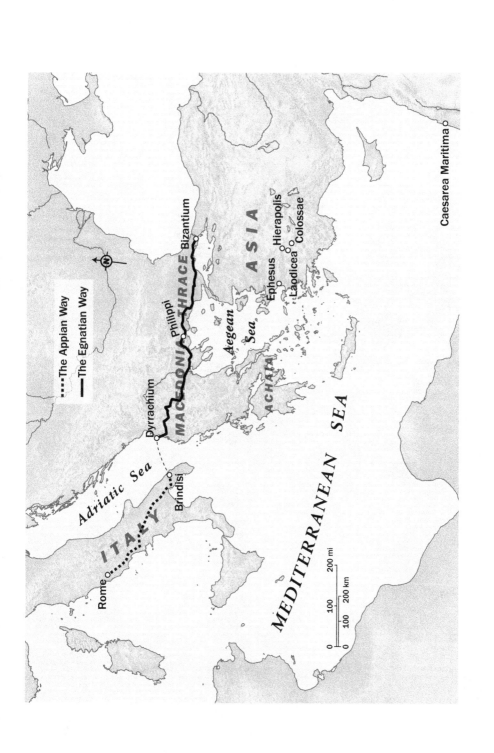